# ATHENIAN
# POLITICAL ORATORY

# ATHENIAN
# POLITICAL ORATORY

## 16 Key Speeches

TRANSLATED BY
# DAVID D. PHILLIPS

### Routledge
NEW YORK AND LONDON

Published in 2004 by
Routledge
29 W 35th Street
New York, NY 10001
www.routledge-ny.com

Published in Great Britain by
Routledge
11 New Fetter Lane
London EC4P 4EE
www.routledge.co.uk

Printed in the United States of America on acid-free paper.

10 9 8 7 6 5 4 3 2 1

Library of Congress Cataloging-in-Publication Data

Phillips, David D., 1971–
  Athenian political oratory: sixteen key speeches / David D. Phillips.
    p. cm.
  Includes bibliographical references and index.
  ISBN 0-415-96609-4 (HB : alk. paper)—ISBN 0-415-96610-8 (PB : alk. paper)
1. Athens (Greece)—History—Sources. I. Title.
  DF285. p47 2004
  938' .5—dc22                                              2004002080

# Contents

# Preface

This book is designed primarily to provide students of Greek history with a collection of translated speeches illustrating political developments between the end of the Peloponnesian War (404 B.C.) and the death of Alexander the Great (323 B.C.). The speeches in this collection were delivered in Athens: some in the Assembly, others in courts of law. All but one were written by residents of Athens; the sole exception, a letter penned by Philip II of Macedon, was read out to the Athenian Assembly by an ambassador. These speeches, therefore, are sources of first importance for Athenian domestic and foreign politics.

I have chosen to focus on three areas where oratory provides especially valuable and copious evidence: the regime of the Thirty Tyrants, the conflict between Athens and Philip, and Athens during the reign of Alexander. Therefore, after a General Introduction that provides readers with the basic facts they need to know before reading the speeches, the book is divided into three parts, with one part dedicated to each of the periods mentioned above. Each part opens with a brief narrative history of the period, followed by the speeches, each of which has its own introduction. Footnotes are appended to provide both an explanation of references and comparison with other relevant passages.

In selecting the speeches for this volume, I have taken into consideration their utility in undergraduate Greek history courses. Accordingly,

I have left out the invaluable *Embassy* and *Crown* speeches of Aeschines and Demosthenes because their length might well deter instructors from assigning them and students from reading them. On the other hand, I have included Demosthenes' Assembly speeches from the decade 351 to 341—including the *Olynthiacs* and *Philippics*, some of the most celebrated speeches from classical antiquity—so that readers can watch Athenian policy toward Macedon as it develops during this crucial period.

Where possible I have endeavored to represent both sides of an issue, as far as the genre allows. Lysias 12 and 13 were delivered by relatives of men killed by the Thirty Tyrants; in Lysias 16 we hear the voice of an accused former supporter of the Thirty. Further, in order to compensate somewhat for the monolithic presence of Demosthenes, I have included one speech by his ally Hegesippus and one by his enemy Philip, not to mention Hypereides 5, which serves as a useful corrective to Demosthenes' pronouncements of selfless patriotism.

I am pleased to record my gratitude to those scholars who have offered useful commentary and advice: Professor Rex Stem of Lousiana State University, Professor H. D. Cameron of the University of Michigan, and Professor K. A. Garbrah of the University of Michigan. I am also indebted to William Germano and Damon Zucca at Routledge for their skill and patience, and to several anonymous readers. All remaining errors, of course, are mine.

For the translations I have used the Oxford Classical Texts of Lysias and Demosthenes by C. Hude and M. R. Dilts, respectively; for Hypereides I have used C. Jensen's Teubner edition. In preparing the translations and footnotes I have consulted a number of excellent commentaries and translations, to which my debt will be obvious. Among these I have found particularly useful C. D. Adams and S. C. Todd on Lysias, J. E. Sandys on Demosthenes, H. Weil on [Demosthenes] 7 and 12, and D. Whitehead on Hypereides. A full bibliography appears at the end of the book.

In the text and footnotes I refer to speeches included in this collection by author, speech number, and section number (e.g., Demosthenes 1.1). Speeches not included in this book are cited by author, speech number and title, and section number (e.g., Demosthenes 54 *Against Conon* 1). The order of speeches has been standardized in the corpus of every orator except Hypereides; Kenyon's OCT, Jensen's Teubner, and Colin's Budé all number Hypereides' speeches differently. One can only hope that the European Union will take cognizance of this situation and impose a uniform standard. For now, although I translate Jensen's text, I use Kenyon's numbering. Other works are cited according to standard scholarly convention. The abbreviation *Ath. Pol.* is used for the pseudo-Aristotelian *Constitution of the Athenians* (Athênaiôn Politeia).

In the following places I diverge from the texts as printed by their respective editors:

Lysias 12.25: stet ἢ δίκαια
Lysias 12.62: del. <οὐ προσηκόντως>
Lysias 13.37: add. τὴν δὲ σῴζουσαν ἐπὶ τὴν προτέραν (Aldus)
Demosthenes 4.49: ἀνοητοτάτους (νοητοτάτους Dilts)
Demosthenes 2.14: stet ἐβοήθησεν
Demosthenes 3.11: ἀτακτοῦντας (τακτοῦντας Dilts)
Demosthenes 3.27: τούτων (τῶν νῦν Dilts)
Demosthenes 3.33: stet ἀσθενοῦσι
Demosthenes 5.16: συμμαχίαι (συμμαίχαι Dilts)
Demosthenes 5.19: del. ἡμῖν πολεμῆσαι
Hegesippus = [Demosthenes] 7.5: τῶν τἀνταῦθα (τἀνταῦθα τῶν Dilts)
Demosthenes 9.6-7: Since these sections are missing from manuscript S, I have printed them in italics; Dilts uses fullsized font (see Dilts p. xvi note 27).
Demosthenes 9.20: add. καὶ τοῖς οὖσιν ἐκεῖ νῦν στρατιώταις πάνθ᾽ ὅσων ἂν δέωνται ἀποστεῖλαι
Demosthenes 9.37: add. οὐδὲν ποικίλον οὐδὲ σοφόν, ἀλλ᾽ ὅτι
Demosthenes 9.65: add. καὶ προέσθαι τῶν ὑπὲρ ὑμῶν λεγόντων τινάς
Hypereides 1 fr. 3: ἀρχείων (ἀρχαίων Jensen)

D.D.P.
Los Angeles, California
October 2003

# GENERAL INTRODUCTION

## I. The Sources

*The Canon of the Attic Orators*

With the exception of Philip of Macedon, all the authors included in this book qualify as "Attic orators"; that is, orators who lived and worked in Athens. By the first century B.C., scholars at Alexandria, Egypt had compiled a canon (list) of the top ten orators from classical Athens. In their canonical (and roughly chronological) order, the Attic orators are Antiphon, Andocides, Lysias, Isocrates, Isaeus, Demosthenes, Aeschines, Hypereides, Lycurgus, and Deinarchus. Several speeches by an eleventh orator, Apollodorus, are preserved in the manuscripts of Demosthenes.

Between antiquity and the present, the great majority of Attic oratory has been lost in transmission. While the fickle finger of Fate has preserved twenty-one speeches under the name of Isocrates and sixty-one ascribed to Demosthenes, Hypereides was entirely lost (except for a few fragments) until the fortuitous discovery of a papyrus in 1847. The body of work ascribed to an author is called his corpus (Latin for "body"); a standard numbering exists for the speeches within the corpus of each orator, with the sole exception of Hypereides. However, not all the speeches preserved in the corpus of an Attic orator were necessarily written by him. For example, two speeches in the present collection come from the corpus of Demosthenes but were written by other authors: number 7 by Demosthenes' political ally Hegesippus, and number 12 by Philip of Macedon. In such cases, by scholarly convention, Demosthenes' name is enclosed in square brackets; where possible I have prefixed to it the name of the actual author, so, to give one example, the speech *On Halonnesus* is designated Hegesippus = [Demosthenes] 7.[1]

## Scholia

Ancient scholars sometimes made notes in the margins of their manuscripts in order to explain difficult passages. These ancient marginal notes are called scholia, and the scholars who made them are called scholiasts. I have occasionally referred to scholia (abbreviated by the Greek letter sigma, Σ) in the footnotes to the translations (for example, at Demosthenes 1.5; Philip = [Demosthenes] 12.3).

## Oratory and History

There is a special difficulty involved in using Attic oratory as a source for history. The men who wrote and delivered the speeches in this collection were concerned with persuading their audiences (whether a jury or the Athenian Assembly), not with making a disinterested statement of the facts. This inherent bias must be kept in mind at all times, and the reader should retain a healthy skepticism.

This is not to say that everything that comes out of a speaker's mouth is a lie. Occasionally, we can catch blatant misrepresentations (Macedon was subject to the Athenian Empire: Demosthenes 3.24; Macedon paid tribute to Athens: Hegesippus = [Demosthenes] 7.12; Athenians do not seek advantage for themselves: Demosthenes 8.42). On the whole, however, the speeches contained in this volume make vital contributions to our knowledge of Greek history in the fifth and fourth centuries B.C. Lysias is one of our chief sources for the reign of the Thirty Tyrants; the Demosthenic corpus is the best source we have for the reign of Philip II; and Hypereides gives us an important and vibrant glimpse into Athenian life and politics during the reign of Alexander the Great.

## The Study of Rhetoric

The goal of the Attic orator was persuasion. How did he aim to accomplish this? In the mid-fifth century B.C., two Sicilians named Corax and Teisias founded the formal study of rhetoric (in Greek, the *technê rhêtorikê*, the "art of speaking"). The new formal rhetoric came to Athens in the person of Gorgias of Leontinoi, who arrived in 427 and made a great impression upon Athenian audiences. The Athenians quickly adapted and became famous (or notorious, depending on your point of view) for their rhetorical ability and generally litigious attitude.[2]

Students of rhetoric were trained to win any argument, regardless of the facts. Summed up in a phrase, the goal of rhetoric was "to make the weaker argument the stronger" (*ton hêttô logon kreittô poiein*: Aristotle, *Rhetoric* 2.24.11; Plato, *Apology* 18b8; cf. Aristophanes, *Clouds* 882–894). The cornerstone of Greek rhetoric was the argument from probability (*eikos*), by which listeners were led to conclusions on the basis of what was (according to the speaker) probable. A classic example posed by teachers of rhetoric goes as follows (see Plato, *Phaedrus* 273a–c): A weak man and a strong man get into a fight. The issue goes to court, and each man tries to convince the jury that the other started the fight. The weak man says, "I am weak and he is strong; therefore it is not probable that I would hit him first." The strong man replies, "I am strong and he is weak; I knew that everyone would naturally suspect me of hitting him first; therefore it is not probable that I did so." A student of rhetoric should be able to take either side of this case, or any case, and persuade his audience.

*Genres of Speeches*

Ancient scholars, beginning perhaps with Aristotle (*Rhetoric* 1.3), divided speeches into three genres, or types:

> Deliberative oratory was pronounced before a political assembly, such as the Athenian Assembly; its goal was to persuade the listener to support the proposal of the speaker or to reject that of his opponents. All the speeches of Demosthenes and Hegesippus in this collection are deliberative.
>
> Epideictic oratory was meant for display (*epideixis*). The most famous incarnation of epideictic oratory was the funeral oration, a eulogy pronounced every year in honor of the Athenians killed in combat (see Thucydides 2.34–46). Funeral orations are preserved in the corpora of Lysias

(speech 2), Demosthenes (speech 60), and Hypereides (speech 6).

Forensic oratory was oratory for the courtroom. The job of the forensic speaker was to convince a jury to convict or acquit. Most of the Attic orators spent at least part of their careers as logographers (*logographoi*, "speechwriters"); a logographer composed speeches for others to deliver in court. The orations of Lysias and Hypereides included in this book are forensic.

*Division of Speeches*

Another element in the study of rhetoric was the division of a speech into its constituent parts:

In the introduction (*prooimion*), the speaker introduces himself to the audience and seeks to win their goodwill.

The narration (*diêgêsis*) sets out the facts according to the speaker.

The proofs (*pisteis*) include the testimony of witnesses, documents such as laws and contracts, and arguments, particularly arguments from probability.

The conclusion (*epilogos*, "epilogue") briefly sums up the speaker's arguments and instructs the listeners as to how they ought to vote.

The quadripartite division outlined above is especially characteristic of forensic oratory. In deliberative speeches the line between narration and proofs is often blurred; however, the section preceding the speaker's proposal (*prothesis*) often contains more narrative, and the section following the proposal generally includes proofs in favor of the proposal. Such was the standard division taught to students of rhetoric. Like great artists in any field, however, the Attic orators did not always adhere strictly to these rules but applied or deviated from them as their purposes dictated.

## II.   Athenian Law and Government

*General Character*

Law and government at Athens were characterized by their participatory and amateur nature. In theory, any adult male Athenian citizen was qualified to play almost any role in government or in a court of law. He could address the Athenian Assembly, making his own motion or offering his opinion on the motions of others. He could appear in court as a litigant or witness, or he could serve on the jury.

In practice, some areas were more specialized than others. Men who habitually addressed the Assembly were called *rhêtores* (singular *rhêtôr*), a word that literally means "speakers," but that I have generally translated as "politicians." Those who had a gift for rhetoric and knew the law well might become logographers, writing speeches for litigants to deliver in court. They did not, however, become lawyers, because the Athenians had no lawyers. As a rule, litigants were expected to plead their own cases; they were, however, allowed to call advocates (*synêgoroi*), who were (at least in theory) friends or family members who would assist the litigant by giving speeches of their own.

## Types of Legal Action

The fundamental distinction between types of legal action at Athens lay between private and public lawsuits. This distinction affected the capacity to prosecute. In a private lawsuit (*dikê idia*, often referred to simply as *dikê*; plural *dikai* [*idiai*]) only the wronged party (or, in homicide cases, a near relative) could prosecute. In a public lawsuit (*dikê dêmosia*, plural *dikai dêmosiai*), any willing Athenian citizen could serve as prosecutor. The chief categories of public lawsuit mentioned in this book are the *graphê* (literally "writing"), *apagôgê* (summary arrest), and *eisangelia* (impeachment). Lysias 13 was delivered in an *apagôgê* for homicide; Hypereides 1 and 4 come from impeachment trials.

## Courts of Law

The great majority of lawsuits were tried in jury-courts (*dikastêria*), which constituted one of the cornerstones of Athenian democracy (see *Ath. Pol.* 9.1). At the beginning of each year, the Athenian state empaneled a pool of 6,000 jurors (*dikastai*), who swore an oath, called the heliastic oath (Hypereides 4.40), affirming that they would vote in accordance with the laws and decrees of the Assembly and the Council of 500.[3] On each day the courts met, jurors were allotted to individual cases. The size of the jury was determined by the type of lawsuit but generally ranged from 201 to 501, with exceptional public cases having juries of up to 2,001. Due to their size and citizen content, Athenian juries were considered to represent the Athenian people. Thus a speaker in court will often tell his jury, "You did *x*," when it was some other manifestation of the Athenian people—usually the Assembly or another jury in a different trial—that performed the act (e.g., Lysias 13.65; Hypereides 1.17).

Some offenses were tried outside the *dikastêria*. For example, the Council of the Areopagus heard trials for intentional wounding and arson, as well as some homicide cases. Depending on the intent of the killer and the status of the victim, a homicide trial could occur in one of five homicide courts (including the Areopagus), or in a jury-court by *apagôgê* (as in Lysias 13).

### Procedure

In an Athenian trial, the prosecutor spoke first, the defendant second. The two sides were given equal amounts of time, which depended on the type of case. Time was measured by a device called the *klepsydra* (water-clock, literally "water-stealer"). The litigant would mount his platform (*bêma*: Hypereides 4.41) and deliver his speech; the clock was stopped for the testimony of witnesses and the reading of documents (Lysias 12.47, 13.22, 16.8). If a litigant had time left on the clock after his own speech, he might call one or more advocates (*synêgoroi*). Hypereides 4, for example, was delivered by Hypereides as *synêgoros* for the defendant Euxenippus. After both litigants had presented their cases, the jury voted; its verdict was determined by a bare majority. Under Athenian law some offenses had penalties set by statute, while others did not. In the latter case, after the jury voted to convict, the prosecution and defense each proposed a penalty, and the jury made its selection, again by majority vote.

### Sycophancy

There existed in classical Athens a class of men who made their living by mounting malicious prosecutions. These individuals were called sycophants.[4] A sycophant would use the threat of litigation to extort money from his target; alternatively, he would take his case to court and attempt to secure a monetary judgment. Athenian defendants commonly accused their prosecutors of sycophantic behavior in an attempt to convince the jury that the accusations against them were baseless (Hypereides 1.2, 4.33; cf. Lysias 13.65).

## Citizens, Metics, and Slaves

The population of Attica was divided into three groups: citizens, metics, and slaves. Under a law enacted in 451/0 on the proposal of Pericles, only the offspring of two Athenian citizens qualified as citizens (*Ath. Pol.* 26.4). Naturalization was extremely rare. Only adult male citizens could attend the Assembly, hold political office, and serve on juries. The citizen body of Athens comprised ten tribes, which were subdivided into demes. Demes were originally geographical units; during the classical period, however, membership in both tribe and deme was hereditary. The official nomenclature of a male Athenian citizen was "*X* son of *Y* from deme *Z*." Thus, for example, the orator Demosthenes was Demosthenes son of Demosthenes from Paeania, while Hypereides was Hypereides son of Glaucippus from Collytus.

Metics were free foreign residents of Athens. They were liable to military service and to some liturgies (see below) but could not own land in Attica without a grant from the state. The orator Lysias was a metic (Part One, The Thirty Tyrants, p. 17). All residents of Attica who were not citizens or metics were slaves. Privately owned slaves worked in the homes, fields, and shops of their masters. Some slaves belonging to individuals lived on their own and enjoyed special status as *chôris oikountes* ("living apart": e.g., Demosthenes 4.36). The city of Athens also owned slaves. Some of these public slaves lived in Athens and assisted in the functioning of government; others, for example, built and repaired roads (*Ath. Pol.* 54.1). Litigants and politicians commonly lobbed accusations of servile or foreign status or ancestry at their opponents in order to prejudice their audiences (Lysias 13.18 with note).

## The Athenian Assembly

All adult male Athenian citizens were qualified to attend and cast votes in the Athenian Assembly. The Greek word for "assembly," *ekklêsia,* produces the words for "church" in various Romance languages: Spanish *iglesia,* French *église,* etc. The Assembly was also often referred to simply as the *dêmos,* or "people." Meetings of the Assembly normally convened on a hill called the Pnyx, located about 500 yards west of the Acropolis and just southwest of the Areopagus.

The Assembly had 40 scheduled meetings per year (*Ath. Pol.* 43.3–4); additional extraordinary meetings could also be summoned. In order to achieve the quorum of 6,000 required to conduct serious business, attendance at the Assembly was rewarded with a payment of three obols (see below, *Money*). Motions brought before the Assembly had first to pass through the Council of 500, which performed a probouleutic function (literally, "deliberating in advance" of the Assembly). While in theory any adult male citizen could mount the speaker's platform (*bêma,* the same word used for a platform in a lawcourt: Demosthenes 1.8; Hegesippus = [Demosthenes] 7.1) and address the Assembly, in practice deliberations were often dominated by established politicians such as Demosthenes, Hegesippus, and Hypereides.

The primary function of the Athenian Assembly in the fourth century was the passage of decrees, including the ratification of treaties (such as the Peace of Philocrates: Hegesippus = [Demosthenes] 7.19). These decrees set policy, both foreign and domestic, for the Athenian state. It was the Assembly that determined Athens' official stance *vis-à-vis* Macedon; thus all the Demosthenic (and pseudo-Demosthenic) speeches in this collection were delivered before the Assembly.

The constitution of Athens forbade the passage of decrees which contravened existing law. The proposer of such a decree was liable to prosecution by a *graphê paranomôn* (public lawsuit for proposing an illegal decree). If the proposer was convicted, his decree was invalidated, and he was subject to additional punishment, usually in the form of a fine (Hegesippus = [Demosthenes] 7.43; Hypereides 4.18).

*Taxation*

Direct taxation in classical Athens came in the form of a property tax called the *eisphora.* In the late fourth century there were two types of *eisphora.* The first, and original, type was a special tax levied in times of war to increase the revenues of the Athenian treasury. Such an *eisphora* had to be decreed by the Assembly; hence Demosthenes goes to great lengths to persuade his countrymen to tax themselves for the war against Philip (Demosthenes 1.20, 2.31, 8.21–23). In addition, from 347/6 to 323/2 the Athenians levied a second *eisphora*, this one a yearly assessment totaling 10 talents (*IG* II² 505, lines 14–17). Both types of *eisphora* fell only on the richest residents of Attica, both citizens and metics; for purposes of tax collection these wealthiest Athenians were organized into groups called symmories (Demosthenes 2.29).

*Liturgies*

The machinery of the Athenian state was oiled primarily by the performance of liturgies. Two hallmark institutions of Athens, her fleet and her cycle of religious festivals, were funded by liturgies. As with the payment of *eisphorai*, the performance of liturgies fell only upon the richest stratum of Athenian society (sometimes called the "liturgical class"), numbering some 1,200 men.

The naval liturgy was known as a trierarchy, and a man performing this liturgy was called a trierarch (Lysias 12.37; Demosthenes 4.36). Every trireme (see pp. 11–12) in the Athenian fleet was assigned to a trierarch, who was responsible for the upkeep of the vessel. Originally a ship's trierarch commanded it in action, but in the fourth century this was not always the case. Since the trierarchy was expensive, sometimes co-trierarchs were appointed. All trierarchs were Athenian citizens.

The most important festival liturgy was the choregy (*chorêgia*). Major Athenian religious festivals included dramatic performances, which required choruses. The task of paying a chorus, as well as paying its director and supplying costumes and other necessities, was assigned as a liturgy; the man discharging this liturgy was called a *chorêgos* (chorus-master: Demosthenes 4.35–36; cf. Demosthenes 9.60). Metics as well as citizens could be called upon to serve as *chorêgoi*.

The performance of liturgies represented a financial burden but also offered the opportunity for prominent Athenians to win good repute. Speakers in the Assembly and courts often made reference to the liturgies they had performed (Demosthenes 8.70; cf. Lysias

13.62), in the hope that their listeners would be impressed and thus persuaded to vote in their favor.

## III.   Some Aspects of Athenian Life

### The Athenian Calendar

Every Greek city-state had its own calendar (see, e.g., Thucydides 2.2). The Athenians used a lunar year, and the new year started at the first new moon after the summer solstice. The twelve months of the Athenian calendar, in order (cf. Demosthenes 3.4), were:

1. Hecatombaeon (roughly July)
2. Metageitnion (August)
3. Boedromion (September)
4. Pyanopsion (October)
5. Maemacterion (November)
6. Poseideon (December)
7. Gamelion (January)
8. Anthesterion (February)
9. Elaphebolion (March)
10. Mounychion (April)
11. Thargelion (May)
12. Scirophorion (June)

Exact correspondences between Athenian days of the year and ours vary from year to year because the Athenian calendar was lunar and ours is solar. For example, the battle of Chaeroneia was fought on Metageitnion 7 = August 2, 338. However, Metageitnion 7 in any other year would correspond with a date in the vicinity of, but usually not exactly, August 2.

### Money

The basic unit of Athenian currency was the drachma (as it was in modern Greece until the introduction of the euro). A table of currency equivalents looks like this:

6 obols (ob.) = 1 drachma (dr.)
100 dr. = 1 mina (mn.)
6,000 dr. = 60 mn. = 1 talent (T.)

These units of currency were also units of weight; thus an Athenian one-drachma coin was (ideally) worth its weight (approximately 0.15 oz.) in silver. The mina weighed a little less than one pound, and the talent weighed about fifty-seven pounds.

Attempts to provide dollar equivalents for Athenian currency tend to mislead; it is more informative to provide some examples of a daily wage. In the fourth century, jurors were paid three obols per day, as were those who attended the Assembly. Hoplites (see below) and sailors on campaign generally received one drachma per day (cf. Demosthenes 4.28 [food allowance only]). One drachma per day was also a common wage paid to skilled workmen. By law, pimps were allowed to charge no more than two drachmas for flute-girls who doubled as prostitutes (Hypereides 4.3 with note).

*Warfare*

Athenian men aged eighteen to sixty years and possessed of sound body were liable to be called up for military service (*Ath. Pol.* 53.4). Depending on their economic status, they served on land as cavalry, hoplites, or light infantry, or on the sea as rowers in the Athenian fleet.

The cavalry was open only to the wealthiest Athenians. The breeding of horses was an ancient mark of nobility, and aristocratic Greeks often gave their children names containing the element *hippos*, "horse" (Hypereides 1.16 with note). Two speeches in the present collection were delivered by men who served in the Athenian cavalry: Mantitheus (Lysias 16.13) and Lycophron (Hypereides 1.16).

The backbone of the infantry of a classical Greek city consisted of its hoplites. The hoplite, who got his name from his large round shield (*hoplon*), wore as defensive armor a helmet, breastplate, and greaves (shinguards). His primary offensive weapon was a thrusting spear between six and eight feet long; he also carried a short sword. A hoplite's equipment weighed around seventy pounds, equivalent to that carried by an American infantryman in World War I. Hoplite equipment was not cheap and had to be provided by the individual soldier; thus the hoplite ranks were filled by middle- to upper-class Athenians. Hoplites fought in a dense rectangular formation called the phalanx.

Poorer Athenians served as rowers in the Athenian fleet, which was by far the finest in classical Greece. The standard warship during this period was the trireme (Demosthenes 1.17, 8.28). Its Greek name, *triêrês*, means "three-fitted," from the ship's three banks of oars. The Athenian trireme had a standard complement of 200 men: 170 rowers plus thirty officers and marines. Athens' navy also included transport vessels for soldiers and for horses (Demosthenes 4.16).

During the classical period, Greek cities and Macedonian kings employed hired mercenaries in addition to citizen soldiers and sailors. As the fourth century progressed, the use of mercenaries by Athens became more and more common; in his speeches against Philip, Demosthenes repeatedly implores the Assembly to levy citizen troops (Demosthenes 4.19, 2.27). Unless engaged in besieging cities, classical Greek armies did not usually take the field year-round; their campaigning season stretched roughly from April to October (Demosthenes 9.48). Philip of Macedon, however, campaigned year-round, in addition to his other innovations in the art of war (Demosthenes 2.23, 9.49–50).

### Agonistic Nature of Greek Society

Society in ancient Greece, and particularly in Athens, was generally agonistic in nature. The word "agonistic" comes from the Greek word *agôn*. The basic meaning of *agôn* is "contest," and it applied equally to political contests in the Assembly, legal contests in the courts, military contests on the field of battle, and contests in other areas, such as athletics and dramatic performance.

In an agonistic society, competition between members is not just ingrained but institutionalized. Interpersonal rivalries dominate many aspects of daily life at all levels of society. Winning brings honor, losing shame. It was, however, possible to take the *agôn* too far; two negative corollaries of the Greek spirit of rivalry were hubris and stasis.

When an individual took his quest for glory too far, the result might be hubris. Hubris is a difficult term to define; it denotes a violation of the proper relationship between man and man or between man and god, often with the goal of glorifying the perpetrator and/or humiliating the victim. For example, Ariston, the speaker of Demosthenes 54 *Against Conon*, prosecuted Conon for simple battery (*aikeia*) but asserted that Conon's actions deserved the more serious charge of hubris. Conon allegedly beat Ariston within an inch of his life, then flapped his elbows and crowed like a rooster over Ariston's prone body. It was not the beating alone, but the combination of the beating and the rooster dance—which in football terms would be deemed "excessive celebration" at the loser's expense—that made the act hubristic.

Speakers in the Assembly and lawcourts of Athens often accused their opponents of hubristic behavior. In the orations included in this collection, the Thirty Tyrants and Philip are favorite targets of such allegations (Lysias 12.98; Hegesippus = [Demosthenes] 7.44; Demosthenes 8.62, 9.1).

If hubris is a violation of the rules of competition by an individual, stasis is competition taken to excess by a group. Stasis (often rendered "civil strife") is dissension between political factions in a city; when left unremedied it can degenerate into outright civil war, such as the conflict between the oligarchs and democrats at Athens in 404/3 (Part One, The Thirty Tyrants; Lysias 12, 13, 16). Perhaps the most famous description of stasis in a Greek city is Thucydides' narration (3.70–85) of the disorder that wracked the city of Corcyra in 427 during the Peloponnesian War. For obvious reasons, stasis within a city weakens it and makes it vulnerable to encroachment from outside; Philip was expert at taking advantage of stasis within Greek cities (Demosthenes 9.12, 50).

# PART ONE
## THE THIRTY TYRANTS

Multiple ancient authors provide us with evidence for the regime of the Thirty Tyrants and its aftermath. Lysias, a prosperous Athenian metic,[1] was present when the Thirty came to power but soon fled to save his life (Lysias 12.8ff.). Xenophon, a moderate oligarch who remained in Athens throughout the reign of the Thirty, treats the period in Book 2, Chapters 3 and 4 of his *Hellenica*, a history of Greece from 411 to 362. The pseudo-Aristotelian *Constitution of Athens* (abbreviated *Ath. Pol.)* covers the Thirty in Chapters 34 through 41. The later narratives of the Thirty in Diodorus (14.3–6, 32–33) and Justin (*Epitome* 5.8–10) both derive ultimately from the fourth-century historian Ephorus, whose work survives only in fragments.

The aforementioned sources are in agreement regarding most events of the reign of the Thirty, but their chronology is not always consistent. The execution of Theramenes, for example, occurs before the seizure of Phyle in Xenophon, Diodorus, and Justin but after it in the *Ath. Pol.* The Spartan garrison arrives at Athens earlier in Xenophon, Diodorus, and Justin and later in Lysias (12.59) and the *Ath. Pol.* The sketch of the reign of the Thirty Tyrants that follows thus represents only one possible reconstruction of the order of events.

### Establishment of the Thirty

In the spring of 404, Athens surrendered to Sparta, ending the Peloponnesian War (431–404). An oligarchic conspiracy had been brewing in Athens during the final days of the war, and when the war ended, the oligarchs sent for the Spartan admiral Lysander. Lysander intimidated the Athenian Assembly into passing a decree moved by

one of the conspirators, Dracontides of Aphidna (Lysias 12.72ff.).
The Dracontides decree entrusted power to a board of thirty men
who were to revise and codify the laws of Athens. The Thirty Tyrants
(as they are now called) included Dracontides; Eratosthenes, the
defendant in Lysias 12; Critias, a student of Socrates and relative of
Plato; and Theramenes, who had played a crucial role in the earlier
oligarchic Revolution of 411. The names of all thirty are given by
Xenophon (*Hellenica* 2.3.2).

### Appointment of Magistrates

Once they were established, the Thirty secured their hold on power
by appointing magistrates friendly to their regime. At the turn of the
new year in midsummer 404 (see General Introduction, p. 10, *The
Athenian Calendar*) they swore in a Council of 500 stacked with their
supporters. Under the Thirty the Council of 500 functioned as a
court of law (Lysias 13.36), displacing the democratic system of jury-
courts (*dikastêria*). The Thirty also chose the Eleven, who were in
charge of the state prison and supervised executions. In addition, the
tyrants created a board of Ten to govern the Peiraeus and established
a corps of 300 attendants called "whip-bearers" (*mastigophoroi: Ath.
Pol.* 35.1).

### Legal Reforms

The Thirty delayed the wholesale revision of the Athenian constitution
but did enact some legal reforms. They annulled the laws of Ephialtes
and Archestratus concerning the Council of the Areopagus. While we
cannot identify Archestratus or the laws ascribed to him, Ephialtes
had carried legislation in 462/1 that had the effect of substantially
curtailing the powers of the Areopagus. By repealing Ephialtes' laws,
the Thirty theoretically returned to the Areopagus all its former privi-
leges. The Thirty may have intended to restore real power to the Areopagus; however, during their brief eight-month reign it was the
Council of 500, not the Areopagus, whose influence expanded.

The Thirty also repealed some of the laws enacted by Solon in
594/3. According to *Ath. Pol.* 35.2, the Thirty rescinded ambiguous

statutes, thus lessening the influence of the democratic jury-courts. A prominent example was Solon's testamentary law, which rendered a will invalid if the testator was insane, senile, drugged, diseased, coerced, bound, or under the influence of a woman (Apollodorus = [Demosthenes] 46 *2 Against Stephanus* 14; cf. Hypereides 3 *Against Athenogenes* 17). These statutory obstacles had made it easy to challenge a will and had produced a number of frivolous lawsuits. By repealing this law and removing the obstacles, the Thirty intended to reduce drastically the number of inheritance cases.

### Attack on Sycophants; Execution of the Generals and Taxiarchs

At the beginning of their reign, the Thirty targeted sycophants (Lysias 12.5; Xenophon, *Hellenica* 2.3.12; see General Introduction, pp. 6–7). Sycophants were generally viewed as a blight on society, and the majority of Athenians approved of the crackdown on sycophancy. The Thirty also took steps to eliminate the opposition to their nascent regime. Shortly before they came to power, an informer named Agoratus had denounced several generals and taxiarchs (tribal hoplite commanders) who were prominent and vocal democrats. The Thirty had these men tried by the Council of 500, convicted, and executed (see Lysias 13).

### Reign of Terror

The popularity of the Thirty did not last long. To secure their regime, they invited their Spartan allies to garrison the Acropolis; Sparta sent Callibius as harmost (garrison commander) with 700 troops. In need of funds, the Thirty began to trump up charges against wealthy Athenians—at first metics, then citizens as well. Lysias and his brother Polemarchus were among the victims of this scheme (Lysias 12.6ff.). Declaring the targeted individuals to be enemies of the state, the Thirty executed some and exiled others, and confiscated their property. During their eight months in power, the Thirty sentenced 1,500 Athenians to death (*Ath. Pol.* 35.4; Aeschines 3 *Against Ctesiphon* 235; Isocrates 7 *Areopagiticus* 67, 20 *Against Lochites* 11).

### Theramenes vs. Critias

The bloody policies of the Thirty alienated many Athenians and brought about a schism within their own ranks. The extreme oligarchs were led by Critias, the moderates by Theramenes, the most vocal opponent of the tyrants' violent methods. Theramenes objected on both moral and political grounds: he condemned the practice of killing men in order to seize their assets, and he advocated a government that distributed power among a greater number of Athenians.

Seeing the people rallying in support of Theramenes, Critias and the rest of the Thirty attempted to appease him by proposing a list of 3,000 Athenian "gentlemen" (*kaloi k'agathoi*) who would have a share in governing the city. Theramenes, however, was not satisfied, since in his opinion the number of "gentlemen" was greater than 3,000. The Thirty delayed publication of the list, and when it was published, they disarmed all Athenians whose names were not on it (*Ath. Pol.* 36–37.1; Lysias 12.40, 95; Xenophon, *Hellenica* 2.3.20).[2] Further, a law was passed whereby the 3,000 could only be put to death by vote of the Council of 500, while those outside the list could be executed by decree of the Thirty alone (Xenophon, *Hellenica* 2.3.51).

### Execution of Theramenes

The conflict between Critias and Theramenes came to a head at a meeting of the Council of 500. Critias accused Theramenes as an enemy of the regime; Theramenes' defense won the applause of the councillors. Realizing that the Council would acquit Theramenes, Critias consulted with the rest of the Thirty, struck Theramenes' name from the list of the 3,000, and condemned him to death. Theramenes was dragged off by the Eleven and forced to drink the fatal hemlock. His last words were a toast to his enemy: "Here's to the fair Critias!" (Xenophon, *Hellenica* 2.3.23–56).

### Resistance under Thrasybulus; Phyle

Soon after the execution of Theramenes, the Thirty took an additional step to consolidate their regime, expelling from the city of Athens all who were not on the list of the Three Thousand. Many exiled

Athenians fled to the neighboring cities of Thebes and Megara, which disobeyed a Spartan directive against accepting Athenian refugees. Among these exiles, resistance to the Thirty arose under the leadership of Thrasybulus, who marched across the border from Boeotia with seventy men and occupied the fortress of Phyle (Lysias 12.52; cf. 13.77–79). The Thirty attempted to dislodge the rebels from Phyle but failed and were forced to retreat to Athens.

### Occupation of Eleusis and Salamis

Sensing a growing threat to their security, the Thirty decided to seize the town of Eleusis, in western Attica, as a possible refuge. On the pretext of conducting a census for defense purposes, the Thirty summoned the Eleusinians for a review. The Eleusinians were placed under arrest by the cavalry, and the next day, at a meeting of the Three Thousand, the entire male population of Eleusis was sentenced to death (Xenophon, *Hellenica* 2.4.8–9; Lysias 12.52, 13.44). This allowed the Thirty to appropriate Eleusis for their own use. Similar measures were taken at Salamis (Lysias *ibid.*).

### Battle of Munychia

In the meantime, emboldened by their success at Phyle, the resistance under Thrasybulus had increased in number from 70 to 1,000 men. The rebels marched on the Peiraeus and seized the hill of Munychia. Hence the democratic rebels are often referred to as "the men of the Peiraeus," while the oligarchic supporters of the Thirty (that is, the Three Thousand) are called "the men of the city" (Lysias 12.92–98). At Munychia the democrats defeated the oligarchs in battle, and Critias, the leader of the Thirty, was killed.

### Ouster of the Thirty

The day after the battle of Munychia, the Three Thousand held a meeting at which they deposed the Thirty. Most of the tyrants retired to their stronghold at Eleusis. The Thirty were replaced by a new board of Ten[3] made up of opponents of the dead Critias (Lysias 12.54–57). The appointment of enemies of Critias suggests that these

Ten were chosen with an eye toward reconciliation with the men of the Peiraeus; if so, the plan backfired, for, rather than coming to terms, the Ten continued to fight the rebels.

### Amnesty of 403

Finally, a settlement between the oligarchs and democrats was brokered by Sparta. The first term of the settlement was an amnesty which historians call the Amnesty of 403. This was a blanket pardon for acts committed during the reign of the Thirty with stated exceptions. The Thirty, the Eleven, the Ten in charge of the Peiraeus, and the Ten who replaced the Thirty were not included in the Amnesty unless they passed a hearing to review their conduct in office. Homicide committed with one's own hand was not covered by the Amnesty (*Ath. Pol.* 31.5). However, conspiracy to commit homicide—for example, procuring a person's execution by informing against him—was covered by the Amnesty (Isocrates 18 *Against Callimachus* 20).

All Athenians swore an oath of reconciliation, which included the clause "I will not bear malice for past wrongs against any citizen except the Thirty and the Eleven, nor against any of these who is willing to give an account of his conduct in the office he held" (Andocides 1 *On the Mysteries* 90). While Xenophon states (*Hellenica* 2.4.43) that the Athenians abided by their oaths, Lysias 13 and 16 provide a more pessimistic account of the diligence with which the Amnesty was enforced.

### Separation of Eleusis from Athens

The second term of reconciliation was the official separation of Eleusis from Athens. Any man of the city who so wished was allowed to move to Eleusis, as most of the Thirty had already done. Residents of Eleusis were barred from holding political office at Athens, and travel between Eleusis and Athens was forbidden, except during the festival of the Eleusinian Mysteries, celebrated annually in honor of the goddesses Demeter and Persephone. This arrangement would last until 401/0, when Athens reabsorbed Eleusis by force of arms and thus reunited Attica.

### Restoration of Democracy

With peace concluded on these terms between the democrats of the Peiraeus and the oligarchs of the city, Athens reverted to a democratic constitution, which remained in effect (with occasional alterations) throughout the Classical period.

# 1

# LYSIAS 12

## *Against Eratosthenes*

### Introduction

Soon after the Thirty Tyrants came to power, two of their number, Theognis and Peison, suggested to their colleagues that some metics were opposed to the new government and that this provided an opportunity to seize their assets. The Thirty chose ten targets, including Lysias and his brother Polemarchus (§§6–7). Lysias was arrested but managed to escape his captors by a combination of bribery and sheer luck (§§8–17). Polemarchus, however, was apprehended by the tyrant Eratosthenes and forced to commit suicide by drinking hemlock (§17).

After the restoration of the democracy, Eratosthenes submitted to a review of his conduct in office (*euthynai*) in order to qualify for the Amnesty of 403 (Part One, The Thirty Tyrants, p. 20). Lysias prosecuted him for the killing of Polemarchus and sought the death penalty (§37). The outcome of the trial is unknown.

In his introduction (§§1–3), Lysias mentions the enormity of the crimes committed by the Thirty, identifies his anger with that felt by the jurors, and expresses the fear that his speech will not do justice to himself and his brother's memory. The narration occupies §§4–25. Here Lysias tells of his family's arrival in Athens (§4) and the brutal treatment they suffered at the hands of the Thirty (§§5–21); he concludes the section by confronting Eratosthenes with the illegal arrest and execution of Polemarchus (§§22–25).

The longest part of the speech consists of proofs (§§26–80). Lysias first refutes Eratosthenes' defense that he opposed the Thirty's plan to arrest metics and was only acting under orders (§§26–34). He then appeals to the jury to set an example by punishing

Eratosthenes and asks for the death penalty, referring to the many heinous acts of Eratosthenes and the Thirty (§§35–42). Sections 43 to 61 summarize the actions of Eratosthenes during the reign of the Thirty. Lysias then digresses to attack another former tyrant, Theramenes. Expecting Eratosthenes to align himself with the moderate Theramenes in order to deflect the jury's hostility, he portrays Theramenes in the worst possible light (§§62–78). The proof section concludes (§§79–80) with an appeal to the jury to punish the Thirty.

In his lengthy conclusion (§§81–100) Lysias meditates upon a fitting penalty for the Thirty (§§81–84) and attacks Eratosthenes' advocates (*synêgoroi*: General Introduction, p. 6) and witnesses (§§85–91). He addresses separately the men of the city (§§92–94) and the men of the Peiraeus (§§95–98), and then appeals to the entire jury to avenge the victims of the Thirty (§§99–100).

### Against Eratosthenes

[1] It is not commencing my prosecution that I find difficult, men of the jury, but bringing an end to my speech. The deeds committed by my adversaries are so enormous and so numerous that, even if I were to lie, I could not bring accusations more terrible than those before you, nor, if I wanted to tell the truth, could I tell the whole truth: either the prosecutor would have to give up or time would run out. [2] I think that we will experience the opposite of what we have experienced previously. In the past, you see, prosecutors had to disclose any existing enmity toward their defendants; but in this case we have to ask the defendants[1] what enmity they felt toward the city which gave them the audacity to commit such crimes against it.

I say this not because I do not carry my own enmity and misfortune, but because all of us possess reasons for anger in great abundance, for our own sakes or for the city's. [3] So I, men of the jury, who have never conducted my own or anyone else's business in public, now stand compelled by what has happened to prosecute this man. As a result, I have frequently fallen into deep despair, fearing that, due to my inexperience, I would conduct this prosecution on behalf of my brother and myself in an unworthy and incapable manner. Nonetheless, I will attempt to instruct you from the beginning in as few words as I can.

[4] My father Cephalus was persuaded by Pericles to move to this country. He lived here for thirty years, and neither he nor we were ever involved in a lawsuit against anyone as prosecutor or defendant; we conducted ourselves under the democracy in such a way as neither to offend against others nor to be wronged by them. [5] But when the Thirty, those depraved sycophants, came to power, they claimed that the city had to be cleansed of unjust men and the remaining citizens had to turn themselves to virtue and justice. That is what they said, but they did not venture to do it, as I will endeavor to recount, speaking first about my own affairs and then about yours.

[6] In a meeting of the Thirty, Theognis and Peison² said that some of the metics³ were displeased with the constitution.⁴ This, they said, was the ideal pretext that would allow them to appear to exact punishment but in reality to make a profit: the city was extremely poor, and the regime needed money. [7] And they persuaded their listeners without difficulty, because, as they saw it, killing people was no big deal, but acquiring money was a very big deal. So they decided to arrest ten men, including two working people, so that they would be able to answer in regard to the rest that these things had been done not for the sake of money but for the benefit of the state—as if they had done anything else from honorable motives.

[8] They divided the houses among themselves and set off. They caught me as I was entertaining friends; they drove my friends away and handed me over to Peison, and the rest of them went to my workshop and started compiling a list of my slaves. I asked Peison if he would be willing to take money and save my life; [9] he responded that he would, if it was a lot of money. So I said that I was prepared to pay him a talent of silver,⁵ and he agreed to do it. Now, I knew that he had no respect for gods or men, but nonetheless, faced with the circumstances, I thought it absolutely necessary to exact a pledge from him. [10] And after he swore, calling down destruction upon himself and his children, that he would take the talent and rescue me, I went into the bedroom and opened the chest. Peison figured out what I was doing and came in; seeing the

contents, he called two of his attendants and ordered them to seize what was in the chest. [11] And when he had, men of the jury, not the amount he had agreed to, but three talents of silver, 400 Cyzicene staters, 100 darics,[6] and four silver bowls, I asked him to give me some money for the road, and he told me I should be happy if I saved my skin.

[12] As Peison and I were leaving, Melobius and Mnesitheides[7] ran into us as they were coming out of the workshop, accosted us on my doorstep, and asked where we were going. Peison said he was going to my brother's in order to inspect the contents of that house. So they told him to be on his way but told me to accompany them to Damnippus'.[8] [13] Peison came up to me and urged me to keep my mouth shut and take heart, since he would follow us there.

At Damnippus' we came upon Theognis guarding some other men; they handed me over to him and went back. In this situation, I decided to take a risk, since I was already facing death. [14] I called Damnippus over and said to him, "You are a friend of mine. I have come to your house, I have done no wrong, and I am being killed for my money. So, since I am suffering this fate, readily do what you can to save me." And he promised that he would. He decided that it was better to inform Theognis, because he believed that Theognis would do anything if someone gave him money. [15] As he was talking to Theognis—I happened to be familiar with the house and knew that it had two doors[9]—I decided to try to save myself there and then. I figured that if I escaped detection, I would be saved; while if I were caught, I reckoned that if Theognis had been persuaded by Damnippus to take money, I would get away nonetheless, and if not, I would be just as dead.

[16] I thought these things through and ran. They were standing guard at the courtyard door. There were three doors I had to go through, and all of them happened to be open. When I got to the house of Archeneus the shipowner, I sent him into town[10] to find out about my brother. When he came back, he told me that Eratosthenes had seized my brother in the street and dragged him off to prison.[11] [17] After receiving this information, the next night I sailed across to Megara. The Thirty gave Polemarchus their customary order, to drink hemlock, without informing him of the charge on which he was about to die; that is how

far he was from standing trial and offering a defense. [18] And when he was carried from the prison dead, although we had three houses, they did not allow his funeral procession to start from any one of them; instead, the family had to rent a hut and lay him out there. And although we owned many cloaks, when we asked, the Thirty gave us none for the burial; instead one of our friends donated a cloak, another a pillow, each donated for Polemarchus' burial whatever he might have.

[19] The Thirty had 700 shields of ours; they had silver and gold in abundance, bronze and jewelry and furniture and women's clothing in amounts they could never have expected to acquire, and 120 slaves as well: they took the best of these for themselves and gave the rest to the treasury. Such were the depths of insatiability and sordid greed to which they sank, and they put their character on display: Polemarchus' wife happened to be wearing gold earrings when Melobius first entered the house, and he grabbed them out of her ears.

[20] We got no pity from them, not in regard to the smallest portion of our property. Instead, they wronged us for our money, treating us as others would treat people out of anger at serious crimes. We, however, did not merit such treatment from the city: we had financed all our assigned choruses, we had paid many war-taxes, we behaved decently and did what we were told. We had not acquired a single enemy, but we had ransomed many an Athenian from the enemies of the city.[12] In these things they demanded that we behave differently as metics than they did as citizens. [21] For they drove many citizens into the hands of the enemy, and they killed many without just cause and denied them burial; many who possessed citizen rights they stripped of those rights, and they kept many men's daughters from their intended betrothals.[13]

[22] And they have sunk to such depths of audacity that they have come to offer their defense and say that they have done nothing evil or shameful. I wish they were telling the truth, for I would have a considerable share of the benefits. [23] But in reality this is not their situation either in regard to the city or to me: for, as I said before, Eratosthenes killed my brother—not because he was personally wronged by him, not because he witnessed him committing a crime against the city, but because he was eagerly serving his own criminal nature. [24] I want to

bring him up here and question him, men of the jury. For this is my way
of thinking: I consider it impious even to discuss the defendant with
someone else for his benefit, but for his harm I consider it righteous and
pious even to address the man himself. So come up here, please, and
answer whatever I ask you.

[25] Did you arrest Polemarchus or not?

*Eratosthenes.* I did what I was ordered to do by the authorities,[14] because
  I was afraid.

Were you in the Council Hall when the discussion about us
  occurred?

*Eratosthenes.* I was.

Did you support those who urged our killing or oppose them?

*Eratosthenes.* I opposed them, so that you would not be killed.

Believing that we were suffering unjustly or justly?

*Eratosthenes.* Unjustly.

[26] So then, you most miserable of all men, you opposed the plan in
order to save us, but you took part in the arrests in order to kill us? And
when our safety was in the hands of the whole lot of you, you claim that
you opposed those who wanted to eliminate us, but when the decision
to save Polemarchus or not was in your hands alone, you dragged him
off to prison? So, for the fact that (as you say) you opposed the killing,
but were of no use, you are asking to be considered a good man, but for
the fact that you arrested Polemarchus and killed him you are asking
not to pay the penalty to me and to this jury?

[27] And in fact, if he is telling the truth when he claims that he opposed Polemarchus' killing, it is not reasonable to believe him when he
says that the task was assigned to him. For they certainly would not
have used the metics to test his trustworthiness. Who was less likely to
be given that order than the person who had argued against it and made
his position clear? For who was less likely to carry out the order than the
one who had opposed what they wanted done? [28] And on top of that,
I think the rest of the Athenians have sufficient cause to place blame for
past events on the Thirty; but as for the Thirty themselves, if they place
blame on their own group, how can you reasonably accept that? [29] If
there had been a more powerful authority in the city, by which the

Thirty had been ordered to kill people in violation of justice, then perhaps you might reasonably pardon Eratosthenes. But, as things are, who in the world will you punish, if the Thirty are going to be allowed to say that they did what the Thirty ordered?

[30] Further, it was not in Polemarchus' house but in the street—where it was possible to save him and do as they had voted—that Eratosthenes arrested Polemarchus and dragged him away. Now, you are angry at all those who entered your homes searching for you or one of your own. [31] And yet, if we have to pardon those who killed others to save themselves, they are the ones who deserve your forgiveness more: for they were at risk if they did not go where they were sent or if they caught people but denied it. Eratosthenes, on the other hand, could have said that he did not run into Polemarchus or that he did not see him: these statements could not be refuted or tested, and so, even if his enemies wanted to catch him lying, they could not.

[32] What you should have done, Eratosthenes, if you really were a good man, is inform those who were going to lose their lives unjustly, rather than arresting those who were to be unjustly killed. But what you actually did proves that you were not distressed but pleased at what happened. [33] Thus these men must cast their votes based on your actions rather than your words, taking what they know to have happened as proof of what was said in that meeting, since it is not possible to provide witnesses to it. For not only were we not allowed to be present there, but we were not even allowed to be in our own homes; thus it is open to them, having done the city all possible harm, to say about themselves nothing but good. [34] However, I am not evading this point; I stipulate, if you like, that you opposed the killing. But I wonder what in the world you did when you supported something, seeing that you killed Polemarchus when you claim to have opposed it!

Tell me now: what would you do if you were his brothers or his sons? Would you vote to acquit? You see, men of the jury, Eratosthenes must prove one of two things: either that he did not arrest Polemarchus or that he did so with justification. But he has admitted that he arrested Polemarchus unjustly, and thus he has made your decision regarding him an easy one.

[35] Furthermore, many people, both citizens and foreigners, have come here to find out what judgment you will render on the defendants. Those who are your fellow citizens will leave knowing either that they will pay the penalty for any crimes they commit, or that, if they achieve their aims, they will be tyrants of the city, while if they fail, they will have the same rights as you do. Those who are foreigners residing in Athens will know whether they are wrong to banish the Thirty from their cities, or right. For, in point of fact, if the actual victims catch the perpetrators and let them go, then certainly the foreigners will conclude that they are wasting their time watching out for you. [36] Isn't this strange? When those generals who won a naval battle asserted that they had been unable to recover their men from the sea due to a storm,[15] you punished them with death, believing that you had to obtain satisfaction from them for the virtue of the dead. The defendants, however, as private citizens did everything they could to make us lose a naval battle,[16] and then, when they came to power, admittedly and of their own free will put many citizens to death without trial.[17] Are you not obliged to punish them and their children with the most extreme sanctions?

[37] As far as I am concerned, men of the jury, I think the charges should be sufficient: for I think it is necessary to prosecute until the defendant is deemed to have committed acts meriting death. This, you see, is the most extreme penalty we can inflict upon them. So I do not know why it is necessary to make a long speech in prosecuting men like this, who could not pay a sufficient penalty even by dying twice for every one of their deeds. [38] In fact, it is not even fitting for him to do what has become customary practice in this city; namely, to make no defense to the charges but use deception as defendants sometimes do by mentioning other things about themselves, demonstrating to you that they are good soldiers or that they captured many enemy ships when they were serving as trierarchs[18] or made enemy cities friendly. [39] Command him to show you where they killed as many of the enemy as of their fellow citizens, or where they captured as many ships as they betrayed of their own, or which city they acquired as great as yours which they made their slave. [40] But, he will respond, they stripped the enemy of as many weapons as they took from you[19]—but, he will say, they captured walls as great as those of their own homeland which

they razed to the ground. These are the people who even dismantled the border fortresses around Attica, and who made it clear to you that they were stripping the Peiraeus of its defenses not because the Spartans ordered them to but because they thought their own regime would thus be more secure.

[41] I have often marvelled at the audacity of those who defend Eratosthenes, except when I consider that it is characteristic of the same people to commit all sorts of evils themselves and to praise similar individuals. [42] You see, this is not the first time that he has acted against the interests of you the people. During the regime of the Four Hundred[20] as well, after attempting to set up an oligarchy in the camp,[21] he fled the Hellespont—a trierarch abandoning his ship!— along with Iatrocles and others whose names I do not need to mention. And when he arrived here, he worked against the proponents of democracy. I will now provide you with witnesses to these events.

*Witnesses*[22]

[43] His career in the meantime I will pass over. But after the sea battle occurred and disaster befell the city,[23] while the democracy was still in power, five men were appointed "ephors" by the so-called "comrades":[24] from there they started the civil strife. The ephors were organizers of the citizens, leaders of the conspirators, and opponents of you the people; and among them were Eratosthenes and Critias. [44] These men put tribe-leaders in charge of the tribes, and they communicated to them whatever was to be approved by vote and whoever was to be elected to office; and whatever else they wanted to do, they had the power to do it. You were thus being plotted against not by the enemy alone, but also by these men, your fellow citizens, so that you could pass no useful measure and lacked many necessities. [45] For they knew well that they would be unable to prevail otherwise, but if you were doing badly, they could. And they believed that you were so eager to rid yourselves of your present misfortunes that you would pay no heed to those to come.

[46] Now, as to the fact that Eratosthenes was one of the ephors, I will bring witnesses before you—not those who conspired with him at the time (for that would be impossible), but those who heard it from

Eratosthenes himself. [47] And yet if those co-conspirators had any sense, they would testify against them and severely chastise their teachers in crime; and, if they had any sense, they would not abide by their oaths to the detriment of their fellow citizens but would break them with ease for the benefit of the city. That is all I have to say regarding them. Please call my witnesses. And you, step up.

*Witnesses*

[48] You have heard the witnesses. And finally, when Eratosthenes took office, he participated in nothing good but in plenty of other things. And yet, if he really were a good man, first, he should not have held office in violation of the law;[25] second, he should have turned informant and told the Council[26] that all the impeachments[27] were false and that Batrachus and Aeschylides[28] were not giving truthful information but were bringing impeachments fabricated by the Thirty and concocted in order to harm their fellow citizens. [49] And in fact, men of the jury, all those who were hostile to you the people were no worse off by keeping silent, for there were others who were saying and doing the worst possible things for the city. And as for all those who claim they were friendly to you, how is it that they did not show it at the time by making the best proposals and by deterring wrongdoers?

[50] Maybe Eratosthenes will say that he was afraid, and for some of you that will be sufficient. But he must take care not to come across in his speech as having opposed the Thirty. Otherwise, it will be immediately obvious that he agreed with their policy and that he enjoyed sufficient influence that he could oppose them without suffering at their hands. He should have displayed this enthusiasm for your salvation, and not for Theramenes, who had committed numerous offenses against you. [51] But Eratosthenes considered the city his enemy and your enemies his friends. I will furnish numerous proofs for both these statements, and I will show you that their disagreements with each other occurred not for your benefit but for their own, to determine who would conduct affairs and rule the city. [52] For if they were engaged in conflict on behalf of the wronged, where was a better opportunity for a man in a position of power to make a display of his goodwill than after Thrasybulus had seized Phyle?[29] But, instead of announcing—or, better yet,

doing—anything good for the men at Phyle, Eratosthenes went with his colleagues to Salamis and Eleusis, dragged 300 citizens off to prison, and, on a single ballot, condemned them all to death.[30]

[53] And when we came to the Peiraeus and the troubles were over[31] and negotiations regarding a reconciliation were underway, both sides[32] held out significant hope that an agreement would be reached, and they showed it. The men of the Peiraeus, although they held the upper hand, allowed the other side to withdraw. [54] The latter returned to the city and expelled the Thirty, with the exceptions of Pheidon and Eratosthenes. As magistrates they elected those most hostile to the Thirty, figuring that those who hated the Thirty would rightly be friendly to the men of the Peiraeus.[33] [55] These included Pheidon, Hippocles, Epichares of Lamptrae, and others who were considered the biggest opponents of Charicles and Critias and their faction. But when they took office, they made the civil war between the men of the city and the men of the Peiraeus much worse. [56] By this they clearly showed that they were not fighting for the men of the Peiraeus or for those who had been unjustly killed, and that what grieved them was not those who had died or those who were about to die, but rather those who were more powerful and getting rich more quickly than they were.

[57] When they gained office and took control of the city, they fought against both sides: against the Thirty, who had committed every evil act, and against you, who had suffered them all. And yet it was clear to all that if the exile of the Thirty was just, your exile was unjust, but if yours was just, then theirs was unjust, for it was their responsibility for those actions and no others which got them expelled from the city. [58] So you should be extremely angry that Pheidon, who was elected in order to reconcile you and bring you home, instead took part in the same acts as Eratosthenes and shared the same opinion: he was ready to use you to injure those more powerful than they were, but, although your exile was unjust, he was unwilling to hand the city back to you. Instead, he went to Sparta and tried to persuade the Spartans to launch a campaign by misinforming them that the city would fall into the hands of the Boeotians and saying other things that he thought would prove especially persuasive.

[59] Unable to achieve these goals, either because the omens were unfavorable[34] or because the Spartans were unwilling, he secured a loan of 100 talents in order to pay mercenaries, and he asked for Lysander to take command, since Lysander was very friendly to the oligarchy and very hostile to Athens, and he especially detested the men of the Peiraeus. [60] Having hired all sorts of men in order to destroy the city, having brought on board other cities and finally the Spartans and as many of their allies as they could persuade, they prepared not to reconcile the city but to eradicate it, which they would have done if not for some good men. And you must show that you will repay those men's favor by punishing their enemies. [61] You know these things yourselves, and I do not see why I have to call witnesses, but I will all the same; for I need to rest, and some of you will prefer hearing the same story from as many people as possible.

*Witnesses*

[62] Let me now inform you about Theramenes in as few words as possible. I ask you now to listen both for my sake and for the city's. And let it not occur to anyone that I am prosecuting Theramenes when Eratosthenes is the one on trial, for I hear that Eratosthenes is going to say in his defense that he was Theramenes' friend and shared in Theramenes' policy. [63] Indeed, I am quite sure that, if he had been an associate of Themistocles, he would claim that he helped build the walls[35]—since in fact, as an associate of Theramenes, he helped tear them down. But I do not consider these men equally worthy. Themistocles built the walls over the objections of the Spartans; Theramenes deceived his fellow citizens and demolished them. [64] Things have thus turned out for the city to be the opposite of what was reasonable. For the friends of Theramenes ought to have died along with him, unless there happened to be one of them who opposed his policy. But now I see people staking their defenses on him, and his associates vying for honors, as though he had been responsible for numerous benefits instead of great evils.

[65] First of all, Theramenes was the man most responsible for the earlier oligarchy, by persuading you to elect the government of the Four Hundred.[36] His father, too, was one of the Commissioners[37] and shared

the same policy; and Theramenes himself, who was deemed most friendly to the revolution, was chosen general by them. [66] And as long as he was held in high esteem, he showed himself faithful to the city. But when he saw Peisander and Callaeschrus and others rising above him, and you the people no longer willing to listen to them, at that point, because he was jealous of them and afraid of you, he joined forces with Aristocrates.[38] [67] Wishing to appear trustworthy to you the people, he prosecuted his closest friends, Antiphon and Archeptolemus, and got them executed;[39] he stooped to such evil that at the same time he reduced you to slavery to keep faith with them and killed his friends to keep faith with you.

[68] Held in esteem and deemed worthy of the highest honors, having proclaimed that he himself would save the city, he himself destroyed it. He claimed to have discovered a great and valuable stratagem—he promised to bring about peace without giving hostages or leveling the walls or surrendering the fleet—but he refused to tell it to anyone and urged you to trust him. [69] And you, men of Athens, while the Council of the Areopagus was taking measures for your safety and many were speaking against Theramenes, although you knew that the rest of mankind keeps secrets because of their enemies, but that he would not even tell his fellow citizens what he intended to say to the enemy, you nonetheless entrusted to him your country, your children, your wives, and yourselves.

[70] But he delivered on none of his promises. So strong was his conviction that the city had to become powerless and weak that he persuaded you to do what the enemy never intended and the citizens never expected. He was not compelled by the Spartans; he invited them to take down the Peiraeus walls and to dismantle the existing constitution— for he knew well that, unless you were deprived of all hope, you would waste no time in punishing him. [71] And finally, men of the jury, he would not allow the Assembly to meet until he had carefully awaited what they[40] called "the right time," and he had summoned Lysander's fleet from Samos, and the enemy was encamped in our territory.

[72] Then, when these things were in place and Lysander and Philochares and Miltiades were present,[41] they held a meeting of the

Assembly concerning the constitution, with the purpose that no speaker would oppose or threaten them, and you would not choose what was best for the city but would ratify what they decreed. [73] Theramenes stood up and instructed you to entrust the city to thirty men and to make use of the constitution being set forth by Dracontides. Even in such a position as you found yourselves, you nonetheless shouted that you would not do it; for you realized that on that day in the Assembly you were deciding between slavery and freedom. [74] Then Theramenes said, men of the jury (and I will present you yourselves as my witnesses to these events), that your noise made no difference to him, since he knew many Athenians who were working for goals similar to his, and his proposals had the backing of Lysander and the Spartans. Lysander stood up after him and said, among many other things, that he held you in violation of the truce and that it would not be a question of your constitution but of your safety, if you did not do as Theramenes commanded.

[75] All those in the Assembly who were good men recognized the plot and the compulsion they were under. Some of them stayed there and kept quiet; others got up and left, content at least in the knowledge that their votes had done no harm to the city. But a few worthless individuals with bad intentions voted as they were ordered. [76] The order had been given to vote for ten men whom Theramenes indicated, ten whom those already appointed as ephors[42] commanded, and ten from those present in the Assembly. They viewed you as so weak, and thought themselves so strong, that they determined the Assembly's agenda in advance.

[77] And you don't have to take my word for these things; you can take his! Everything I have just said, Theramenes said when he was making his defense before the Council.[43] He reproached those who had been exiled from the city on the ground that they had been restored to their homes thanks to him, while the Spartans had not cared a bit; and he reproached those who participated in the regime on the ground that they were treating him so poorly despite the fact that he was responsible for everything that had been done in the ways I mentioned earlier, had proven his trustworthiness many times with his actions, and had received oaths from them.

[78] Theramenes is responsible for all these evil and shameful acts and more, past and recent, small and great; and they will have the gall to advertise themselves as his friends, although Theramenes died not for you but for his own vices—a fitting penalty under the oligarchy (for he had already brought it down), which would have been equally fitting under the democracy. Twice he reduced you to slavery, scorning what was present, longing for what was absent, and employing the most attractive slogan[44] to establish himself as a teacher of the most horrendous deeds.

[79] Concerning Theramenes I have brought sufficient accusations. For you, though, the time has come to remove pardon and pity from your minds and to punish Eratosthenes and his colleagues. Do not be stronger than the foe in battle but weaker than your enemies at the ballot. [80] Do not feel more gratitude toward the defendants for what they promise to do than anger for what they have done. Do not plot against the Thirty when they are absent but let them go free when they are present. And do not render worse assistance to yourselves than Fortune did when she handed the defendants over to the city.

[81] These are my accusations against Eratosthenes, and against his friends, the men upon whom his defense will rely and with whom he has committed these acts. In fact, though, it is not an equal contest between the city and Eratosthenes: he was both prosecutor and judge of the condemned,[45] while now we play the roles of prosecution and defense. [82] Furthermore, the defendants executed innocent men without trial, while you consider deserving of a lawful trial those who destroyed the city, upon whom, even if you were willing to break the law, you could not impose a punishment worthy of their crimes against the city. For what could they suffer which would constitute the fitting penalty for their actions? [83] If you were to execute them and their children, would we receive sufficient recompense for the killings of our fathers and sons and brothers whom they put to death without trial? What if you were to confiscate their visible property?[46] Would that set things right for the city from which they have stolen so much, or for the individuals whose houses they looted? [84] Since, then, even if you did all these things, you could not punish the defendants sufficiently, how is it not shameful for you to omit any form of retribution whatsoever that someone wishes to exact from them?

I think Eratosthenes would have the gall to do anything: with a jury composed of none other than his own victims, he has now come to defend himself before the very people who witnessed his depravity; so great is either his contempt for you or his trust in others. [85] You must be attentive to both these possibilities. Consider that the defendants could not have done what they did without the cooperation of others, nor would they now have ventured to come forward unless they expected to be rescued by the same people. And these men have come not to render assistance to the defendants,[47] but in the belief that, if you get hold of those responsible for the greatest evils and acquit them, they themselves will enjoy considerable amnesty for the acts they have already committed and license to do whatever they want in the future.

[86] We should also wonder at the men who will serve as advocates for the defense. Will they base their pleas on their own noble character, declaring that their virtue carries more weight than the depravity of the defendants? (I wish they were as eager to save the city as the defendants are to destroy it!) Or will they give skillful speeches for the defense and declare that the defendants' actions were of great value? Regardless, not one of them has ever endeavored to speak on your behalf or in the interests of justice.

[87] Their witnesses are also worth observing: in testifying for the defense, they denounce themselves. They obviously think you are extremely forgetful and stupid, if they believe that you the people will let them rescue the Thirty with impunity, when thanks to Eratosthenes and his colleagues it was dangerous even to attend the funerals of the dead.[48] [88] And yet, if these men are saved, they could destroy the city again; but those whom they killed have reached the end of their lives and are past taking vengeance upon their enemies. Is it not terrible that, while the friends of those unjustly executed risked dying along with them, the funerals of those who destroyed the city will obviously be well attended, since so many are prepared to come to their aid?

[89] Further, I consider it much easier to respond on behalf of what you suffered than to defend what these men have done. And yet they say that Eratosthenes has committed the fewest evils of any of the Thirty, and for that reason they think he should be saved; but he has committed the most crimes against you of all the rest of the Greeks, and for that

they do not think he ought to die? [90] You must indicate what opinion you have concerning these matters. If you convict the defendant, your anger at his actions will be clear. But if you acquit him, you will be seen as yearning for the same things as the defendants, and you will not be able to say that you were merely following the Thirty's orders, [91] because now no one is forcing you to vote contrary to your judgment.[49] I therefore counsel you not to acquit the defendants and thereby convict yourselves. Nor should you consider the ballot secret:[50] for you will be making your verdict clear to the city.

[92] Before I step down, I want to say a few words to both groups, the men of the city and the men of the Peiraeus, so that you have as warnings in your minds as you cast your votes the disasters you suffered because of these men. First, those of you who are men of the city, consider that you were ruled so harshly by the defendants that you were compelled to fight against your brothers, sons, and fellow citizens. Although you lost the war, you stand on equal footing with the victors; while if you had won, you would be slaves to the defendants. [93] And the defendants would have increased their own estates as a result of their activities, while yours have been diminished by civil war. They did not see fit for you to share their profits, but they did force you to share their discredit; they held you in such contempt that they endeavored to win your trust without sharing their benefits, thinking that you would be friendly to them if they let you share in their disgrace.

[94] Now, to repay them for this, take heart, to the extent that you can, and exact vengeance for yourselves and for the men of the Peiraeus. Bear in mind that you used to be ruled by these utter degenerates; bear in mind that now you live as citizens, fight the enemy, and deliberate for the good of the city with the best of men. Remember the mercenaries whom the defendants installed on the Acropolis as defenders of their regime and your enslavement. [95] There are many more things I could say to you, but this is enough.

Those of you who are men of the Peiraeus, first remember your weapons: after fighting many battles in foreign territory, you had those weapons taken away not by the enemy, but by the defendants, in time of peace. Then recall that you were drummed out of the city that your fathers handed down to you; and then, when you were in exile, they ordered the cities to surrender you. [96] To repay them for this, express your anger, just as you did when you were in exile. Remember as well the other evils you suffered at their hands: they snatched up some from the agora and others from the temples, and violently put them to death; still others they dragged from the arms of their children, parents, and wives, and forced to become their own killers.[51] They did not even allow them to receive proper burial, believing their own regime to be more secure than divine retribution.

[97] Those of you who managed to escape death faced danger in many places and wandered into many cities, being drummed out everywhere;[52] you lacked basic necessities; some of you had left your children behind in a hostile homeland and others in foreign territory; and despite numerous opposition you arrived at the Peiraeus. Confronted by many grave dangers, you acquitted yourselves as noble men; you freed your children at home and restored to their country those abroad. [98] But if you had been unlucky and failed at these objectives, you would now be in exile, fearing that you would suffer as you did before. And, owing to the character of the defendants, neither temples nor altars, which offer sanctuary even to criminals, would have availed you, the victims. As for your children, those who were here would have suffered the hubris[53] of the defendants, and those in foreign lands would have been enslaved for petty debts, with no one to come to their aid.[54]

[99] But in fact I do not wish to speak of what would have happened, when I am unable to describe what the defendants have done: that would require not one prosecutor or two, but many. All the same, I am not lacking in zeal: on behalf of the temples, which the defendants either sold or befouled with their entrance; on behalf of the city, which they brought low; on behalf of the dockyards, which they demolished; and on behalf of the dead—since you could not defend them when they were alive, help them now that they are gone. [100] I believe that they are listening to us and will know it when you cast your votes, and, as they see it, those who acquit the defendants will have confirmed their death sentence, while those who punish the defendants will have taken revenge for them.[55]

I will end my prosecution here. You have heard; you have seen; you have suffered; you have them in your hands. Render your verdict.

# 2

# LYSIAS 13

*Against Agoratus*

## Introduction

In the winter of 405/4, the Athenians dispatched Theramenes to Sparta with the goal of bringing an end to the Peloponnesian War. He remained abroad for several months; when he returned, he was confronted by a group of democrats led by certain generals and taxiarchs and opposed to the terms of peace he brought back (§§5–16). In order to help ensure the ratification of the treaty, Theramenes and his fellow oligarchs hatched a plot against the democratic leaders, enlisting a man named Agoratus to serve as informer (§§17–18).

In order that Agoratus appear coerced and therefore trustworthy, the oligarchs first sent his friend Theocritus to a meeting of the Council of 500. Theocritus informed the Council of a conspiracy against the state; the Council responded by issuing a decree authorizing the arrest of Agoratus (§§19–22). A first attempt to apprehend Agoratus was foiled by men who volunteered to stand surety for him, but the second attempt succeeded. Agoratus was then brought before the Council, where he disclosed the names of his sureties, of the generals and taxiarchs who led the resistance to Theramenes' proposed treaty, and of certain other citizens (§§23–30). The men denounced by Agoratus were arrested, tried by the Council of 500 in the presence of the Thirty Tyrants, and executed (§§34–43).

Around 398 (§83 with note), the family of the taxiarch Dionysodorus prosecuted Agoratus for his killing, using the procedure called *apagôgê* (summary arrest: §§85–87). Dionysius, the victim's brother, brought the indictment and probably served (at

least nominally) as lead prosecutor. The man who delivered
Lysias 13, whose name we do not know, was the victim's first cousin,
as well as his wife's brother (§§1, 41). The outcome of the trial is
unknown.

The prosecution of Agoratus violated the Amnesty of 403. The
terms of the amnesty shielded informers, allowing homicide prosecutions only against those who had killed with their own hands
(Part One, The Thirty Tyrants, p. 20). Yet Agoratus was clearly
accused of homicide as an informer (§2); and the Eleven, whose
jurisdiction included *apagôgê*, accepted the case against Agoratus,
requiring only that Dionysius alter the indictment so that it contained
the phrase "in the act" (§§85–87). In writing this speech, Lysias
clearly recognized the difficulty of proving that Agoratus, who was
on trial some five years after the death of Dionysodorus, had been
caught "in the act" of anything; he therefore resorts to contortions of
logic which are less than persuasive. But the fact that the Eleven
granted the trial of Agoratus despite the Amnesty of 403 shows that
the Athenians did not always obey the Amnesty to the letter and that
resentment against the former oligarchs and their followers remained
(cf. Lysias 16).

In the introduction (§§1–4) the speaker plays upon the jury's
presumed desire for revenge against the Thirty; he explains the
source of his personal hostility toward Agoratus, who caused the
death of Dionysodorus, his brother-in-law and cousin. The narration
(§§5–48) begins at the conclusion of the Peloponnesian War:
Cleophon, champion of the democracy, is contrasted with
Theramenes, leader of an oligarchic conspiracy (§§5–12). The
speaker goes on to relate the plot in which the oligarchic conspirators
suborn Agoratus and procure the executions of the generals and
taxiarchs (§§13–42). At §§43–48, where the narration ends, the
speaker discusses the further crimes of the Thirty, for which he holds
Agoratus responsible, since Agoratus set their regime in motion.

The proofs occupy §§49–91. First (§§49–57) comes a refutation
of Agoratus' anticipated arguments. Documents prove that Agoratus denounced the generals and taxiarchs; Agoratus cannot plead
duress, since he had the opportunity to flee; blame cannot be thrown

onto Menestratus. Next (§§58–82) the speaker attacks Agoratus' character. He is compared negatively with one of his sureties, Aristophanes. His victims were much better men than he and his brothers, all infamous malefactors of servile origin. His claim to have acquired citizenship as a reward for the assassination of Phrynichus is false. When he attempted to join the democrats at Phyle, he was rebuffed.

Lastly, the speaker anticipates and rejects Agoratus' arguments that the prosecution is too late, that the phrase "in the act" does not apply, and that Agoratus is covered by the Amnesty of 403 (§§83–90). The proof section concludes with an appeal for the death penalty (§91).

In the conclusion (§§92–97), the speaker tells the jury that it is their duty as well as his to punish Agoratus. He reminds them of their sufferings under the Thirty and places the blame on Agoratus. He warns them against voting to acquit and thereby aligning themselves with the Thirty; instead they should convict Agoratus, thus avenging the dead and gaining a reputation for justice.

### Against Agoratus

[1] It befits all of you, men of the jury, to avenge the men who died because they were loyal to you the people; and it befits me especially, since Dionysodorus was my brother-in-law[1] and cousin. I therefore have the same hatred for the defendant Agoratus that you the people have. He committed such deeds that I have good reason to hate him now, and you, God willing,[2] will justly punish him. [2] During the reign of the Thirty, he killed my brother-in-law Dionysodorus and many others whose names you will hear, men loyal to you the people, by informing against them. In doing so, he inflicted a great private loss upon me and each of Dionysodorus' relatives, and publicly he did the entire city no little harm, in my opinion, by robbing it of men such as these. [3] So for my part, men of the jury, I consider it just and righteous for me and for all of you to take vengeance to the extent that each of us is able; and if we did so, I think we would be treated better by both gods and men.

[4] You must hear the whole thing from the beginning, men of Athens, so that you may know, first, how your democracy was overthrown and by whom; and second, how these men died at the hands of Agoratus, and in particular, what injunctions they issued when they were about to die. If you possessed accurate knowledge of all these things, you would more gladly and righteously convict the defendant Agoratus. I will begin my narration of events from the point where it is easiest for me to instruct you and for you to learn.

[5] Not long after your ships were destroyed[3] and things in the city had become less secure, the Spartan ships arrived at the Peiraeus, and at the same time peace negotiations were opened with the Spartans. [6] At this time, those who desired a revolution in the city were conspiring, thinking that they had hit upon an ideal opportunity and that this was the exact time to establish the government that they wanted. [7] As they saw it, the only things standing in their way were the leaders of the people and the generals and taxiarchs.[4] So they wanted to get these men out of the way somehow, in order to accomplish their desires with ease.

First they attacked Cleophon[5] in the following manner. [8] When the first meeting of the Assembly on the topic of the peace was held, the ambassadors from Sparta said that the Spartans were prepared to make peace on condition that a portion of the Long Walls be demolished, to the extent of ten stades on each side.[6] At that time, men of Athens, you could not bear to hear of demolishing the walls; and Cleophon stood up and responded, on behalf of all of you, that there was no way that could be done.

[9] After that, Theramenes, who was plotting against you the people,[7] stood up and said that if you elected him ambassador with full powers to negotiate peace, he would see to it that you would not have to destroy any part of the walls or diminish the city in any other way; he told you that he thought he could even get some other benefit for the city from the Spartans. [10] You believed him and elected him ambassador with full powers—the same man whom you had rejected the previous year at his candidacy examination when he had been elected general,[8] believing him to be unfriendly to you the people. [11] At any rate, he went to Sparta and stayed there for a long time, leaving you behind under siege,

knowing that you the people were in dire straits and that many of you lacked necessities on account of the war and its disasters. He thought that if he kept you in the condition you were in, you would be gladly willing to make peace on any terms at all.

[12] The men who remained here plotting to overthrow the democracy then put Cleophon on trial. The pretext was that he had not returned to camp to rest,[9] but the truth was that he had spoken on your behalf against destroying the walls. So those who wanted to set up an oligarchy stacked the jury,[10] went into court, and got him executed on this pretext.

[13] Later, Theramenes arrived from Sparta. Some of the generals and taxiarchs, among them Strombichides[11] and Dionysodorus, approached him, as did some other citizens friendly to you (as they would later show), and took great offense. For he had come bearing a peace treaty with which we are all familiar from experience: we lost many good citizens, and we ourselves were driven into exile by the Thirty. [14] Among its terms was, in place of the dismantling of the Long Walls to a distance of ten stades, the demolition of the entire Long Walls; and instead of getting some other benefit for the city, we had to surrender our fleet and take down the wall around the Peiraeus.

[15] These men, witnessing what was called by the name "peace" but was in fact the overthrow of the democracy, refused to allow this to occur. It was not that they took pity on the walls, men of Athens, if they were to fall, or mourned the loss of the ships, if they were to be handed over to the Spartans: these things did not concern them more than each one of you. [16] What they realized was that in this manner you the people would be overthrown. It is not (as some say) that they were not eager for peace; rather, they wanted to make a peace that was better for the people of Athens than this one. They thought they could do it, and they would have, if they had not been destroyed by Agoratus here.

[17] Theramenes and the rest of the men conspiring against you realized that there were men who were going to prevent the overthrow of the democracy and take a stand on behalf of freedom. So they chose, before the Assembly could meet to debate the peace,[12] to endanger these men by slander, so that there would be no one in the Assembly to oppose them on behalf of you the people. [18] This is the plot they

hatched. They persuaded the defendant Agoratus to inform against the generals and taxiarchs. He had absolutely nothing on them, men of Athens. (Certainly they were not so lacking in intelligence and friends that, when they were engaged in such serious business, they would call upon Agoratus, a slave and the descendant of slaves, as a trustworthy ally!)[13] But the conspirators decided that Agoratus would make a suitable informer.

[19] They wanted him to appear to be informing against his will, rather than voluntarily, so that his denunciation would seem more credible. But I think you will realize from what happened that he informed willingly. They sent into the Council Theocritus, called the son of Elaphostictus.[14] This Theocritus was a comrade and close friend of Agoratus. [20] The Council sitting before the establishment of the Thirty had been corrupted and was, as you know, extremely eager for oligarchy. Here's the proof: most of the men serving on that Council also served on the subsequent Council under the Thirty. Why am I telling you this? So that you know that all the decrees which came through that Council were passed not with good intentions toward you but for the overthrow of your democracy, and so that you pay attention to them as such.

[21] So Theocritus went before that Council, in secret, and informed them that men were gathering in opposition to the government then being formed. He said that he would not mention specific names, since he had sworn the same oaths as the men in question; there were others who would name names, but he would never do so. [22] And yet, if his denunciation were not planned, how would the Council not have forced him to name names rather than making a denunciation without names? As it was, though, the following decree was issued.

*Decree*

[23] When this decree had been passed, chosen members of the Council went down to the Peiraeus to get Agoratus; they found him in the agora[15] and sought to take him away. But Nicias and Nicomenes[16] and some other bystanders, seeing that things in the city were not going as well as they could, refused to let them seize Agoratus. They rescued

Agoratus from arrest, offered to stand surety for him, and agreed to bring him before the Council. [24] The councillors wrote down the names of the sureties who were obstructing the arrest, then went back to the city.

Agoratus and his sureties went to sit at the altar on Munychia,[17] and when they had taken their seats, they debated what they should do. The sureties and everybody else thought they should get Agoratus out of the way as quickly as possible. [25] They brought two boats to anchor along shore, and they begged Agoratus by all means to leave Athens. They volunteered to sail with him until things calmed down; they told him that, if he were brought before the Council, he might be tortured and forced to give the names of whichever Athenians were suggested to him by those who wanted to work some evil in the city.

[26] They made these requests and had prepared boats, and they were ready to sail away with him; but Agoratus here was unwilling to listen to them. And yet, Agoratus, unless some arrangement had been made for you and you trusted that you would suffer no harm, why would you not leave town? Boats were prepared, and your sureties were ready to set sail with you. You still could have done it: the Council did not have control over you yet. [27] But in fact the situation for you and for your sureties was not the same. First of all, they were Athenian citizens, so they had no fear of being tortured.[18] Second, they were ready to leave their homeland and sail away with you, believing that this would be better than having many good citizens unjustly destroyed by you. But as for you, first, you risked torture if you stayed behind; and second, you would not be leaving your homeland.[19] [28] Thus in every way it benefited you more than them to sail away—unless you had something to rely on. Now you pretend you were unwilling, but you willingly killed many good Athenians. And as to the fact that it was all set up as I say, there are witnesses, and the actual decree of the Council will bear witness against him.

*Witnesses; Decree*

[29] So when this decree was passed and the men from the Council came to Munychia, Agoratus voluntarily got up from the altar; and yet now he says he was torn away by force. [30] And when they were

brought before the Council, Agoratus listed first the names of his sureties, then the names of the generals and taxiarchs, and then the names of some other citizens. This was the start of the whole evil business. I think even he will admit that he listed these names; if not, I will catch him lying in the act.[20] Now answer me.

*Cross-Examination*

[31] They wanted him, men of the jury, to list the names of even more men: the Council was so utterly eager to work some evil that they decided Agoratus had not yet told the whole truth in his accusations. Now, all these men he denounced voluntarily, under no duress. [32] And when the Assembly met in the theater on Munychia,[21] some people were so strongly concerned that a denunciation of the generals and taxiarchs take place in the Assembly as well (for the others the denunciation in the Council alone was deemed sufficient) that they brought Agoratus there before the Assembly too. Answer me, Agoratus; I don't think you will deny what you did in the presence of all Athenians.

*Cross-Examination*

[33] He admits it himself; but all the same the decrees of the Assembly will be read to you as well.

*Decrees*

So, then, I think you know pretty well that Agoratus here listed the names of those men, both the ones in the Council and the ones in the Assembly, and that he is their killer. But I think I can demonstrate to you in brief that he was the cause of all the city's ills, and that not a single person should pity him. [34] When the men denounced by Agoratus had been arrested and imprisoned, at that point Lysander came sailing into your harbors, your ships were surrendered to the Spartans, the walls were demolished, the Thirty came to power[22]—in short, what conceivable disaster did not befall the city? [35] And when the Thirty had been installed, they immediately put these men on trial in the Council, although the Assembly had decreed that they be tried "in a jury-court, by a jury of 2,000." Please read the decree.

*Decree*

[36] Now, if they had been tried in a jury-court, they would easily have been acquitted, for you had all realized by that point that the city was in such deep trouble that you could no longer do anything to help. As it happened, however, they brought them to trial before the Council sitting under the Thirty. The kind of trial that followed, you yourselves know. [37] The Thirty were seated on the benches where the members of the Executive Committee now take their seats.[23] Two tables were set up in front of the Thirty. The councillors had to cast their votes not into urns,[24] but in the open, onto the tables: votes to convict went on the farther table, votes to acquit on the nearer, so how could any of the defendants possibly be acquitted? [38] To put it briefly, all those who went into the Council House to be tried were condemned to death, and not a single person was acquitted except this man Agoratus: they let him off as a benefactor. In order that you may know how many people met their deaths at his hands, I want to read you their names.

*Names*

[39] When the death sentence had been passed on them, men of the jury, and they had to die, they summoned people to the prison: one man sent for his sister, another for his mother, another for his wife, another for whatever female relative he had, so that they could say their last good-byes to their families before they died. [40] In particular, Dionysodorus summoned to the prison my sister, who was his wife. She got the message and came, dressed in a black cloak, which made sense, given that her husband had fallen victim to such disaster. [41] In the presence of my sister, Dionysodorus disposed of his estate as he saw fit; concerning the defendant Agoratus, he named him responsible for his death, and he enjoined me and his brother Dionysius here and all his friends to get revenge on Agoratus for him. [42] And, believing that his wife was pregnant by him, he enjoined her, if she bore a child, to tell it when it was born that Agoratus had killed its father and to command it to take vengeance for him upon Agoratus as his killer. To prove that I am telling the truth, I will now bring forward witnesses to these events.

*Witnesses*

[43] These men, then, men of Athens, were denounced by Agoratus and executed. I think you know pretty well that, once the Thirty got them out of the way, many terrible things befell the city afterward; because he killed these men, the defendant is reponsible for all those things. Now, it grieves me to recount the disasters which befell the city, [44] but I have to do it, men of the jury, at the present moment, so that you know exactly how much Agoratus deserves your pity. You know, of course, about the citizens who were taken from Salamis, how many and how good they were, and what sort of doom they met at the hands of the Thirty. And you know about the men of Eleusis, that many of them met this same disastrous end.[25] You also remember the men here in Athens who were dragged off to prison on account of private feuds. [45] They had done the city no wrong, yet they were forced to die the most shameful and dishonorable of deaths. Some of them left behind elderly parents, who expected that their children would support them in their old age and bury them when they died. Others left behind unmarried sisters,[26] and still others left little children still in need of much care.

[46] What sort of opinion, men of the jury, do you think they have of Agoratus? How do you think they would cast their votes, if it were up to them, robbed as they were of the sweetest things in life thanks to the defendant? You remember, too, how the walls were demolished, and the ships were surrendered to the enemy, and the dockyards were destroyed, and the Spartans occupied our Acropolis, and all the power of the city was broken, so that our city was no different from the lowliest. [47] On top of that, you lost your personal property, and finally, you were all collectively driven out of your homeland by the Thirty.[27] This is what those good men realized, men of the jury, when they refused to allow peace to be made. [48] They wanted to render a good service to the city; but you, Agoratus, killed them, by denouncing them for conspiring against the city, and you bear responsibility for all the evils that befell the city. Therefore, jurors, remember now both your own private misfortunes and the common misfortunes of the city, and punish the person responsible for them.

[49] I myself wonder, men of the jury, what in the world he will have the gall to say to you in his defense. He has to prove that he did not

denounce these men and is not responsible for their deaths, which he would never be able to prove. [50] First of all, the decrees of the Council and of the Assembly bear witness against him: they explicitly declare, "Regarding those whom Agoratus has denounced." Also, the verdict passed by the Thirty acquitting him explicitly reads, "because he was deemed to have given a truthful report." Read them, please.

*Decrees; Verdict*

[51] There is, therefore, no way he could prove that he did not make denunciations; what he has to do is show that he informed with justification, because he witnessed these men committing acts that were immoral and disadvantageous to you the people. But I don't think he would even try to prove that. Obviously, if they had done some harm to the Athenian people, the Thirty would not have feared the downfall of the democracy and avenged the democracy by executing them; actually, I think, they would have done the exact opposite!

[52] But perhaps he will claim that he committed all these evil deeds against his will. In my opinion, though, men of the jury, even if someone has committed such great evils as to defy exaggeration completely against his will, you should not on that account fail to retaliate. Also keep these facts in mind: Agoratus here, before he was brought before the Council, when he was sitting at the altar on Munychia, could have been rescued: boats had been prepared, and his sureties were ready to take the trip with him. [53] And further, Agoratus, if you had listened to them and had been willing to set sail with them, you would not have killed so many Athenians, willingly or not. But, as it turned out, you listened to those who persuaded you at that time, and you expected to obtain a considerable reward from them by merely reporting the names of the generals and taxiarchs. For that you deserve no pardon from us, because the men you killed received none from you. [54] Now, Hippias of Thasos and Xenophon of Curium[28] were summoned before the Council on the same charge as the defendant, and they were executed—one, Xenophon, after being tortured on the rack, and Hippias just as he was. Since they had destroyed no Athenian, the Thirty did not deem them worthy of saving; but they let Agoratus go, because in their judgment he had done what they most wanted.

[55] I hear he is also going to throw some of the blame for these denunciations onto Menestratus. Here's how the Menestratus affair
happened. This Menestratus was denounced by Agoratus, arrested, and
thrown into prison. Hagnodorus of Amphitrope,[29] one of Menestratus'
fellow demesmen, was the brother-in-law of Critias, one of the Thirty.
When the Assembly was meeting in the theater on Munychia,[30]
Hagnodorus, wishing to save Menestratus while simultaneously destroying as many of the other denounced men as he could, brought
Menestratus before the Assembly; and they worked out a grant of
immunity for him as provided by the following decree.

*Decree*

[56] When this decree was passed, Menestratus turned informer and
added still more citizens to the list. So the Thirty let him go as they had
Agoratus, deciding that he had given a truthful report. Much later,
however, you got him in court on a homicide charge; you justly condemned him to death and handed him over to the executioner, and he
was nailed to the board.[31] [57] And if Menestratus got the death
penalty, surely Agoratus will be justly executed, since, by denouncing
Menestratus, he was responsible for Menestratus' death; and who bears
more responsibility for the deaths of those denounced by Menestratus
than the one who placed Menestratus under such duress?

[58] Not at all similar, it seems to me, was the behavior of Aristophanes
of Cholleidae, who stood surety for the defendant, provided the boats at
Munychia, and was ready to sail away with him.[32] Insofar as it was up to
him, Agoratus, you were saved, and you would not have killed a single
Athenian, nor would you yourself have confronted such dangers. [59] But,
as it was, you had the gall to denounce the man who saved your life; and,
by denouncing him, you killed both him and the rest of your sureties.
Since Aristophanes was not of pure Athenian descent, some people
wanted him tortured, and they convinced the Assembly to pass this decree.

*Decree*

[60] Afterwards, those who were conducting affairs at the time approached Aristophanes and asked him to make denunciations and save

himself rather than risking going to trial for usurpation of citizen rights and suffering the extreme sanction. He absolutely refused. So true was he to his fellow prisoners and to the people of Athens that he chose to die rather than to make denunciations and destroy people unjustly. [61] So, even though he was facing death because of you, Agoratus, this is how Aristophanes behaved. You, on the other hand, had no information on those men; but you were persuaded that if they were destroyed, you would get a share in the government then being formed, so you denounced and killed many good Athenians.

[62] Now I want to show you, men of the jury, what sort of men you were robbed of by Agoratus. If there were not so many of them, you would be able to hear about each of them individually; but, as it is, I will tell you about all of them collectively. Some of them served repeatedly as generals and handed the city over to their successors in command having made it greater. Others held other important offices and performed many trierarchies[33] without incurring a single shameful accusation from you. [63] Some of these men survived and were rescued. Even though the defendant tried to have them killed like the rest and a death sentence had been imposed upon them, Fortune and divine providence preserved them. They fled from here without being arrested or waiting to stand trial, returned from Phyle, and are honored by you as noble men.

[64] It is men like these whom Agoratus killed and drove into exile. And who is Agoratus? You should know that he is a slave and the descendant of slaves, so that you can see what sort of person committed these outrages against you. The defendant's father was Eumares, and Eumares was the property of Nicocles and Anticles. Would the witnesses please come forward?

*Witnesses*

[65] It would take considerable effort, men of the jury, to recount all the other evil and shameful practices of the defendant and his brothers. But as for his sycophancy[34]—all the private prosecutions he mounted as a sycophant, all the public lawsuits he brought, all the denunciations he made—I do not need to discuss these individually. You have all as a

group convicted him of sycophancy in both the Assembly and the courts and fined him countless drachmas;[35] [66] so on that count, at least, you have all given sufficient testimony. And, even though this is the sort of person he is, he has ventured to seduce the wives of citizens and to corrupt free women; he has been caught as a seducer, and the penalty for that is death.[36] To prove that I am telling the truth, call the witnesses.

*Witnesses*

[67] Agoratus, men of the jury, was one of four brothers. Of these, the eldest was caught by Lamachus in Sicily making secret signals to the enemy[37] and was nailed to the board.[38] The second brother kidnapped a slave from here and went to Corinth; he was then caught kidnapping a female slave from there and died incarcerated in prison. [68] The third brother was summarily arrested here by Phaenippides as a clothes-stealer;[39] you tried him in a jury-court, sentenced him to death, and handed him over to be nailed to the board. I think Agoratus himself will admit that I am telling the truth, and I will also provide you with witnesses.

*Witnesses*

[69] How, then, does it not befit all of you to convict the defendant? If each of his brothers was found deserving of death for only one offense, then surely, since Agoratus has committed many offenses, both publicly against the city and privately against each of you, for each of which the laws provide capital punishment, you absolutely must condemn him to death.

[70] Now, he is going to try to deceive you, men of the jury, by telling you that he assassinated Phrynichus during the reign of the Four Hundred: he claims that in return the Assembly made him an Athenian citizen.[40] This is a lie, men of the jury: Agoratus did not assassinate Phrynichus, and the Assembly did not make him an Athenian citizen. [71] Phrynichus, men of the jury, fell victim to a plot by the co-conspirators Thrasybulus of Calydon and Apollodorus of Megara.[41] They came upon him as he was walking; Thrasybulus hit Phrynichus and knocked him down, and Apollodorus didn't even touch him. At this point a commotion arose, and they ran away. Agoratus here had not been brought into

the plot, was not present, and had no knowledge of the affair. The decree itself will make it clear to you that I am telling the truth.

*Decree*[42]

[72] That Agoratus did not assassinate Phrynichus is clear from the decree itself. Nowhere does it provide that "Agoratus is to be an Athenian citizen," as it does for Thrasybulus and Apollodorus. And yet if Agoratus had assassinated Phrynichus, his grant of Athenian citizenship should have been inscribed on the same pillar as Thrasybulus' and Apollodorus'. But people got their names added onto the pillar as "benefactors" by giving money to the proposer. This decree will prove that I am telling the truth.

*Decree*

[73] The defendant, however, held you in such utter contempt that, although he was not an Athenian, he served as a juror, attended the Assembly, and brought all manner of public lawsuits, adding to his name that he was "from Anagyrous."[43]

There is still another important indication that he did not assassinate Phrynichus, for which act he claims to have been made an Athenian citizen. This Phrynichus established the Four Hundred, and when he was killed, the majority of the Four Hundred went into exile. [74] Do you think that if the Thirty and the then-sitting Council, who themselves had all been among those exiled Four Hundred, got their hands on Phrynichus' killer, they would have let him go or would have punished him for Phrynichus and for their own exile? I think they would have punished him.

[75] So if Agoratus pretends to have assassinated Phrynichus when he did not, as I assert, then he does wrong. If, however, you dispute this, Agoratus, and you claim that you did assassinate Phrynichus, then it is clear that you got yourself released from liability for Phrynichus with the Thirty by committing even greater evils against the people of Athens; for you will never persuade anyone that the Thirty would have let you off for killing Phrynichus unless you did great and irreparable harm to the Athenian people. [76] So if he claims to have assassinated

Phrynichus, keep these things in mind and punish him for what he did. If he denies it, ask him on what basis he claims to have been made an Athenian citizen. And, if he is unable to show you, punish him for serving as a juror, for sitting in the Assembly, and for launching sycophantic prosecutions of a number of people, attaching his name as that of an Athenian.

[77] I also hear that he is preparing to say in his defense that he went to Phyle and took part in the return from Phyle,[44] and that this is his most powerful argument. It happened like this. The defendant did go to Phyle; and yet how could there ever be a more foul human being? He knew that some of the men at Phyle were among those he had forced into exile, and still he had the gall to go to them. [78] As soon as they saw him, they placed him under arrest and immediately led him off for execution to the place where they cut the throats of the other thieves and criminals they apprehended. The general Anytus,[45] however, said they should not do it, telling them that they were not yet in a position to punish any of their enemies: for the time being they should keep calm, but if they ever returned home, then they could punish those who did them wrong. [79] By saying this, Anytus caused Agoratus to escape at Phyle: the men had to listen to their general if they were going to save themselves. There is something else. It will be clear that no one took meals with the defendant or shared a tent with him, nor did the taxiarch[46] station the defendant with his tribe; not a single person spoke to Agoratus, just as though he were accursed. Please call the taxiarch.

*Testimony*

[80] When the two sides were reconciled[47] and the men of the Peiraeus conducted their procession to the Acropolis, Aesimus[48] led the way, and the defendant was audacious enough to show up there too. He took up arms, came along, and marched in the parade with the hoplites toward the city. [81] But when they were at the gates and halted under arms before entering the city, Aesimus spotted him. He went up to him, grabbed his shield, flung it away, and told him to go to the crows,[49] saying that Agoratus, being a killer, could not take part in the procession to Athena. That is how he was kicked out of the procession by Aesimus. To prove that I am telling the truth, I will bring forth witnesses.

*Witnesses*

[82] This, men of the jury, is how he was treated by the hoplites both at Phyle and in the Peiraeus. Nobody spoke to him because he was a killer, and Anytus was the reason he was not executed. So if in his defense he brings up his trip to Phyle, you should retort by asking him if Anytus was responsible for saving his life when others were prepared to punish him, and if Aesimus flung away his shield and refused to allow him to participate in the procession.

[83] Do not, therefore, accept these assertions of his, and do not accept it if he claims that we are seeking to punish him long after the fact. I don't think there is any statute of limitations[50] for offenses such as these; I think that, whether someone seeks punishment immediately or after some time, the defendant has to show that he did not do what he is charged with. [84] So let Agoratus demonstrate either that he did not kill those men or that he killed them with justification because they were doing some harm to the Athenian people. And if he should have been punished long ago and we are late in punishing him, he gets the benefit of the time he lived when he did not deserve to, while the men he killed are no less dead.

[85] I hear he is also going to rely on the fact that the phrase "in the act"[51] has been added to the arrest warrant.[52] This, I think, is the silliest thing of all: the argument that without the addition of "in the act," he would be liable to summary arrest, but, since it was added, he thinks he gets some relief. All this amounts to is an admission that he did kill but was not "in the act," and a reliance on this argument—as though, if he was not "in the act," even though he did kill, he must be acquitted on that account. [86] It seems to me, at least, that the Eleven, who accepted this arrest warrant, did not think they were cooperating with Agoratus, who was even then relying on this argument. They were entirely correct to compel Dionysius, in making out the arrest warrant, to add the phrase "in the act." Really, how could he not be "in the act?" By denouncing individuals first in the presence of 500 people, then again in the presence of all Athenians,[53] he killed them, and he caused their deaths.

[87] Certainly, Agoratus, you don't think that "in the act" applies only if someone knocks a person down by striking him with a club or a knife,

since, by your reasoning, nobody will appear to have killed the men you denounced, for nobody struck them or cut their throats: they were forced to die by your denunciation. Is not, then, the person who is responsible for their deaths "in the act"? And who else is responsible but you, who denounced them? So how are you, the killer, not "in the act"?

[88] I hear that he also intends to discuss the oaths and the treaty, and to say that his trial violates the oaths and the treaty which we men of the Peiraeus concluded with the men of the city.[54] Well, by relying on these arguments, he practically admits to being a killer: he presents as obstacles the oaths or the treaty or the timing or the phrase "in the act," but, in regard to the actual issue, he has no confidence that he will mount a good defense. [89] But for you, men of the jury, it is not fitting to accept what he says about these things. Instead, make him defend himself by arguing that he made no denunications and that the men are not dead. Further, I believe that the oaths and the treaty have no bearing on us with regard to the defendant. The oaths, you see, were sworn between the men of the city and the men of the Peiraeus. [90] Thus, if the defendant had been in the city and we had been in the Peiraeus, the treaty would have some relation to him. But, as it is, he was in the Peiraeus, along with me and Dionysius and all these men who are seeking to punish him. Therefore, nothing stands in our way, since no oath was sworn by the men of the Peiraeus to the men of the Peiraeus.

[91] In every conceivable way, it seems to me, he deserves more than one death. He claims to have been adopted by the people, but he clearly abused the people—whom he claims as his father—by compromising and betraying the men who were making the people greater and more powerful. How would a person who beat his birth father and furnished him with none of life's necessities, and who stripped his adoptive father of the goods in his possession, not deserve to be punished with death on that account as well, in accordance with the law on abuse?[55]

[92] It befits all of you, men of the jury, to avenge those men, just as it befits each one of us. With their dying breaths they enjoined us and all their friends to get revenge for them on this man, Agoratus, as their killer, and to do him harm to whatever extent each of us could. So, if they have clearly done good for the city or for you the people, as you

yourselves agree, then by necessity you are all their friends and inti-
mates; and so they laid this injunction no more upon us than upon each
one of you. [93] Therefore it is neither right nor lawful for you to let
this man Agoratus go. Since, at the time they died, you were unable to
help them due to the circumstances, right now, men of Athens, now
when you are able, punish their killer.

And be mindful, men of Athens, that you do not perform the most
cruel act of all. You see, if you acquit this man Agoratus, that is not the
only thing you will accomplish: you will also, by the very same vote,
condemn to death those men whom you agree were friendly to you.[56]
[94] By letting go the man responsible for their deaths, you do nothing
other than determine that they met their deaths justly at his hands. This
would cause them the most terrible suffering of all, if the very people
whom they enjoined as their friends to avenge them were to cast the
same votes to condemn them as the Thirty did.

[95] By the Olympian gods, men of the jury, do not, in any way or
manner, condemn to death those men who did you many a good deed
and were killed for that very reason by the Thirty and by this man
Agoratus. Remember all those terrible things, both those common to
the city and those affecting you personally, which befell each of you
when those men died, and punish the person responsible. It has been
proven to you in all respects—based on the decrees, the denunciations,
and everything else—that Agoratus bears responsibility for their deaths.

[96] In addition, it also befits you to vote in opposition to the Thirty.
Those whom they sentenced to death, you should acquit; and those
whom they did not sentence to death, you should convict. The Thirty
condemned to death these men, who were your friends, and whom you
should acquit. Agoratus, though, they acquitted, because he was judged
to have destroyed these men eagerly; it befits you to convict him. [97]
Thus, if you vote in opposition to the Thirty, first, you are not voting
the same way as your enemies; second, you will have avenged your
friends; and third, you will be judged by all men to have cast a just and
righteous vote.

# 3

# LYSIAS 16

## For Mantitheus

### Introduction

An Athenian selected for public office had to undergo a candidacy examination called a *dokimasia* (often translated "scrutiny"). The candidate was asked (*Ath. Pol.* 55.3–4): "Who is your father and what is his deme? Who is your father's father? Who is your mother? Who is your mother's father and what is his deme? Do you have an ancestral Apollo and a Zeus of the Courtyard, and where are their sanctuaries? Do you have a family tomb, and where is it? Do you treat your parents well? Do you perform the sacrifices? Have you served on the assigned military campaigns?" Witnesses were called to verify the candidate's answers. Then the examiner asked, "Does anyone wish to accuse this man?" If an accuser came forward, he gave a speech, then the candidate spoke in his own defense. Finally, the body hearing the *dokimasia* voted to accept or reject the candidate.

At some point between 394 and 389/8 (§15 with note), a man named Mantitheus was a candidate for the Council of 500. He appeared before the outgoing Council for his examination (§1). An unknown accuser challenged his candidacy; the substance of the complaint was that Mantitheus had served in the cavalry under the Thirty Tyrants (§3). Mantitheus replied by giving this speech, written for him by Lysias. We do not know whether Mantitheus was approved or rejected.

Mantitheus was not the only Athenian whose conduct under the Thirty was an issue at his *dokimasia*: the anonymous speaker of Lysias 25 *Defense on a Charge of Overthrowing the Democracy*, Evander (Lysias 26 *Against Evander*), and Philon (Lysias 31 *Against Philon*) all faced the same problem. Despite the apparent protection of the

Amnesty of 403, an Athenian who had supported the oligarchy of the Thirty could find that it was still counted against him ten (in the case of Mantitheus) or twenty (in the case of Evander) years later.

Lysias was famous for his portrayal of character (*ēthopoiia*), and this speech is a prime example. Mantitheus comes across as a cocky young aristocrat, but capable of backing up words with action. In the introduction (§§1–3) he expresses confidence in himself, asks the Council to approve his candidacy, and promises to disprove the allegation that he served in the cavalry under the Thirty. Lysias then inverts the normal order of elements within a speech.[1] After the introduction come the proofs (§§4–8). Since Mantitheus was abroad during the beginning of the oligarchy, the Thirty would not have trusted him (§§4–5). The board on which cavalrymen's names were written is less reliable than the reports of the phylarchs (§§6–7). If Mantitheus had served in the cavalry under the Thirty, he would not deny it (§8).

Mantitheus then moves on to the narration, which summarizes his life (§§9–17). He has behaved honorably toward his family (§§10) and in public (§§11–12). His military record is admirable: he has performed all assigned tasks and volunteered for hazardous duty (§§12–17). In the conclusion (§§18–20) Mantitheus asks the Council to judge him on his record, not on his appearance; he counters the accusation that he is too young for politics by referring to his family tradition of public service and to his desire to gain honor in the eyes of his countrymen.

### For Mantitheus

[1] If I were not aware, councillors,[2] that my prosecutors wanted to harm me in every conceivable way, I would feel quite a bit of gratitude to them for this prosecution, for I believe that the people responsible for the greatest benefits to victims of unjust slander are those who force them to undergo an examination of their lives. [2] I have such complete confidence in myself that I expect that, even if someone happens to dislike me, when he hears me speak about what I have done, he will change his mind and think much better of me in the future. [3] This is what I ask, councillors. If I demonstrate to you just this one thing, that I am

friendly to the existing government and that I have been compelled to undergo the same risks as you, I ask for no additional consideration on that account. But if I have also clearly lived a moderate life in other respects, quite contrary to the opinion and the words of my enemies, then I ask you to approve my candidacy and to think the worse of my accusers. First, I will prove that I did not serve in the cavalry and was not even in Attica during the reign of the Thirty, and that I had no share in the government at that time.

[4] Before the disaster in the Hellespont,[3] our father sent us abroad to live with Satyrus in Pontus.[4] We were not in Attica when the walls were demolished or when the constitution was changed; we came home only five days before the men from Phyle returned to the Peiraeus.[5] [5] Arriving as we did at such a critical moment, it was not likely that we would desire to share other people's dangers. The Thirty, likewise, clearly were not disposed to share political power with people who had been abroad and had committed no crimes; they preferred to disenfranchise even those who had helped them overthrow the democracy.

[6] Also, it is silly to inspect the board[6] for those who served in the cavalry. Many men whom everybody knows served in the cavalry are not on it, and some men who were out of the country are listed on it. Here is the best way to find out: when you returned from exile, you decreed that the phylarchs[7] should report those who had served in the cavalry, so that you could recover their allotments from them.[8] [7] As for me, nobody could ever show that I was reported by the phylarchs or was handed over to the commissioners[9] or paid back an allotment. Further, this was easy for everyone to determine, since, if the phylarchs could not demonstrate who was in possession of allotments, they had to pay the fines themselves. So you would be much more justified in trusting these documents than the boards: anyone who wanted to could easily get his name erased from the boards, while on these documents the phylarchs were compelled to report the names of the cavalrymen.

[8] Furthermore, councillors, if I had served in the cavalry, I would not deny it, as though I had done something terrible; instead, I would ask to have my candidacy approved, after demonstrating that no citizen has

ever been harmed by me. For this is the standard of judgment I see you employing; and I see that many men who served in the cavalry then are sitting on the Council, and many have been elected generals and hipparchs. So I do not want you to think that I am making this defense for any reason other than the prosecution's conspicuous audacity to lie about me. Please come up here and testify.

*Testimony*

[9] On the topic of the actual accusation, I do not see what more I need to say. But it seems to me, councillors, that while in other trials defendants should stick to a discussion of the charges alone, in candidacy examinations it is right to give an account of one's entire life. So I ask you to listen to me with goodwill; I will make my defense in as few words as I can.

[10] First of all, due to the setbacks suffered by both my father and the city, not much property was left to me, but I married off two sisters, giving each a dowry of thirty minae.[10] I divided my father's estate with my brother in such a way that he admits possessing a greater share of the patrimony than I do.[11] As for my relations with all others, I have lived my life in such a way that not one charge has arisen against me concerning any person at any time.

[11] That is how I have conducted my private life. Concerning public matters, I think the greatest indication of my good character is this: all those young men who spend their time playing dice and drinking and engaging in that kind of wanton behavior, you will see, do not get along with me; and it is they, for the most part, who are making up stories and telling lies about me. And it is obvious that, if we shared the same objects of enthusiasm, they would not have such a low opinion of me. [12] Furthermore, councillors, no one could show that I was ever involved in any shameful private or public lawsuit or impeachment; and yet you often see other men engaged in those sorts of trials.

Look, too, at how I offer myself to the city for military service and for hazardous duty against the enemy. [13] First, when you concluded the alliance with the Boeotians and we had to render assistance at Haliartus,[12]

I was put on the cavalry roll by Orthobulus. But when I saw that everyone thought that the cavalry should be in no danger and believed that
the risk was with the hoplites, while other people were breaking the law
by mounting horses without passing their examinations, I approached
Orthobulus and told him to erase me from the cavalry roll. I thought it
was shameful for me to procure safe duty for myself when the rank and
file were going to risk their lives. Please come up here, Orthobulus.

*Testimony*

[14] So then, when all my demesmen were marshalled for departure,
I knew that some of them were good and enthusiastic citizens but in
need of supplies. I proposed that those who could afford it furnish the
necessities to those who were in need. And not only did I recommend
this to the rest, but I myself gave two men thirty drachmas each,[13] not
because I was wealthy, but to provide an example to the rest. Please
come up here.

*Witnesses*

[15] After that, councillors, when we left for Corinth[14] and everybody
knew in advance that it was going to be risky, when other men were
shirking danger, I made sure that I was stationed in the first rank to
fight the enemy.[15] Our tribe was extremely unlucky and had the most
men killed in action, yet I held my position longer than that pompous
man from Steiria who has rebuked everyone for cowardice.[16] [16] A few
days after that, we occupied some fortified positions in Corinth, so that
the enemy could not pass by. Since Agesilaus[17] had penetrated into Boeotia,
our commanders voted to detach some divisions to bring aid. Everybody was afraid—and rightly so, councillors: it was a frightful thing,
having been happy to escape with our lives a little earlier, to go face
another danger—but I went up to my taxiarch[18] and urged him to send
our division without casting lots.

[17] So, if some of you get angry at those who see fit to conduct the
city's affairs but run away from danger, you would not be justified in
having that opinion of me: not only did I enthusiastically follow my

orders, but I dared to risk my life. And I did not do this because I did not consider fighting the Spartans to be a fearsome task. I did it so that, if I ever found myself in trouble without just cause, you would think the better of me and I would receive all my rights. Would the witnesses to these things please come up.

*Witnesses*

[18] At no time have I ever been absent from any other expedition or garrison duty; my entire life I have consistently been among the first to depart and the last to retreat. And it is on such grounds that you should examine those who lead their lives as citizens ambitiously and decently, rather than hating someone if he happens to have long hair.[19] Habits such as this harm neither private individuals nor the common good of the city; but all of you benefit from those who are willing to risk their lives against the enemy. [19] So, councillors, it is not right to love or hate someone based on his appearance; you should instead examine him based on his deeds. Many men who speak quietly and dress respectably have been the cause of great evils, while others who disregard such things have done you many good services.

[20] I have already heard, councillors, from certain individuals who are also angry at me because I ventured to speak in the Assembly when I was too young. But, in the first place, I was forced to give a public speech in defense of my own affairs. Second, I seem even to myself to have been more disposed to ambition than was necessary. I thought of my ancestors, who never ceased conducting the city's affairs; [21] and, at the same time, I saw that men like them (for I must tell the truth) are the only ones you find worthy. So, seeing that this is your opinion, who would not be inspired to act and speak on behalf of the city? What's more, why would you be annoyed at such men? For, you see, it is you, and no one else, who are their judges.

# PART TWO
## PHILIP AND ATHENS

### Sources

The corpus of Demosthenes, an Athenian politician who led the resistance to Macedon, is our most fruitful source for the activities of Philip of Macedon and the Athenian response. In addition to the ten speeches from the Demosthenic corpus included in this volume, Demosthenes' speeches *On the Crown* and *On the False Embassy* (orations 18 and 19, respectively) are especially important. Also vital are the speeches of Demosthenes' political rival Aeschines, particularly *On the False Embassy* (oration 2) and *Against Ctesiphon* (oration 3). Additional sources include book 16 of Diodorus' *Bibliothêkê Historikê (Library of History)*, composed in the first century B.C.; Justin, *Epitome* 7–9; the surviving fragments of Theopompus of Chios' *Philippica* (*FGrHist* 115 F 24–396: fourth century B.C.); several preserved passages of Philochorus' *Atthis* (*FGrHist* 328: fourth or third century B.C.); and a number of Athenian inscriptions recording decrees of the Assembly.

### Preliminary: Greek Affairs, 404–362

Victory in the Peloponnesian War catapulted Sparta to the hegemony of Greece, which she would enjoy until the battle of Leuctra (371). In 395, hostilities flared up anew, with Sparta facing a coalition of Corinth, Athens, Thebes, and Argos in the Corinthian War. Nearly a decade of inconclusive warfare followed, until in 387/6 Artaxerxes II Mnemon, Great King of Persia, dictated terms that confirmed the Spartan hegemony in Greece (Xenophon, *Hellenica* 5.1.31).

During the war, however, the Athenians had rebuilt their fleet, and in 378/7 they founded a new league, the Second Athenian Confederacy. Established with the express purpose of defending the liberty and autonomy of its members against Sparta, the Confederacy was led by Athens, but decisions were to be made jointly by the Athenian Assembly and by a congress (*synedrion*) of representatives of the allied states (Diodorus 15.28; *IG* II$^2$ 43 = Tod, no. 123 = Harding, no. 35). In 376, the Athenian and Spartan navies met near the island of Naxos; the Athenians won the battle and thus reestablished the maritime supremacy that Athens had enjoyed prior to 404 (Demosthenes 9.23 with note).

The Spartan hegemony came to an end in 371, when Sparta lost the battle of Leuctra to a resurgent Thebes. During the resulting Theban hegemony of nearly a decade (371–362), Thebes launched repeated invasions of the Peloponnese, was active in Thessaly and Macedonia, and built a navy intended to rival Athens'. The supremacy of Thebes came to an end when her great general Epaminondas was killed at the battle of Mantinea in 362. The result, according to Xenophon in the conclusion to his *Hellenica* (7.5.27), was that "even more confusion and disorder occurred in Greece after the battle than before."

### Philip's Early Reign, 359–357

Our focal point now shifts north to Macedonia. In 359 the Macedonian king Perdiccas III was killed in action against the Illyrians. Perdiccas' brother Philip II, aged 22, succeeded to the throne, possibly as regent for Perdiccas' infant son (Justin 7.5.9) but more likely in his own right. Philip faced serious threats both foreign and domestic: the Paeonians and Illyrians were poised to invade Macedonia, and two Macedonian nobles, Pausanias and Argaeus, threatened to usurp the throne.

Philip moved quickly and decisively to neutralize these threats. A Paeonian invasion was averted by bribery. Philip deprived the pretenders of their backing: he paid Berisades, king of western Thrace, to desert the cause of Pausanias; and he minimized Athenian support for Argaeus by assuring the Athenians that he had no designs on the city of Amphipolis, which the Athenians claimed as theirs despite not having controlled it since 424. He then defeated Argaeus in battle. By engineering the assassination of one of his half-brothers (Archelaus) and the exile of two others (Arrhidaeus and Menelaus), Philip cemented his hold on the Macedonian throne.

In 358, Philip turned the tables on his barbarian neighbors, defeating first the Paeonians, then the Illyrians. Under the terms of peace, the Illyrian king Bardylis surrendered all his lands east of Lake Lychnitis. As a result of his success in Illyria, Philip gained two wives (by his death in 336 he would have seven): Audata, daughter of Bardylis; and Olympias, a princess of the Molossians of Epirus, who was to become the most powerful of Philip's wives and the mother of Alexander the Great.

### Amphipolis and Pydna, 357

Having secured his northern and western borders by his conquests in Paeonia and Illyria, in 357 Philip began to expand eastward into Thrace and the Chalcidice. First he laid siege to Amphipolis. With the wary Athenians, who recalled his disclaimer of 359, he secretly agreed to trade Amphipolis for the city of Pydna on the Macedonian coast (Demosthenes 2.6–7, 23 *Against Aristocrates* 116; Hegesippus = [Demosthenes] 7.27; Theopompus *FGrHist* 115 F 30). But when Philip captured Amphipolis, he reneged on his agreement and declared the city autonomous; he then marched on and took Pydna. The Athenians responded by declaring war on Philip, but their embroilment in the Social War (see below, pp. 70–71) prevented them from making a serious effort against Macedon.

### Poteidaea and Crenides/Philippi, 357–356

In the winter of 357, Philip secured a defensive alliance with the Chalcidic League, a federation of cities in the Chalcidice led by Olynthus, by promising to transfer control of the city of Poteidaea from Athens to the League. This time good to his word, Philip besieged Poteidaea early in 356, captured the city in the fall, and handed it over to the League (Demosthenes 4.35; 1.9, 12; 6.20). The Athenian garrison at Poteidaea was released without ransom. Also in 356, the inhabitants of Crenides, located northeast of Amphipolis near the coast, appealed to Philip for help against the Thracian king Cersobleptes. Philip took control of the city (and with it the productive gold and silver mines of nearby Mt. Pangaeum) and renamed it Philippi in his own honor.

Meanwhile, the western Thracians, Illyrians, and Paeonians formed a coalition against Philip and secured an alliance with Athens ($IG$ II$^2$ 127 = Todd, no. 157 = Harding, no. 70). The Athenians, however, were still occupied with the Social War, and Philip made short work of the barbarians. According to Plutarch (*Alexander* 3), on a single day in August 356, Philip received news of three triumphs: his general Parmenio had defeated the Illyrians, his horse had won an Olympic victory, and his wife Olympias had given birth[1] to a son, Alexander.

### Methone, 355–354

In the following year, 355, Philip set his sights on the city of Methone, the sole remaining Athenian possession on the Macedonian coast. During the assault on Methone, while inspecting his artillery, Philip lost his right eye to an enemy arrow (Theopompus *FGrHist* 115 F 52; Justin 7.6.15; Demosthenes 18 *On the Crown* 67). Unlike Harold II at Hastings, Philip survived and won, capturing the city in 354.

### Social War, 357–355

Since 357, meanwhile, the Athenians had been fully occupied with the Social War (the name comes from Latin *socius* "ally"). In 357, Chios, Rhodes, Cos, and Byzantium, four of Athens' most important allies in the Second Athenian Confederacy, were induced to rebel by Mausolus, satrap of Caria (Demosthenes 15 *On the Liberty of the Rhodians* 3). The rebels twice defeated Athens at sea in 356, encouraging further defections from the Confederacy.

The issue was decided when the Athenian admiral Chares managed to alienate the Great King of Persia, the bloodthirsty and effective

Artaxerxes III Ochus (r. 358–338), by supporting Artabazus, the maverick satrap of Hellespontine Phrygia. Ochus responded by issuing an ultimatum to Athens: if the Athenians did not recall Chares, Ochus would join the Social War on the side of Athens' revolting allies. The Athenians complied and made peace with the rebels in 355, formally recognizing the autonomy of 75 cities (Aeschines 2 *On the False Embassy* 70).

### Initial Stages of the Third Sacred War, 355–352

The outbreak of the Third Sacred War (355–346) would provide Philip with his next opportunity to assert his presence in Greece. The Amphictyonic Council, which oversaw the oracle of Apollo at Delphi, declared war on Phocis in 355. In 354 the Boeotians defeated the Phocians at Neon in East Locris; the Phocian supreme commander Philomelus was killed in the battle and replaced by the talented Onomarchus. When Onomarchus concluded an alliance with Pherae in Thessaly, other Thessalians invited Philip to intervene in their defense, thus bringing Philip into the war.

For the next two years (353–352), Thessaly served as the prime battleground of the Third Sacred War. Onomarchus and the Phocians defeated Philip in 353, but the next year Philip got his revenge at the Battle of the Crocus Field, crushing the Phocians and driving 6,000 of them off a cliff into the sea. Onomarchus was among the casualties. In the aftermath of the battle, Philip gained several Thessalian cities, including Pherae, whose tyrants were deposed (Demosthenes 1.13, 6.22), and Pagasae (Demosthenes 4.35, 1.9). The Thessalians rewarded Philip by electing him archon for life of the Thessalian League, a position which carried with it command of the Thessalian armed forces.

Philip then drove south at the head of an army of Macedonians and Thessalians with the goal of joining forces with the Boeotians and bringing an end to the war. Determined to keep Philip out of central Greece, the Phocians and their allies, including Athens, occupied the pass of Thermopylae.[2] When Philip arrived at Thermopylae and found it fortified by his opponents, he withdrew.

Thracian Campaign, 352–351

Philip then went on campaign in Thrace against the Thracian king Cersobleptes. By Maemacterion (November) 352 (Demosthenes 3.4), he was engaged in the siege of Heraion Teichos, which he eventually captured. Cersobleptes renewed his alliance with Athens by ceding the Chersonese peninsula, apart from the city of Cardia, to the Athenians.[3] Nonetheless, Philip got the better of Cersobleptes, who surrendered his son to Philip as a hostage. At some point in 351, illness forced Philip to return to Macedonia (Demosthenes 4.10, 1.13, 3.5).

### Eubulus and the Theoric Fund

In the aftermath of the Social War, under the leadership of a politician named Eubulus, the Athenians pursued a recovery-oriented policy that limited their activities abroad. As a result, Athens enjoyed an upswing in prosperity: both domestic and foreign revenues increased, and the Athenian fleet and its dockyards were upgraded. Eubulus also carried an important reform concerning the theoric fund, a fund in the Athenian state treasury from which money was disbursed to poor Athenians to allow them to attend religious festivals. Eubulus authored a law mandating the allocation of any annual treasury surplus to the theoric fund. Besides propelling Eubulus to instant popularity among lower-class Athenians, this measure had the effect of decreasing military expenditures: since all budget surplus now had to be transferred into the theoric fund, it could not be spent on defense. Eubulus' law would thus serve as an obstacle to Athenians such as Demosthenes (1.19–20; 3.10–13) who wished to beef up the Athenian military for a confrontation with Philip.

### Rise of Demosthenes

Eubulus, however, was not without opposition. A young politician, Demosthenes son of Demosthenes of the deme Paeania, was rising to prominence. In his earliest speeches before the Athenian Assembly, Demosthenes opposed Eubulus' policy, advocating Athenian intervention at Megalopolis and Rhodes. Gradually, Demosthenes came to believe that Macedon represented the prime threat to Athenian interests. In 352 he labeled Philip Athens' Public Enemy Number One (23 *Against Aristocrates* 121). The following year, alarmed by Philip's penetration to Thermopylae and aggression in Thrace, he urged active opposition to Macedon in the *First Philippic* (oration 4).

### Olynthian War, 349–348

Philip next targeted the Chalcidice, home of the Chalcidic League headed by Olynthus (above, p. 69). In summer 349, facing a Macedonian invasion, the Chalcidic League appealed to Athens for military aid. During the ensuing months, Demosthenes delivered the three *Olynthiacs* (speeches 1 to 3) in the Athenian Assembly. In response, Athens dispatched two expeditions to Olynthus. The first, commanded by Chares, totaled 38 triremes and 2,000 peltasts.[4] The second, under Charidemus, consisted of 18 triremes, 4,000 peltasts, and 150 cavalry (Philochorus *FGrHist* 328 F 49–51).

In the meantime, Philip had taken some outlying cities and was closing in on Olynthus. By summer 348, Olynthus was near collapse. A final call for help was sent to Athens; the Athenians assembled a third relief force, but it was delayed by bad weather. In the fall, Olynthus was betrayed from within (Demosthenes 8.40, 9.56), and Philip marched into the city. The triumphant Macedonian king leveled Olynthus and sold its people into slavery (Demosthenes 9.26). With Olynthus at his feet, Philip now controlled the Chalcidice.

### Revolt of Euboea, 348

As Philip was campaigning in Chalcidice, closer to home the Athenians were simultaneously confronted by a revolt on the island of Euboea, which may have been engineered in part by Philip in order to distract the Athenians from affairs in the north. An attempt to support the Eretrian tyrant Plutarchus against the rebels proved disastrous, and in the summer of 348 a peace was made by which Athens recognized the independence of the entire island save Carystus, which remained a member of the Second Athenian Confederacy.

### Peace of Philocrates, 346

Despite the loss of Euboea, which seriously compromised Athenian security, Athens rejected Macedonian peace offers in 348 and 347. Several factors would induce the Athenians to change their minds in 346. First, an attempt to attract the cities of Greece into a coalition against Philip failed miserably. Then, Phalaecus of Phocis reneged on an agreement to transfer control of Thermopylae to the Athenians and Spartans. Suspecting that Phalaecus had been negotiating with Philip behind their backs, the Athenians feared that Philip would gain control of Thermopylae and thus have a clear path into central Greece.

Accordingly, the Athenians reversed their policy and sought peace with Philip. For his part, Philip wanted to end hostilities in Greece so that he could pursue his ultimate goal, the conquest of Asia Minor. In Gamelion (February) 346, the Athenians dispatched their first embassy to Philip. The ten ambassadors, including Philocrates, Demosthenes, and Aeschines, met with Philip at Pella. Philip made an offer of peace and alliance and promised not to invade the Chersonese while negotiations were open.

The ambassadors brought Philip's offer back to Athens in Elaphebolion (April). At a meeting of the Assembly on Elaphebolion 18, representatives of the allied *synedrion* of the Second Athenian Confederacy urged the Athenians to sign a peace with Philip which included a three-month waiting period during which any Greek city could become an Athenian ally and thus be included in the peace (Aeschines 3 *Against Ctesiphon* 69–70). Philip's negotiators, however, advocated a treaty of peace and alliance to take effect immediately. The next day (Elaphebolion 19) the Assembly met again and passed a motion by Philocrates to conclude a peace and alliance with Macedon effective immediately, without the three-month moratorium recommended by Athens' allies.

The resulting Peace of Philocrates contained two provisions. First, Philip and the Second Athenian Confederacy each kept the territories they held at the signing of the treaty (such an arrangement is often designated for convenience by the Latin phrase *uti possidetis*, literally "as you possess"). Second, Philip and the Athenians agreed to cooperate to keep the seas clear of pirates and safe for interstate commerce.

In order to receive Philip's oath ratifying the treaty, the Assembly sent a second embassy (comprising the same ten ambassadors as the first), which reached Pella in Mounychion (May). There they found representatives of other Greek cities waiting to negotiate with Philip, but the king himself was away, having resumed hostilities against Cersobleptes (above, p. 72). Philip finally returned in mid-June and swore the oath affirming the Peace of Philocrates (Demosthenes 18 *On the Crown* 32). He then marched south, keeping the Athenian ambassadors with him until they received the oaths of Philip's allies at Pherae, only a short distance from Thermopylae (Demosthenes 19 *On the False Embassy* 158).

When the second embassy returned home in Scirophorion (July), Demosthenes accused his colleagues of taking Macedonian bribes and questioned the sincerity of Philip's desire for peace. Aeschines and Philocrates supported Philip and counterattacked Demosthenes; in a famous incident Philocrates mocked Demosthenes, telling the Assembly, "No wonder, Athenians, that Demosthenes and I are of differing opinions: he drinks water; I drink wine" (Demosthenes 19 *On the False Embassy* 46; cf. 6.30). With Philip now at Thermopylae, the Assembly rejected Demosthenes' allegations and broadened the terms of the Peace of Philocrates to include Philip's descendants.

### End of the Third Sacred War, 346

Philip invited the Athenians to support him by sending troops to Thermopylae, but Demosthenes and his associate Hegesippus convinced the Assembly to refuse. An embassy was dispatched from Athens to report this decision to Philip. Before it arrived, however, Phalaecus handed over Thermopylae to Philip. Philip then crossed the pass and received the surrender of Phocis (Demosthenes 5.20; 6.7; 9.11), which ended the Third Sacred War.

The Amphictyonic League now met to determine the punishment of Phocis. One delegate proposed to descopulate every adult male Phocian (thus repeating the slaughter at the Crocus Field) and to enslave the women and children. Aeschines, present among the Athenian ambassadors, urged more lenient treatment. The final settlement imposed by the Amphictyons broke the power of Phocis but spared her people. The towns of Phocis were dissolved into villages with a maximum population and a minimum distance between them. The Phocians were disarmed and deprived of their horses. Phocis was sentenced to pay a yearly indemnity of 60 talents to Apollo and expelled from the Amphictyonic Council, with her two votes given to Philip. The Amphictyons further expressed their gratitude to the Macedonian king by granting him the right to consult the oracle first and by appointing him to preside over the Pythian Games of 346 (Demosthenes 5.22, 9.32). Philip conducted the games and then returned to Macedonia.

### Aftermath of the Peace

The Athenians were displeased with the way the war had ended. They did not receive the benefits they expected from Philip (Demosthenes 5.10) and resented his new Amphictyonic perquisites. Some politicians wanted to annul the Peace of Philocrates immediately and declare war. In response, late in 346 Demosthenes delivered his oration *On the Peace* (speech 5), in which he urged his countrymen to keep the peace and not to give the Amphictyonic League an excuse to declare a new Sacred War on Athens. The Athenians listened to Demosthenes, and war was averted for the time being. The Peace of Philocrates would remain technically in effect until 340, but its fragility was already evident.

### Philip's Activities, 345–344

When he returned to Macedonia following the Pythian Games of 346, Philip reorganized his kingdom by transplanting peoples and redistributing its population. "And so," in the words of Justin (8.6.2), "out of many clans and tribes he established one kingdom and people." The year 345 saw a successful Macedonian campaign against the Illyrians. In 344, under his authority as archon for life of the Thessalian League, Philip set about the reorganization of Thessaly.

He divided the entire region into four tetrarchies (Demosthenes 9.26). According to Demosthenes 6.22, he also established a decadarchy (board of ten), possibly at Pherae to replace the traditional tyrants.

Most disturbing to Athenian interests was Philip's intervention in the Peloponnese, where he supported Messene and Argos against Spartan encroachment (Demosthenes 6.15). Athens responded by dispatching Demosthenes and other envoys to the Peloponnese in order to stir up opposition to Philip. Philip sent the Athenians a letter of protest; Demosthenes countered by issuing his *Second Philippic* (speech 6) in the Assembly, accusing Philip of violating the peace and calling for its rectification (*epanorthôsis*: e.g., Demosthenes 6.34).

## Mission of Python, 343

Philip now attempted to mollify his Athenian critics. Early in 343, he sent to Athens an embassy led by Python of Byzantium which offered to amend the Peace of Philocrates (Hegesippus = [Demosthenes] 7.20–23). In response, the Athenians sent a delegation to Philip headed by the hard-line anti-Macedonian Hegesippus. These envoys demanded two drastic alterations to the peace. The first was that the *uti possidetis* clause be stricken and replaced with language stating that each party (Athens and Macedon) should "have its own possessions" (Hegesippus = [Demosthenes] 7.18). In other words, Athens desired not only recognition of what she possessed, but restoration of all places she claimed as rightfully hers, including—and especially— Amphipolis. Second, the Athenians proposed to transform the Peace of Philocrates into a common peace including all the Greeks, not just themselves, Philip, and their respective allies (Hegesippus = [Demosthenes] 7.30). Philip rejected the first proposed amendment but was receptive to the second.

## Prosecutions of Philocrates and Aeschines, 343

Meanwhile, at Athens, public opinion had turned against the supporters of the Peace. Hypereides, an anti-Macedonian hawk allied with Demosthenes, brought an impeachment[5] against Philocrates on the ground that he had been bribed by Philip to propose measures against Athenian interests (Hypereides 4.29). Philocrates fled the country and was condemned to death *in absentia*. Later in the year, Demosthenes brought Aeschines to trial for his role in procuring the Peace. Demosthenes accused Aeschines of receiving Macedonian bribes and called for a death sentence. Both Demosthenes' (19 *On the False Embassy*) and Aeschines' (2 *On the False Embassy*) speeches from this trial survive. Demosthenes fell thirty votes short of a conviction, but the *Embassy* case cemented his position at the forefront of Athenian politics. At the end of 343, the Athenians sent another embassy to the Peloponnese (as they had the previous year) to agitate against Philip (Demosthenes 9.72). The hawks Demosthenes and Hegesippus were among the ambassadors; the dove Aeschines was not.

### Halonnesus Affair, 342

In 343 and 342, thanks to the efforts of Demosthenes and other anti-Macedonian politicians, Athens succeeded in gaining allies against Philip, including Corinth, Achaea, and Messenia. In 342, Philip again offered to amend the Peace of Philocrates and convert it into a common peace; as an added incentive he offered to give Athens the small island of Halonnesus. Led by Hegesippus (whose speech *On Halonnesus* is preserved as [Demosthenes] 7), the Athenians rejected Philip's overtures. They refused the gift of Halonnesus because the offer was improperly worded (Hegesippus = [Demosthenes] 7.5–6), and continued to insist upon the restoration of "their own possessions," particularly Amphipolis (*ibid.* 26ff.).

By this point, if not before, the Athenians were also demanding that Philip return territory captured from Cersobleptes in 346 while peace negotiations were ongoing (*ibid.* 37; cf. Demosthenes 8.64; Philip = [Demosthenes] 12.8). Cersobleptes was an Athenian ally but not a member of the Second Athenian Confederacy and not a signatory to the Peace of Philocrates. While Philip's activities against Cersobleptes might be questioned from an ethical standpoint, they did not violate the Peace (*pace* Hegesippus and Demosthenes). Further, the *uti possidetis* clause of the Peace confirmed Philip's possession of all Thracian cities he took before swearing the oath of peace.

Recognizing that the Athenians were no longer engaging in serious diplomacy, Philip refused their demands.

## Philip in Thrace, 342–341

Philip now returned to Thrace with the intent of conquering the entire region. Western Thrace was already under Macedonian dominion; Philip now added the center and east to his empire and concluded an alliance with the Getae in the north. After the desultory fighting of 352 and 346, now Philip finally deposed Cersobleptes, as well as another Thracian king, Teres (Philip = [Demosthenes] 12.8–10). Philip's expansion eastward in Thrace constituted a serious threat to Athenian interests. Athens imported significant quantities of grain from the Black Sea; if Philip could take Byzantium and control the Bosporus, he could strangle the Athenian grain supply and thus starve Athens into submission.[6]

## Macedonian Intervention in Euboea, 343–341

At the same time, Philip was also pursuing intrigues in Euboea. In 343 and 342 he dispatched several expeditions to install and support two tyrants, Cleitarchus of Eretria and Philistides of Oreus (Demosthenes 8.36, 9.57–62). Macedonian control of Eretria proved ephemeral, however: in 341 the Athenians allied with Chalcis and expelled first Philistides, then Cleitarchus (Philochorus FGrHist 328 F 159–161).

## Diopeithes in the Chersonese, 342–341

The Chersonese peninsula was another hot spot in the cold war between Athens and Macedon. Athens claimed the entire peninsula; but the city of Cardia, an ally of Philip, refused to accept Athenian hegemony. The Athenians rebuffed Philip's proposal to submit the Cardia question to arbitration (Hegesippus = [Demosthenes] 7.41–44) and in 342 sent the general Diopeithes to the Chersonese with mercenaries and additional Athenian cleruchs (settlers). In response to a Cardian appeal, Philip dispatched a Macedonian garrison to defend his ally.

Diopeithes exacerbated the situation by extorting payments (euphemistically called *eunoiai*, "benevolences": Demosthenes 8.24) from the merchant traffic in the Hellespont, assaulting Macedonian-held cities on the Thracian coast, and seizing and torturing a Macedonian envoy to Athens before ransoming him back to Philip for a sum of nine talents (Philip = [Demosthenes] 12.3). Outraged by Diopeithes' conduct, Philip sent a letter of complaint to Athens. Demosthenes responded with his speeches *On the Chersonese* (oration 8) and the *Third Philippic* (oration 9). He won over the Assembly, and the Athenians prepared to engage in open warfare against Philip. Reinforcements were sent to Diopeithes; Hypereides and Demosthenes were dispatched to the eastern Aegean to secure alliances there; and in Anthesterion (February) 340, Athens' allies convened and pledged support for the coming war (Aeschines 3 *Against Ctesiphon* 98).

### Perinthus and Byzantium, 340

In the summer of 340, Philip drove from the Chersonese northeast along the coast of the Propontis toward Perinthus and, ultimately, Byzantium. Along the way, he dispatched a letter, preserved as speech 12 in the Demosthenic corpus, complaining of Athens' violations of the Peace of Philocrates and announcing his intention to retaliate. Philip began the siege of Perinthus first; after facing stiff resistance for several months, he left some troops there to continue the siege and advanced with the rest of his forces to assault Byzantium.

In the fall, the Macedonian navy captured a convoy of 230 grain transports gathering in the Bosporus under an armed Athenian escort. Fifty ships from neutral states were released; as for the remaining 180 Athenian vessels, Philip confiscated their cargoes and used their timbers to build siege engines (Theopompus *FGrHist* 115 F 292; Philochorus *FGrHist* 328 F 162; cf. Justin 9.1.6). In response, the Athenians destroyed the pillar on which the Peace of Philocrates was inscribed and mobilized the fleet (Philochorus *FGrHist* 328 F 55). War was now official.

In the meantime, the Macedonian sieges of Byzantium and Perinthus continued. The Byzantines withstood the besieging forces at first by themselves, then with help from Athens; a nighttime assault failed when the Byzantines were awakened by the barking of their dogs. In the winter or spring of 340/39, Philip lifted the sieges and withdrew.

### Scythian Campaign, 339

Philip now headed north to Scythia, where he decisively defeated the Scythian king Atheas, taking 20,000 horses and a like number of women and boys as prizes of war. On its return, however, the Macedonian army was attacked by the Triballi. Philip himself sustained a serious wound to the leg that forced him to return to Pella to convalesce (Justin 9.2–3).

### Athenian War Preparations, 340–339

Athens was now preparing for a showdown with Philip. In 340, the financing of the Athenian navy was reoganized by the new Superintendent of the Navy, Demosthenes (Aeschines 3 *Against Ctesiphon* 222). The following year, Eubulus' law concerning the theoric fund (above, p. 72) was finally repealed (Philochorus *FGrHist* 328 F 56a), and budget surplus was redirected to defense.

### Outbreak of the Fourth Sacred War, 339

The final confrontation between Philip and the Greeks would again be occasioned by a Sacred War. At the spring *pylaia* (meeting of the Amphictyonic Council) of 339, while Philip was still campaigning in Scythia, the representatives of the Locrian town of Amphissa proposed to fine Athens 50 talents for improperly rededicating spoils seized from the Persians in 480. Aeschines, one of the Athenian delegates, succeeded in deflecting the Council's anger by accusing the Amphissans of sarilegiously cultivating Apollo's sacred land. At an extraordinary meeting held in the summer, the Amphictyons declared war on Amphissa. Command of the forces of the Amphictyonic League in this Fourth Sacred War (339–338) was initially given to

Cottyphus of Thessaly but transferred to Philip in the fall after his return from Scythia.

### Approach of Philip and Athenian–Theban Alliance

Late in 339, Philip marched south into central Greece. Approaching Thermopylae, as he had in 352 and 346, Philip discovered that the Thebans, in support of Amphissa, had garrisoned the city of Nicaea at the southern mouth of the pass. He therefore circumvented Thermopylae by marching through the mountains west of the pass, then turned east and seized Elatea in Phocis. From Elatea Philip issued two demands to the Thebans: the immediate surrender of Nicaea and cooperation in an invasion of Attica, either active (by sending troops) or passive (by allowing Philip unobstructed travel through Boeotia).

When they learned that Philip was at Elatea, only two days' march from the Attic border, the Athenians panicked (Demosthenes 18 *On the Crown* 169). At an emergency meeting of the Assembly held at dawn the next day, they swallowed their pride. Realizing that the sole hope of salvation lay with the despised Thebans, Demosthenes proposed and carried a motion for the immediate dispatch of an embassy, including himself, to Thebes to seek an alliance against Philip. A generous Athenian offer won the Thebans over: Thebes was granted sole command of the allied army and joint command of the navy; Athens would bear two-thirds of the war's expenses and would recognize the Theban-led Boeotian League (Aeschines 3 *Against Ctesiphon* 142–143).

### Battle of Chaeroneia, August 2, 338

The winter of 339/8 witnessed some desultory fighting between the Boeotian–Athenian forces and the Macedonians. On the diplomatic front, each side sent envoys to other Greek cities to solicit alliances. Euboea, Achaea, Corinth, Megara, Leucas, Corcyra, and Acarnania reaffirmed their commitment to resist Philip (Demosthenes 18 *On the Crown* 237; Aeschines 3 *Against Ctesiphon* 95–98; *IG* II$^2$ 237 =

Tod, no. 178 = Harding, no. 100). A last attempt by Philip to negotiate peace was quashed by Demosthenes, who threatened sanctions
against any Athenian or Boeotian who introduced a peace proposal
(Aeschines 3 *Against Ctesiphon* 149–150).

The decisive battle between Philip and the Greek coalition was
fought at Chaeroneia in Boeotia on Metageitnion 7 = August 2,
338. Philip's Macedonians routed the opposition; all 300 members of
the elite Sacred Band of Thebes were slain. Either Philip or the
Thebans later erected on the battlefield a monument called the Lion
of Chaeroneia, under which were buried 254 men, presumably the
identifiable members of the Sacred Band.

### Terms Imposed on Thebes and Athens

After Chaeroneia, the cities of Greece capitulated to Philip one by one.
Philip showed little mercy to Thebes, where the terms of peace
included the dissolution of the Boeotian League, the replacement of the
democratic government of Thebes by an oligarchy, the restoration of all
exiles, and the installation of a Macedonian garrison on the Cadmeia.

Athens received more lenient treatment. She was forced to disband the Second Athenian Confederacy, but she was allowed to keep
Lemnos, Imbros, Scyros, Delos, and Samos, and she received the city
of Oropus on the Attic-Boeotian border, which had been a Theban
possession. On these terms, Philip granted Athens not only peace
but an alliance as well (Diodorus 16.87.3). He provided further evidence of his goodwill by releasing without ransom 2,000 Athenian
prisoners of war and by conveying to Athens the remains of her
1,000 men killed at Chaeroneia under a Macedonian honor guard.
Philip's magnanimity resulted from a number of considerations, including the prominence of Athens, the desire to avoid another
lengthy and difficult siege, and the usefulness of the Athenian navy
for his planned campaign in Asia Minor (see below).

### Foundation of the League of Corinth, 337

Philip next received the surrenders of Megara and Corinth, then
marched into the Peloponnese, where he continued his policy of

protecting Sparta's neighbors (e.g., Demosthenes 6.13–15) by granting portions of Spartan territory to Argos, Messenia, Megalopolis, and Tegea.

Early in 337, at the instigation of Philip, the mainland Greeks (with the exception of Sparta) and a number of the islanders established a federal organization that scholars call the League of Corinth. League policy was determined by majority decision of a Council of the Greeks, to which each member state contributed a number of representatives proportional to the size of its army and navy. The League decreed a Common Peace covering all the Greeks: members were bound by oath to keep the peace with each other and Philip, to defend any member under invasion, to respect the autonomy and constitutions of all members, to abstain from acts of revolution, and to promote free trade and combat bringandage and piracy (*IG* II² 236 = Tod, no. 177 = Harding, no. 99; [Demosthenes] 17 *On the Treaty with Alexander*). Philip was elected *Hêgemôn* (Leader) of the League, which promptly declared war on Persia (with the stated purpose of avenging Xerxes' destruction of Greek temples in 480) and appointed Philip commander-in-chief of its armed forces.

### Assassination of Philip, 336

Accordingly, in the spring of 336, Philip raised an army and a navy and sent an advance force of 10,000 men to Asia Minor. Before he could join them, however, he was assassinated at the wedding of his daughter Cleopatra in Aegae. What Philip had left undone—the conquest of the Persian Empire—was left to his son and heir, Alexander III (the Great).

# 4

# DEMOSTHENES 4

*First Philippic*

## Introduction

Athens had been officially at war with Philip since his seizure of Amphipolis in 357, but other priorities, particularly the Social War, made more pressing demands on Athenian attention. In 352, however, Philip's aggressive activities put the Athenians on alert. On the Greek mainland, Philip advanced as far as Thermopylae before turning back; and in the Chersonese, an area vital to Athenian interests, he besieged Heraion Teichos (Part Two, Philip and Athens, p. 72). In 351, Demosthenes responded by delivering before the Athenian Assembly a call to arms now known as his *First Philippic*.

In his introduction,[1] (§1) Demosthenes begs the indulgence of his listeners for rising to speak first rather than yielding to more established politicians. The narrative (§§2–12) surveys the present situation and reassures the Athenians that all is not lost, provided that they are willing to stop delaying and act. Then comes Demosthenes' proposal (*prothesis*: §§13–30). He calls for the mobilization of a fleet of fifty triremes[2] plus support vessels, and an army numbering 2,000 infantry and 200 cavalry, with twenty-five percent of each consisting of Athenian citizens. The total estimated cost is ninety-two talents (§§16, 21, 28).

Demosthenes then gives proofs in support of his proposal (§§31–50). Auxiliary forces have proven ineffective and should be replaced by a standing army (§§31–36). A dilatory and reactive policy is harmful to Athens (§§37–41). Progress is only possible if the Athenians resolve to oppose Macedon actively (§§42–43) and with citizen forces (§§44–47). Philip is a wily enemy; unless the Athenians resist him abroad, they will have to do so on their own soil (§§48–50).

In his conclusion (§51), Demosthenes expresses apprehension about the popularity of his plan but confidence in its effectiveness.

### First Philippic

[1] If the task before us, men of Athens, were to discuss some novel issue, I would have held off until most of the usual speakers had expressed their opinions, and if I approved of something they said, I would have kept quiet, but if not, then I would have ventured to say what I think. But since it has fallen to us now again to examine a topic about which they have often spoken previously, I believe that I could reasonably be pardoned even for being the first to stand up. For if they had offered the necessary counsel earlier, there would be no need for us to deliberate now.

[2] First of all, men of Athens, you should not be disheartened by present circumstances, even if they seem to be in altogether bad shape. For what was worst about our situation in the past is best for the future. And what is that? The fact, men of Athens, that your affairs are in bad shape when you have taken none of the necessary steps: if you had done everything you ought to and were still in this situation, there would be no hope for improvement. [3] Second, you must keep in mind, either hearing it from others or—for those of you who know— remembering it yourselves, what power the Spartans possessed not long ago, and how nobly and properly you behaved, doing nothing unworthy of the city, but rather withstanding the war against them[3] on behalf of justice.

Why do I mention this? So that you may know, men of Athens, and see that, if you are on your guard, there is nothing you must fear, but if you are negligent, nothing turns out as you wish. As examples you may use the then-existing strength of the Spartans, which you bested because you paid attention to your affairs, and the present hubris[4] of this man,[5] which throws us into confusion because we pay no attention to what we ought to.

[4] Now, if anyone among you, men of Athens, thinks that Philip is hard to fight, looking at the size of his existing forces and the fact that

the city[6] has lost all its territories, he is thinking correctly. But let him also consider this: once, men of Athens, we held Pydna and Poteidaea and Methone and the entire surrounding region as our own; and many of the tribes[7] that are now on his side were autonomous and free, and wanted to be on friendly terms with us more than with him.

[5] If Philip had held the opinion then that it was difficult to fight the Athenians, who possessed so many fortified bases of operations against his country, while he was bereft of allies, he would have achieved none of his present accomplishments, nor would he have acquired such considerable power. But he knew well, men of Athens, that all those places are prizes of war, lying up for grabs; he knew that by nature the property of the absent belongs to those who are present, and the property of the negligent belongs to those who are willing to work hard and take risks. [6] This is the way of thinking that has allowed him to conquer, and now to possess, all these places, some of them held as possessions taken in war, others won over as allies and friends. For, as you know, all men are willing to ally with and pay attention to those whom they see to be prepared and willing to do what they must.

[7] Now, if you too, men of Athens, are willing to adopt a similar way of thinking now—even if you were not before—and if each of you stands ready to act where he is needed and can provide useful service to the city, casting off all pretense of incapacity, the man of means by paying the war-tax,[8] the man of military age by serving—to put it all together in simple terms, if you are willing to become your own masters and stop expecting that each of you can do nothing himself and his neighbor will do everything for him, then you will get back what is yours, God willing;[9] you will recover what you have lost through neglect; and you will punish Philip. [8] You must not believe that his present circumstances are fixed and immortal, as though he were a god. There are people who hate and fear and envy him, men of Athens, even among those who now seem entirely friendly toward him. You must suppose that all the characteristics present in any other group of men are present among his men as well. All these characteristics currently lie concealed, having no opportunity for expression due to your sloth and neglect—which, I tell you, you must now put aside.

[9] You see the situation, men of Athens: the man has become so incorrigible that he gives you no choice whether to act or to keep quiet; he makes threats and issues, they say, contemptuous remarks. And he is not one to hold what he has conquered and stop there; no, he is constantly extending his reach somewhere and hedging us in, surrounding us on all sides as we sit here and delay. [10] So when, men of Athens, when will you do what you must? When what happens? "When, by Zeus, there is some necessity." Well, how are we supposed to interpret current events? I should think that, for free men, the most powerful necessity is a feeling of shame at the state of their affairs.

Or, tell me now, do you really want to go around asking each other, "Is there any news?" Could there be anything more newsworthy than a man from Macedon subduing Athenians in war and administering the affairs of the Greeks? "Is Philip dead?" "No, by Zeus, but he is sick."[10] [11] What difference does it make to you? After all, if something does happen to him, you will quickly create another Philip, if this is how you attend to your affairs: Philip has grown so great not so much as a measure of his own strength as of your negligence. [12] And there is also this. If something should happen to Philip—if our good fortune, which has always taken better care of us than we have of ourselves, should accomplish this too for us—know this: if you were on the scene, you could take control of all chaotic conditions and manage them to your liking; but, as you are now, even if opportunities should hand you Amphipolis,[11] you could not take it, far removed as you are in your preparations and mindsets.

[13] On the assumption that you have been persuaded and realize that you must all be ready and willing to do your duty, I will cease discussing that. Now I will attempt to address the type of armament by which I think you will rid yourselves of these problems, and its size, and the sources of revenue, and the rest, and my opinion of the best and quickest way to prepare them. I ask only this of you, men of Athens: [14] that you make your judgments only when you have heard it all and not in advance; and, if anyone thinks I am proposing a fundamentally novel armament, let him not suppose that I am putting off our business. For it is not those who have talked about acting "quickly" and "today" who speak most to the purpose (for we could not prevent what has already happened by sending

aid now); [15] it is, rather, the one who demonstrates what armament we can provide, how large, and from what sources, so that it will be able to hold out until we are either persuaded to bring an end to the war or overcome our enemies. That is how we can avoid misfortune in the future. Now, I think I can tell you this, but I will not stand in the way if someone else volunteers something. This is the magnitude of my promise; the event will soon provide the test, and you will be the judges.

[16] First, men of Athens, I say that we must equip fifty triremes;[12] and then we must possess such a mindset that, if necessary, we will board them ourselves[13] and set sail. In addition to these, I call for the outfitting of triremes for horse transport for half of our cavalry,[14] and a sufficient number of boats. [17] These, I think, must be at hand to meet those lightning expeditions of his from his own country to Thermopylae and the Chersonese and Olynthus and wherever he wishes.[15] It is necessary to implant it in his mind that you may perhaps rouse yourselves from your excessive negligence, as you did on Euboea, and earlier (as they say) at Haliartus, and lastly, just recently, at Thermopylae.[16] [18] Even if you should not actually carry this out, as I say you must, it will not be easy for him to dismiss you with complete contempt. Either he will be afraid, knowing that you are prepared for him (and he will have accurate intelligence: there are people, you see—and more than there ought to be—who report all our activities to him), and he will keep quiet; or he will overlook these things and be caught off guard, with no one to prevent you from sailing against his own country, given the opportunity.

[19] These are the decisions which I say all must make, and the preparations that I consider proper. But before you do that, men of Athens, I tell you that you must mobilize a force that will fight and harass Philip nonstop. I am not talking about ten or twenty thousand mercenaries, or those paper forces.[17] Let it come from the city:[18] whether you elect one general or more than one, and whether you elect this man or whomever, it will obey and follow him. [20] I also recommend that you furnish this force with provisions.[19] Now, what shall this force be? How large? From where will it get its provisions? How will it be willing to do these things?[20] I will tell you, going through each of these questions separately. I do propose mercenaries—and make sure that you do not do what has often hurt you in the past: you think that whatever you do will be less

than you need, and in your decrees you choose the largest proposal, but, when the time comes for action, you do not even carry out the small one. What you need to do instead is put into effect the smaller proposal, provide it with support, and add more if it turns out to be too little.

[21] I propose a total of 2,000 soldiers. Of these, I say, 500 must be Athenians, from whatever age-group you decide is right.[21] They shall serve for an appointed period, and not a long one, but as long as you decide is right, relieving each other in rotation. I recommend that the rest be mercenaries. Along with these, there shall be 200 cavalry, at least fifty of whom shall be Athenians, as with the infantry, serving in the same manner; and there shall be horse-transports for them. [22] All right; what else besides this? Ten fast triremes.[22] Since Philip has a navy, we need fast triremes as well, so that our force may sail in safety. Now, where will the provisions for these men come from? I will tell you that too, and I will show you, when I instruct you as to why I think a force of this size will suffice and why I urge the inclusion of citizens in it.

[23] This is a sufficient size, men of Athens, because at present it is impossible for us to provide a force capable of meeting Philip in the field; instead we have to plunder and wage that kind of war at first.[23] This force, then, must be neither overly large (for we could not afford to pay or feed it) nor completely insignificant. [24] I recommend that citizens be present and sail along for this reason: I hear that, sometime in the past, the city supported a mercenary force at Corinth, commanded by Polystratus, Iphicrates, Chabrias, and others, and you yourselves served alongside them.[24] And I know from hearsay that these mercenaries, posted beside you, and you beside them, defeated the Spartans. But ever since your mercenary contingents have served all by themselves, they conquer your friends and allies, and your enemies have become more powerful than they should be. These mercenaries cast only a passing glance at the city's war and go sailing off to Artabazus[25] or wherever instead; and their general follows them, which makes sense: it is impossible to command without providing pay.

[25] What, then, do I recommend? Take away the excuses from both the general and the troops by providing pay and stationing citizen soldiers alongside them to serve, as it were, as inspectors of the generals'

conduct. The way we handle our affairs now is laughable. If someone were to ask you, "Are you at peace, men of Athens?" you would say, "Not us, by Zeus: we are fighting Philip." [26] Didn't you just elect from among yourselves ten taxiarchs, generals, and phylarchs, and two hipparchs?[26] So what do these people do? With the exception of one man—whichever one you send out to the war—the rest of them assist the Sacral Commissioners[27] in marshalling your processions. You elect your taxiarchs and phylarchs for the agora, like those who fashion clay figurines,[28] not for war. [27] Shouldn't your taxiarchs, men of Athens, come from you, your hipparch come from you, your officers be your own, so that your forces truly belong to the city? But instead, your hipparch has to sail to Lemnos,[29] while Menelaus[30] is to be hipparch of the men fighting for the city's possessions. In saying this, I am not blaming the man, merely pointing out that this person, whoever he might be, should have been elected by you.

[28] Now, perhaps you think that I have spoken correctly so far, but you really want to hear about the money, how much it will be and where it will come from. I will proceed to that right now. As for the money: the provisions for this force—rations only[31]—come to ninety talents and a little more.[32] For the ten fast ships,[33] forty talents: twenty minae per ship per month. Another forty talents for the 2,000 soldiers, so that each soldier receives ten drachmas per month for rations. And, for the cavalry, 200 in number, if each man receives thirty drachmas per month, that comes to twelve talents. [29] And if anyone thinks this is a small starting point, the provision of rations for the soldiers, his conclusion is incorrect. I know clearly that, if this goes into effect, the army will procure the remainder on its own from the war, without harming any Greek or ally, and thus it will have full pay. I am prepared to sail along as a volunteer and suffer any penalty if things do not turn out this way. So, what is the revenue source of the money that I am urging you to spend? This I will now tell you.

*Revenue Schedule*[34]

[30] This, men of Athens, is what we[35] have been able to come up with. And when you vote your resolutions, if you approve this, you will

be voting to fight Philip not only with decrees and letters but with actions as well.

[31] I think that you would come up with a better plan for the war and for the entire armament if you considered the location, men of Athens, of the country where you will be fighting, and if you took into account that it is by getting the jump on us with regard to the winds and the seasons of the year that Philip has accomplished most of his achievements: he watches for the etesian winds[36] or the winter and then attacks when we would be unable to get there. [32] So, keeping this in mind, we should fight the war not with auxiliary forces (since we show up too late for everything) but with an armed force operating nonstop. You have ready to use as winter quarters for this force Lemnos, Thasos, Sciathos, and the islands in that area, which are provided with harbors, grain, and everything the army needs. And, during the time of year when it is easy to sail close to shore and the winds are safe, it will be easy to take up positions right by the land and the entrances to the commercial ports.[37]

[33] How and when to use this force will be determined according to circumstances by its commander, appointed by you. What I have drafted in my proposal is what needs to come from you. If you provide these things, men of Athens, preparing first the money that I propose, then the rest—the soldiers, the triremes, the cavalry, the entire complete force—and if you bind them by law to remain at war, serving as your own paymasters and quartermasters in financial matters, while demanding from the general an account of his operations, then you will stop constantly deliberating on the same topics and making no progress. [34] In addition, men of Athens, in the first place you will deprive Philip of his greatest source of revenue. What is that? He fights you with the resources of your own allies, plundering those who sail the sea. What else? You yourselves will be out of range of misfortune; it will not be as it was in the past, when he invaded Lemnos and Imbros and made off with your citizens as prisoners-of-war;[38] when he detained the vessels off Geraestus and exacted an unspeakable amount of money;[39] and, most recently, when he disembarked at Marathon and left the country with the sacred trireme[40]—while you can neither prevent these things nor render aid by the time you prescribe.

[35] Now, why in the world do you think, men of Athens, that the festivals of the Panathenaea and the Dionysia[41] always occur at the appropriate time, whether experts or laymen are allotted to superintend them—festivals upon which more money is spent than on any of our naval expeditions, and which involve more commotion and preparation than anything I can imagine—while all your naval expeditions show up too late: the one to Methone, the one to Pagasae, the one to Poteidaea?[42] [36] It is because all those festivals are regulated by law; each of you knows far in advance who will be chorus-leader[43] or gymnasiarch[44] for his tribe, and what he is going to get when and from whom, and what he is supposed to do. In these matters nothing is neglected from lack of examination or definition. But when it comes to war and its preparations, everything is undisciplined, unrevised, undefined.

This is why it is not until we have heard something that we appoint trierarchs and hold property exchanges[45] for them and look into sources of revenue; after that we resolve to embark the metics and the independent slaves,[46] then ourselves, then our substitutes. [37] And, while these delays occur, the goal of our expedition is lost. We waste the time for action on preparation, but the opportunities for action do not wait for our sloth and pretended incapacity; and the forces we think are there for us in the meantime are proven unable to act at the moment of crisis. And Philip has reached such a level of hubris that he is now sending the Euboeans letters like this.

*Reading of the Letter*[47]

[38] Most of what was just read, men of Athens, should not be true, but it is, unpleasant as it may be to hear. Now, if all the things one passes over in speaking to avoid causing pain are also passed over by the facts, then we should give public speeches aimed at providing pleasure. If, however, pleasant speech, when it is out of place, becomes a liability in action, it is shameful for us to lie to ourselves, to put off everything disagreeable and thereby be too late for every event, [39] and not even to be able to learn that those who fight wars the right way must not follow the situation but rather be ahead of the situation. Just as one might expect a general to lead his army, so those who sit in deliberation must

take the lead in affairs, so that what they decide gets done and they are not forced to catch up to the results.

[40] But you, men of Athens, although you possess the greatest power of all men—in triremes, hoplites, cavalry, monetary income—up to this very day you have never used any of these for any necessary purpose. You fight Philip exactly as barbarians box. When one of them takes a punch, he always feels for the blow, and if you hit him somewhere else, there go his hands; as for blocking or looking you in the eye, he does not know how and does not want to. [41] You do the same thing. If you hear that Philip is in the Chersonese, you vote to send aid there; if he is at Thermopylae, there; if he is somewhere else, you run at his heels up and down, taking your orders from him. On your own you have not come up with a single useful plan for the war; you do not see anything coming before it happens, before you learn that something has occurred or is in the process of occurring. Maybe that was possible before, but now things have reached an absolute crisis, so it is no longer allowed.

[42] I think that some god, men of Athens, has inspired this meddle-someness in Philip out of shame for the city at what is going on. For, if Philip were willing to hold what he has conquered and seized already and keep quiet, doing nothing more, I think some of you would be content with behavior that would have resulted in our public conviction of dishonor, cowardice, and all the most disgraceful charges. As it is, though, by constantly attacking someone and reaching for more, perhaps Philip might yet provoke you, if you have not completely given up. [43] It surprises me that none of you is concerned or angry, men of Athens, seeing that our goal at the beginning of the war was to punish Philip, but now at the end it is to avoid being injured by Philip. But surely it is obvious that he will not stand still unless someone stops him. So are we going to wait for that too? If you send off empty[48] triremes and the hopes inspired by someone or other, do you think everything is fine?

[44] Will we not man the ships? Will we not set out ourselves, with at least some portion of our own soldiers, now, even if we did not before? Will we not sail against Philip's land? "Where, then, will we put in?" someone just asked. The war itself, men of Athens, will find the

vulnerable parts of his affairs, if we make the effort. But if we sit at home listening to the speakers abusing and blaming each other, no part of what we need will ever get done. [45] Wherever, I think, a part of the city joins in the expedition—even if it is not the entire city—the goodwill of the gods and of Fortune fights at their side. But wherever you send a general and an empty decree and the hopes expressed on the platform,[49] nothing that you need happens; instead, your enemies laugh at you, while your allies stand in mortal fear of such expeditions.

[46] It is impossible, impossible, for one man ever to be able to accomplish for you everything that you want. It is, however, possible to make promises and claims, and to accuse this man and that; and as a result our interests are lost. For whenever a general commands miserable unpaid mercenaries, and there are men here who lie to you without scruple about what that general does, and you vote at random based on what you hear, tell me, what are we supposed to expect?

[47] How, then, will these things cease? When you, men of Athens, appoint the same men as soldiers, as witnesses to the conduct of the generals, and as jurors at their reviews[50] when they come home, so that you may not just hear about your business, but be there and see it. Our affairs have now reached such depths of disgrace that each of the generals is tried two and three times in your court on capital charges, but not one of them has the courage to risk death even once against the enemy. They prefer the death of kidnappers and clothes-stealers[51] to a fitting one: a criminal dies as the result of a conviction; a general dies fighting the enemy.

[48] Now, some of us go around saying that Philip, together with the Spartans, is plotting the destruction of Thebes and breaking up the constitutional governments.[52] Some say that he has sent envoys to the Great King;[53] some say he is fortifying cities in Illyria; we all go around, each of us making up his own story. [49] Now I think, men of Athens, that, by the gods, he is drunk on the greatness of his deeds and has many such dreams in his mind, seeing the utter lack of people to stop him and elated by his accomplishments. But, by Zeus, he certainly does not deliberately act in such a way that the most foolish among us know what he is about to do—and most foolish indeed are the inventors of stories.

[50] However, if we cast aside all that and know that the man is our enemy, that he deprives us of our own property and has treated us with hubris for a long time, that all the things we ever expected someone to do for us have been discovered to be against us, that the future depends on us, and that if we are not willing to fight him now on his ground, we may be forced to do so on ours—if we know these things, we will have made the necessary decisions and rid ourselves of idle talk. For it is not necessary to speculate about what will happen in the future, only to know well that it will be bad unless you pay attention and are willing to do your duty.

[51] Now, I have never chosen at any other time to seek popularity by saying what I was not convinced would be beneficial; now too, I have simply told you everything I think openly and without reservation. I only wish that, just as I know that it benefits you to hear the best proposal, I knew it was also beneficial to the one who proposed it; I would be much happier. But as things are, although it is unclear what will happen to me as a result, I nonetheless choose to propose these measures, confident that, if you carry them out, they will be to your benefit. But let whatever will benefit all be victorious.

# 5

# DEMOSTHENES I

*First Olynthiac*

## Introduction

When Philip invaded the Chalcidice in summer 349, ambassadors from the Chalcidic League, headed by the city of Olynthus, came to Athens to plead for assistance (Part Two, Philip and Athens, p. 73). Demosthenes recommended support for Olynthus and delivered three orations, the *Olynthiacs*, in the Athenian Assembly in 349/8. The present speech, first in the series, was probably given soon after the arrival of the ambassadors.

The introduction to the *First Olynthiac* (§1) urges the Assembly to listen to all who come forward in order that it may choose the best course of action. In the narrative (§§2–15), Demosthenes advises the Athenians to take advantage of their circumstances. They can yet turn Philip's strength to their own advantage (§§2–4). The Olynthians realize their situation (§5). If the Athenians respond with speed and determination, they can reverse their earlier mistakes in dealing with Philip (§§6–9). On the other hand, if Athens continues to delay and Philip takes Olynthus, soon he will be on the borders of Attica (§§10–15).

Demosthenes offers his proposals at §§16–20. Two expeditionary forces are required: one to relieve Olynthus, the other to harass Macedonia (§§17–18). These can be financed either by redirecting the theoric fund to support the military (§19) or by levying a universal war-tax (*eisphora*) (§20). The proofs then follow (§§21–27). Philip's position in the Chersonese, Thessaly, and Thrace is insecure (§§21–23). By supporting Olynthus, Athens can fight the war far from home; if Olynthus falls, no other Greek city can withstand Philip (§§24–26). If the war is carried into Attica, the Athenians will suffer (§27). In conclusion (§28), Demosthenes urges each Athenian to do his part to keep the war away from their homes.

*First Olynthiac*

[1] Men of Athens, I think you would pay a large sum of money if what would benefit the city regarding the matters you are presently considering were to become clear. Now, as this is the case, you should be willing to pay eager attention to those wishing to advise you. Not only might you listen and accept it if someone has come with a useful plan formulated, but I also consider it part of your good fortune that many of the necessary proposals may occur to some people on the spur of the moment, thus simplifying your choice of the advantageous plan from all those presented.

[2] The present crisis, men of Athens, practically tells you in an audible voice that you must come to grips with those affairs[1] yourselves, if you are at all concerned with their preservation. We seem to me, though, to possess I don't know what attitude toward them. Here is what I think: we must approve the proposed auxiliary force immediately and prepare as quickly as possible to dispatch it from here (so as not to experience the same thing as before);[2] and we must dispatch an embassy to announce these decisions and to be present as events occur. [3] For our greatest fear is this. The man[3] is a scoundrel and clever at handling his affairs. Sometimes he makes concessions when it so happens, sometimes he issues threats—and he could reasonably be found credible— and sometimes he slanders us and our absence. The fear is that he may take an element of our vital interests, turn it to his own use, and detach it from us.

[4] But in spite of that, men of Athens, it is reasonable to say that the very aspect of Philip's affairs that is hardest to fight against is also the best for you. The fact that this one man is master of all things open and secret, simultaneously serving as general, despot, and treasurer, and that he is with his army wherever it goes, gives him a significant advantage in waging war quickly and in an opportune manner. But when it comes to the agreement which he would gladly make with the Olynthians, the opposite holds true. [5] For it is clear to the Olynthians that now they

are not fighting for their reputation or for a portion of their country, but to stave off the destruction and enslavement of their homeland. They know what Philip did to those Amphipolitans who handed their city over to him and to those men of Pydna who welcomed him.[4]

Tyranny, I think, is generally an object of mistrust to constitutional governments, especially when they inhabit neighboring lands. [6] So, men of Athens, having come to this realization and bearing in your minds all other proper considerations, I tell you that now, if ever before, you must be resolute and indignant and devote yourselves to the war, by paying the war-tax[5] eagerly, going on campaign personally,[6] and leaving nothing undone. You no longer have any rationale or excuse not to be willing to do your duty. [7] Right now what everybody has been talking about—that we had to provoke the Olynthians to fight Philip—has occurred of its own accord, and in the manner most advantageous to you. For if the Olynthians had undertaken the war at your persuasion, they might be unreliable allies and maintain their resolve only up to a point. But since their hatred of Philip arises from their own grievances, we can expect the enmity they feel due to their fears and sufferings to be steadfast.

[8] When such an opportunity falls in your path, men of Athens, you absolutely must not let it go and experience the same thing you have experienced repeatedly in the past. If, when we had returned from rendering aid to the Euboeans,[7] and Hierax and Stratocles of Amphipolis stood on this very platform[8] urging us to set sail and take possession of their city, we had exhibited the same enthusiasm on our own behalf as we did for the preservation of Euboea, you would have taken possession of Amphipolis then and rid yourselves of all the subsequent complications.[9] [9] And again, when Pydna, Poteidaea, Methone, Pagasae,[10] and the rest (not to waste time mentioning them one by one) were reported under siege, if back then we had rendered aid in person[11] to one of them, the first, enthusiastically and in a manner befitting us, we would now be dealing with an easier and considerably humbler Philip. But as it is, by constantly abandoning the present and thinking the future will work out well on its own, we, men of Athens, have caused Philip to grow, and we have made him as powerful as no previous king of Macedon has ever been.

But at this very moment an opportunity, this opportunity with the Olynthians, has come to our city on its own, and it is no less significant than those previous ones. [10] In my opinion, men of Athens, if a just auditor were appointed to assess what the gods have done for us, even though many things are not as they should be, nonetheless he would feel very grateful to them, and with good reason. The fact that we have suffered significant losses in the war can be rightly chalked up to our own negligence; but, as for the fact that this did not happen to us a long time ago, and that we have been presented with an alliance which will balance things out, if we are willing to make use of it, I would chalk that up as a kindness done by the gods' goodwill.

[11] In fact, I think it is like making money. If, you see, a person saves whatever he gets, he is very thankful to Fate; but if he spends it without realizing it, he expends his memory along with his money. It works the same way in politics. Those who do not make correct use of their opportunities do not remember it even if they received something useful from the gods in the past, because each previous event is judged in light of the most recent result. For this reason, men of Athens, you absolutely must think of the future, so that we may rectify this situation and erase the bad reputation caused by our past actions.

[12] If we abandon these people too, men of Athens, and Philip reduces Olynthus, somebody tell me what will be left to prevent him from marching wherever he likes. Is anyone among you, men of Athens, taking into account and observing the manner in which Philip has grown great from his original weakness? First he took Amphipolis, after that Pydna, next Poteidaea, then Methone. Then he advanced on Thessaly. [13] Next he took Pherae, Pagasae, Magnesia; having set everything up to his liking, he went to Thrace.[12] There, after expelling some kings and installing others, he fell ill. He convalesced but was not inclined to remain idle: immediately he attacked the Olynthians—I omit his expeditions against the Illyrians and Paeonians and Arybbas[13] and wherever one might mention.

[14] "So," you might say, "why are you telling us this now?" So that you recognize and perceive two things, men of Athens: first, the unprofitability

of constantly neglecting your affairs one by one; and second, the meddlesomeness[14] that Philip exhibits throughout his life, and that does not allow him to be content with his accomplishments and stay quiet. If he is resolved that he must constantly achieve something greater than he already has, while we are resolved not to come to grips with any of our affairs with authority, then consider how in the world you expect these things to turn out. [15] By the gods, who among you is so stupid that he does not realize that the war there will come here, if we neglect it? And in fact, if that happens, I am afraid, men of Athens, that, just as those who recklessly take out high-interest loans profit in the short run but are soon deprived of their capital as well, so we too will prove to have paid a high price for our easy living: thanks to our total pursuit of pleasure, we will later be compelled to do many difficult things against our will, and we will risk losing our possessions in our own country.

[16] Perhaps you might say that criticism comes easy and anyone can do it, but the job of an advisor is to clarify what must be done in regard to the present situation. I am not unaware, men of Athens, that, if something does not turn out as you wish, you often take out your anger not on those responsible, but on those who spoke last on the issue. Nonetheless, I do not think that, out of consideration for my personal safety, I should shrink from saying what I believe is best for you.

[17] I say that you must come to the aid of your interests in two ways: by preserving the cities[15] for the Olynthians and dispatching the soldiers to do it; and by ravaging Philip's territory both with triremes[16] and with additional soldiers. [18] If you neglect either of these, I fear that our expedition will be in vain. If you only attack his territory, he will wait that out until he brings Olynthus to terms, then return to his own country and fight us off without difficulty. If you only render aid to Olynthus, he will see that his home front is not in danger, press his siege and keep watch on the situation, and in time defeat the besieged. It is thus absolutely necessary that our auxiliary force be sizable and in two parts.

[19] Those are my recommendations for the auxiliary force. Now, as to revenues, you have money, men of Athens, in amounts available to no

other people; but you appropriate it as it pleases you.[17] Now, if you allocate this money to the soldiers on campaign, you need no additional source of revenue; but if you do not, you do need an additional source of revenue, or, to put it better, you have a complete lack of revenue.

"What then?" you might say. "Are you proposing that these funds be allocated to the military?" By Zeus, no. [20] I believe that troops need to be equipped, that a military fund should exist, and that there should be one and the same system for receiving the money and performing one's duty.[18] You, however, think you should receive the money pretty much as you do now, without complications, for the festivals. There is, in fact, another option, I think; namely, for everyone to pay the war-tax:[19] a large tax if we need a large fund, a small tax if we need a small fund. Money is needed, and without it none of our needs can be realized. Some people propose one source of revenue, others another; choose whichever of these you think suits you, and while the opportunity is here, get a handle on your business.

[21] Another thing worthy of your consideration and calculation is the situation in which Philip now finds himself. His present situation is not, as it appears and as one might say if he did not examine things carefully, in good shape or in the best possible state for him. Nor would he ever have undertaken this war if he had thought he would have to fight; he expected that he would carry everything before him on his mere approach, and in that he was mistaken.

This is the first thing that disturbs him by having turned out contrary to expectation, and it depresses him considerably; and then there is the Thessalian problem. [22] This is an area that is by nature always treacherous for all mankind, I suppose; and just as it always has been, so it is now to a high degree for Philip. In fact, they have voted to demand Pagasae back from him,[20] and they have prevented him from fortifying Magnesia. I personally just heard from some sources that they will no longer allow him to reap the revenues of their harbors and markets: they think they should use that income to administer the government of Thessaly rather than letting Philip take it. And if Philip is deprived of these funds, the means of support for his mercenaries will be severely constrained.

[23] What is more, we have to believe that the Paeonian and the Illyrian[21] and, in a word, all those people would rather be autonomous and free than slaves. They are unaccustomed to obeying anyone, and, as they say, the man is hubristic. And, by Zeus, perhaps that is not unbelievable: in senseless men, undeserved success often serves as the stepping-stone to wrong thinking; that is why it is often more difficult to keep good things than to get them. [24] Thus, men of Athens, you must consider his bad timing your opportunity and lend your enthusiastic support to the situation. You must send ambassadors where they are needed; you must serve in person; you must spur on all the rest. Consider this: if Philip got an opportunity like this against us, and a war arose on our borders, how eager do you think he would be to attack you? Are you, then, not ashamed if, having the opportunity, you will not have the courage to do to him what he would do to you if he could?

[25] In addition, men of Athens, let it not escape you that the choice before you now is whether you will fight in his territory or he will fight in yours. If the Olynthians' resources hold out, you will fight the war there and ravage his land, while reaping without fear the benefits of this land which you possess as your own. But if Philip takes Olynthus, who will prevent him from marching here? [26] The Thebans? It may be too harsh to say, but they will readily join in the invasion.[22] What about the Phocians? They are not even capable of protecting their own land unless you help them. Anybody else?

"But, my friend, Philip will not wish to invade." Surely he would be among the strangest of people, if what he now blurts out despite accusations of stupidity, he will not do when he actually can. [27] To be sure, the magnitude of the differences between fighting here and fighting there requires, I believe, no further discussion. If you yourselves had to serve abroad for only thirty days, taking as much produce of the land as was necessary for the army's use—I mean with no enemy in Attica—I think the losses incurred by the farmers among you would be greater than your expenditures on the entire war up to this point. And if war actually comes here, how much must we expect to lose then? In addition, there is the hubris and, on top of that, the disgrace of our situation, which to sensible men, at least, is a loss second to none.

[28] Viewing all these things together, we must send aid and push the war there: the wealthy, so that, by spending a little to defend what they rightly possess, they may enjoy the remainder without fear; those of military age,[23] in order to gain combat experience in Philip's territory and become fearsome guardians to keep their own country inviolate; the politicians, in order to make the reviews of their conduct easy, since the circumstances confronting you determine likewise your behavior as judges of their actions.[24] May things turn out well on every account.

# 6

# DEMOSTHENES 2

*Second Olynthiac*

## Introduction

The *Second Olynthiac* was delivered in 349, soon after the *First*, but it cannot be dated with precision. From the speech itself we can discern no concrete change in the state of affairs at Athens or Olynthus since the delivery of the *First Olynthiac*; it is possible, but not definite, that between the two speeches the first Athenian relief expedition under Chares had set sail (Part Two, Philip and Athens, p. 73). Here Demosthenes repeats in brief the proposals given in the *First Olynthiac*, adding the suggestion that an embassy be sent to Thessaly to secure an alliance (§11) and urging his countrymen to resolve their internal conflicts (§§27–30).

In the introduction (§§1–2) Demosthenes presents events at Olynthus as an opportunity for Athens and evidence of the gods' goodwill. The narration (§§3–10) concentrates on the deceitful conduct of Philip, which renders his power insecure. In the brief proposal section (§§11–13), the orator reiterates his plea to send help to Olynthus as quickly as possible, stressing the necessity of citizen service.

In his proofs (§§14–30), Demosthenes downplays the power of Philip. On its own, Macedon carries little weight (§14). Philip's goals are not compatible with those of his subjects (§§15–16). Philip's soldiers do not deserve their superior reputation, and the men who frequent his court are of low character (§§17–19). His weakness is ripe for exploitation; the Athenians must take advantage immediately, recalling the vigor of their ancestors rather than indulging their recent penchant for delay (§§20–26). A war-tax must be levied; the Athenians must take charge of affairs before engaging in accusations

(§27). Rivalries at home must be subordinated to interests abroad (§§28–30). The conclusion (§31) summarizes the orator's proposals and ends on a hopeful note.

### Second Olynthiac

[1] There are many instances, men of Athens, where I think one could see the goodwill of the gods being openly displayed toward our city, and not least in the current situation. For men have arisen to fight Philip who both inhabit a neighboring land and possess some military strength, and, most important of all, are of such a mindset concerning the war that they consider agreements with him to be untrustworthy and to mean the ruin of their country. This looks in all respects like some supernatural and divine benefaction. [2] So we must see to it, men of Athens, that we do not appear to treat ourselves worse than circumstances treat us. It is a mark of shameful men—rather, of the most shameful men—openly to abandon not only cities and places that we once controlled, but even the allies and opportunities provided to us by Fortune.

[3] Now, to discuss Philip's strength in detail, men of Athens, and to impel you to do your duty by using such arguments is not, I believe, the right course. Why not? Because, it seems to me, everything one could say on that topic involves glory for him and poor conduct by us. The more his performance has exceeded his merit, the more impressive everyone considers him; but the worse your conduct of affairs has compared with your duty, the greater the shame you have incurred.

[4] But I will pass over these things. If one truly examined the issue, men of Athens, he would see that Philip has grown great on our account, not his own. Now, there are things for which Philip owes gratitude to the politicians acting on his behalf, and for which you ought to exact punishment; but, as I see it, now is not the time to discuss them. But there is something to be said quite apart from these things, which is better for all of you to have heard, and which, men of Athens, would clearly constitute a serious reproach against him, if you are willing to scrutinize matters correctly; and this I will endeavor to say.

[5] Now, you might say that calling someone a faithless oath-breaker without providing evidence of his conduct constitutes groundless abuse, and rightly so. But to go through everything Philip has ever done and expose him on those grounds happens to require only a few words; and I believe it is in your interest to have them said for two reasons. First, it shows him to be a person of low character, as is actually the case. Second, it allows those who are exceedingly afraid of Philip, as though he were invincible, to see that he has exhausted all the deceptive means by which he rose to greatness and that his activities have reached an absolute end.

[6] I too, men of Athens, would consider Philip extremely fearsome and impressive if I saw him growing in power by right conduct. As it is, however, my observations and investigations lead to this conclusion. Originally, when certain individuals wanted to drive out of Athens the Olynthians who wanted to negotiate with you, Philip won us over in our foolishness by offering to hand over Amphipolis and by concocting that secret that was such a popular topic of conversation.[1] [7] Next he won the friendship of the Olynthians by capturing Poteidaea, which belonged to you—wronging his former allies—and handing it over to them. Now, most recently, he has won over the Thessalians by promising to hand over Magnesia and undertaking to fight the Phocian war on their behalf.[2]

There is absolutely no one who has dealt with him whom he has not cheated. This is how he has gained power, by deceiving and taking advantage of the ignorance of those who do not know him. [8] So, just as he has risen to greatness by these means, because everybody thought that he would do something to benefit them, in the same way and by these same means he ought to be brought back down, now that he has been exposed in doing everything for his own purposes. This, men of Athens, is the state of crisis in which Philip's affairs find themselves. Otherwise let someone come forth and show me—or, rather, you—that what I say is not the truth, or that those whom Philip deceived at first will trust him in the future, or that those who have been undeservedly enslaved would not now gladly be free.

[9] And in fact, if any of you believes that things are as I have said, but thinks that Philip will retain control of his affairs by force, because

he has already seized forts, harbors, and similar places, he is incorrect. When affairs are held together by goodwill, and all the allies in a war have the same interests, people are willing to work together, bear misfortunes, and persevere. On the other hand, when someone has grown strong, as Philip has, by greed and vice, the first excuse, even a small slip, upsets and dissolves everything. [10] It is impossible, impossible, men of Athens, for an unjust oath-breaking liar to acquire secure power. Such things hold out for one brief period; they flourish brilliantly on hope, perhaps, but in time they are detected and collapse upon themselves. Just as, I think, the lowest part of a house, a boat, and other similar things has to be the strongest, so too the beginnings and grounds of actions should be true and just. This is not the case now with Philip's actions.

[11] I say that we must come to the aid of the Olynthians; the best and speediest proposal gets my approval. We must send an embassy to the Thessalians to instruct some of them in these matters and to urge on others; for in point of fact they have now voted to demand Pagasae back and to hold negotiations regarding Magnesia. [12] See to it, now, men of Athens, that our ambassadors not only make speeches but also have some action to point to; namely, that you have taken the field in a manner worthy of the city and are on top of things. All speech, if it is not accompanied by action, appears pointless and empty, especially when it comes from our city: the more utterly ready we appear to use it, the less everybody trusts it. [13] You have to display a considerable shift and a great change, by paying the war-tax, by going on campaign, by doing everything readily,[3] if anyone is going to take you seriously. And if you are willing actually to see these things through properly, not only, men of Athens, will Philip's alliances be shown to be insecure and undependable, but also the elements of his own authority and power will be exposed in their weakness.

[14] As a rule, you see, the power of the Macedonian kingdom is not insignificant when it acts as an accessory to something else. It once served this purpose for you, in the time of Timotheus, against the Olynthians; then again, when it joined with the Olynthians against Poteidaea, their cooperation amounted to something; now it has come to the aid of the Thessalians, reduced to disorder by civil strife, against

their tyrannical house.⁴ Wherever one adds even a small force, I think, it always helps; but on its own Macedon is weak and full of defects.

[15] And in fact Philip has made it even more insecure for himself than it naturally was by all these activities, these wars and expeditions, which one might believe made him great. Do not think, men of Athens, that Philip and his subjects find joy in the same things. Philip yearns for glory and has made this his pursuit. He has deliberately chosen to suffer whatever may happen in the course of his actions and dangers, preferring the glory of accomplishing what no other Macedonian king ever has to a life spent in safety. [16] His subjects, however, have no share in the resulting honor. Constantly hammered by these expeditions up and down, they suffer grief and endure constant hardships: they are not allowed to spend time at their occupations or on their own concerns; and they cannot even dispose of whatever they produce however they can, since the trading stations in the country are closed due to the war.

[17] From those factors one could gauge without difficulty the opinion of the majority of Macedonians toward Philip. Now, he is surrounded by mercenaries and Foot Companions⁵ who have the reputation of being impressive and well-trained in the arts of war; but, as I just heard from someone who has been in that country, a man who is utterly incapable of lying, they are no better than anyone. [18] Any man among them who is experienced in war and its trials, he said, Philip pushes away out of rivalry: he wants to receive the credit for everything done, for, in addition to all his other traits, his spirit of rivalry too is insurpassable. And anyone who is possessed of self-control or generally civilized, and who cannot bear the daily intemperance of the life, the drunkenness, and the indecent dancing,⁶ gets pushed aside and is held of no account. [19] The people who are left around Philip are brigands and flatterers and the sort of men who get drunk and dance dances that I hesitate to name before you here.⁷ The truth of these things is obvious, since in point of fact the people whom everyone tried to drive out of Attica for having morals considerably lower than jugglers'—the notorious Callias the public slave and men like him, actors in farces and writers of disgusting songs which they create at their companions' expense in order to get a laugh—these are the people Philip loves and keeps around him.

[20] And even if you consider these things unimportant, men of Athens, to sensible people they are powerful indicators of Philip's delusional state of mind. At present, I think, his prosperity overshadows these things—successes are good at covering up such causes of reproach—but if he slips up in the least, then these flaws of his will receive an accurate examination. And I think, men of Athens, that things will become clear before long, if the gods will it and you so resolve. [21] Just as in the human body, while a person is healthy, he feels nothing wrong, but when disease strikes, all parts are affected, whether there is a fracture or a sprain or some other weakness, so it is with cities and tyrants: so long as they wage war abroad, their defects are invisible to the majority, but when they become entangled in a war on their own borders, that makes everything perfectly clear.

[22] Now, if any of you, men of Athens, seeing Philip's good fortune, considers him a formidable enemy on that account, he is reasoning like an intelligent man: Fortune carries great weight; or, rather, Fortune is everything, throughout all human affairs. Even so, if someone were to give me the choice, I would choose the fortune of our city—provided that you yourselves were willing to do your duty even to a slight extent—over that of Philip: I see that you have many more grounds for enjoying the goodwill of the gods than he does. [23] As I see it, though, we sit here and do nothing; but one who sits idle cannot order his friends to do something for him, much less the gods. It is no surprise that Philip, who campaigns and toils in person, is present at everything, and passes by no opportunity or season,[8] is getting the better of us, who hang fire and pass decrees and receive reports. That does not surprise me. The opposite would be surprising: if we, doing none of the things that people at war ought to do, had the advantage over someone doing all those things.

[24] Here is what does surprise me. Once, men of Athens, you stood up to the Spartans on behalf of the rights of the Greeks.[9] You often had the opportunity to achieve great personal gain, but you refused. Instead, so that others might obtain their rights, you expended your own resources in paying war-taxes[10] and took the lead in facing danger on campaign. But now you hesitate to go on campaign and delay levying a war-tax to defend your own possessions! Time and again you have saved

the rest of the Greeks, collectively and individually in turn; now you have lost what belongs to you, and you just sit there.

[25] That is what surprises me; and in addition to that, the fact that not one of you, men of Athens, is able to calculate how long you have been fighting Philip and what you have been doing while this time has passed. You must know. You have been procrastinating, hoping that someone else will act, accusing each other, mounting prosecutions, hoping some more, doing pretty much the same things you are doing right now: that is how all this time has passed. [26] Are you, then, so senseless, men of Athens, that you expect the city's situation to improve from pathetic to prosperous by means of the same policies that reduced it from prosperous to pathetic? That is neither logical nor natural; for in all cases it is naturally much easier to preserve what one has than to acquire it.[11]

But now, because of the war, none of our previous possessions is left to preserve, and we have to acquire. This is now a job for us to do ourselves. [27] I say that you must pay a war-tax. You must go on campaign in person with enthusiasm.[12] You must not bring accusations against anyone before you gain control of the situation; and then you must judge men based on their actual deeds, honor those deserving of praise, and punish wrongdoers. You must take away their excuses and remove your own deficiencies as well; for you cannot examine the deeds of others in a harsh light unless you have done your own duty first.

[28] Why do you think, men of Athens, that all the generals you dispatch avoid this war and find their own wars—if I must tell part of the truth about the generals too? Because in this case the prizes over which the war is fought are yours (if Amphipolis were captured, you would immediately take it for yourselves), while the risks are limited to the commanders, and there is no pay. But elsewhere the dangers are lesser, and the income goes to the commanders and their soldiers: Lampsacus, Sigeum, the ships they ransack.[13] So they each go where their profits are.

[29] As for you, when you look at the pathetic state of your affairs, you put the commanders on trial; but when you give them a hearing and hear these pleas of necessity, you let them go. And the result is that you argue and divide yourselves into factions,[14] some of you convinced of

one thing, others of another, and meanwhile our public affairs are in pathetic shape. In the past, men of Athens, you used to pay war-taxes by symmories;[15] now you conduct politics by symmories. The leader of each side is a politician; there is a general under him, and then the Three Hundred, who come to shout. The rest of you are assigned, some to this side, some to that.[16] [30] You must now let this go; even now you must become your own masters and make deliberation, speech, and action common prerogatives. If you assign some of you to give orders, as if in a tyranny, and others to be forced to serve as trierarchs, pay the war-tax, and fight on campaign, and still others only to vote to condemn the aforementioned, taking absolutely no part in their hardships, then not a single one of our needs will be accomplished in time: whichever group has been wronged will come up short, and then you will have them to punish instead of the enemy.

[31] This is what I propose, in short. Everyone must pay as war-tax an equal proportion of his assets. Everyone must serve abroad in turn, until you have all served.[17] To everyone who comes forward you must give a hearing, and you must choose the best of all proposals you hear, not whatever this or that man proposes. If you do these things, not only will you praise the proposer for the moment, but you will also praise yourselves afterward, when your entire situation is in better shape.

# 7

# DEMOSTHENES 3

## *Third Olynthiac*

### Introduction

Demosthenes delivered the *Third Olynthiac* some time after the first two, in late 349 or early 348. By this point the Athenians had dispatched at least one relief effort to Olynthus (§35 with note). Demosthenes, however, had lost some of his confidence: while in the first two *Olynthiacs* he urged both the defense of Olynthus and the punishment of Philip, he is now willing to forgo the second goal, concentrating only on the first (§2). He now openly suggests (cf. the more guarded statements at 1.19) the repeal of Eubulus' law governing the theoric fund (Part Two, Philip and Athens, p. 72) and the redirection of those funds to the military (§11).

In the introduction (§§1–2) Demosthenes notes the inconsistency between the speeches being given in the Assembly and the current state of affairs. The time when Athens could both protect her allies and attack Philip is past; now the safety of the allies must be her paramount concern. The narration (§§3–9) urges the Athenians to learn from their previous mistakes and defend Olynthus by a substantial show of force. Failure to do so will result in shame and leave Attica vulnerable.

In his proposals (§§10–13), Demosthenes recommends the appointment of a commission of lawgivers to repeal Eubulus' law on the theoric fund as well as certain statutes governing the military. The present situation dissuades politicians from proposing the correct course of action; Eubulus himself should propose the repeal of his own law in order to clear the way.

Next Demosthenes offers his proofs (§§14–32). The Athenians must stop deceiving themselves and act immediately, or they will have only themselves to blame (§§14–20). The orator contrasts the glorious achievements of Pericles and other fifth-century politicians with the popularity-courting demagoguery of his contemporaries (§§21–29). In the past the people controlled the politicians; now the situation is reversed (§§30–32). In his conclusion (§§33–36), Demosthenes reiterates his call to action and proposes a uniform system of pay for service.

### Third Olynthiac

[1] Entirely different judgments present themselves, men of Athens, when I look at our situation and at the speeches I hear: I see the speeches concerning themselves with punishing Philip, while our situation has reached the point where we must see to it that we avoid suffering harm first. The people who make these speeches, it seems to me, simply err by presenting you with a subject for your deliberation that is not the real one. [2] Now, I know all too well that it was once possible for the city both to keep a secure hold on her own possessions and to punish Philip: it was in my own time, not long ago, that both these possibilities existed. Now, however, I am persuaded that in the first instance it is a sufficient start for us to preserve our allies. If we secure this, then we will be able to examine whom to punish and how. But before the beginning is correctly established, I believe it is pointless to utter a single word about the end.

[3] Now, if ever, the present crisis calls for considerable care and deliberation. What I find most difficult is not what advice I should offer regarding the present situation; rather, I am at a loss, men of Athens, as to the manner in which I should speak to you about it. I am persuaded by what I know from my own eyes and ears that most of our affairs have gotten away from us because we are unwilling to do our duty, not because we do not understand what it is. And I call upon you to bear with me if I speak freely, and to look at whether I am telling the truth, and whether I do so with the goal of improving our future; for you see that it is due to certain individuals' quest for popularity in public speaking that present circumstances have degenerated completely.

[4] I consider it necessary first to speak to you briefly about past events. You remember, men of Athens, two or three years ago, when the

news was brought to you that Philip was in Thrace besieging Heraion Teichos. It was then the month of Maemacterion.[1] Amidst many speeches and much commotion in the Assembly, you voted to launch forty triremes, to man them yourselves[2] with men up to the age of forty-five, and to impose a war-tax of sixty talents.[3] [5] After that, the rest of that year passed, then Hecatombaeon, Metageitnion, Boedromion.[4] While it was still barely Boedromion, after the Mysteries,[5] you dispatched Charidemus with ten ships, empty,[6] and five talents of silver. For, when news of Philip's illness or death was reported (both versions reached you),[7] you thought the time for your assistance had passed, men of Athens, and you dismissed the expedition. But that was the exact time: if we had sent aid there then, as we had decreed, and with enthusiasm, Philip would not have survived to trouble us now.

[6] What was done then cannot be changed. Now, however, the opportunity of another war has presented itself; this is why I have mentioned these things, so that you do not have the same experience. How shall we use this opportunity, men of Athens? If you do not render aid "with all strength according to your ability,"[8] see how completely you will have managed the war in Philip's interest. [7] There were the Olynthians, in possession of a respectable force, and the state of affairs was such that Philip did not feel confidence in them, nor they in him. We made peace with them, and they with us. This served as a stumbling-block to Philip and an annoyance, that a great city reconciled with us should be on the lookout for opportunities against him. We thought we should provoke them to war by all means;[9] and now the very thing that everyone was talking about has somehow or other been achieved.

[8] What is left, then, men of Athens, except to render aid with strength and enthusiasm? I don't see what. Apart from the shame that would surround us if we should dishonorably surrender one of our interests, I see that there would be no small fear of the consequences, with the Thebans disposed toward us as they are, the Phocians' funds exhausted, and no one to prevent Philip, once he has reduced his present goal,[10] from putting pressure on the situation here.[11] [9] Now, if any of you is putting off doing his duty until then, he must want to see the terrors of war at close range when it is possible to hear of them occurring elsewhere, and to seek allies for himself when it is possible now to render

aid to others. I think we all know pretty well that if we throw away the present opportunity, that is where the situation is headed.

[10] "Well," you might say, "we have all decided that we must render aid, and we will; but tell us how." Now, do not be surprised, men of Athens, if what I say is unexpected to most of you. You must appoint lawgivers. With these lawgivers, though, do not enact any law (you have enough already), but repeal those laws which are presently doing you harm. [11] I mean those concerning the theoric fund—I put it as plainly as that—and some of those concerning soldiers on campaign. Some of these laws distribute military funds as theoric allotments to those who stay at home; others confer immunity upon those who evade service and thus lower the morale of those who want to do their duty. When you have repealed these laws and made the way safe for offering the best proposals,[12] then look for someone to propose what you all know is to your advantage.

[12] But before you do that, do not look to see who will be willing to offer the best proposal on your behalf, only to face ruin at your hands. You will not find him, especially since the sole result will be that the man who makes the proposal and the motion will come to some unjust harm; rather than improving matters at all, he will actually make offering the best proposal an even more fearsome prospect in the future than it is now. In fact, men of Athens, we should demand that the same men who made these laws[13] repeal them: [13] it is not right that those who made the laws enjoy popularity for what has harmed the entire city, while he who now offers the best proposal is punished with hatred for what will improve conditions for us all. Before you prepare the way, men of Athens, you should never expect any man to be so powerful among you as to pay no penalty for breaking these laws, or so foolish as to expose himself to obvious harm.

[14] And you should certainly not fail to recognize as well, men of Athens, that a decree is worthless unless there is added to it your willingness to carry out its terms with enthusiasm. If decrees were sufficient in themselves either to compel you to do your duty or to carry out the terms written in them, you would not have decreed many things but done few, or rather none, of them; nor would Philip's hubris[14] have

lasted such a long time: he would have been punished for it long ago, if it were up to the decrees. [15] But this is not how things work. In terms of order, action comes after speaking and voting, but in terms of force it comes first and is stronger. This, then, we must add; we have the rest. There are those among you, men of Athens, who have the ability to say what must be said, and you are of all men the keenest critics of the spoken word; now you will also have the ability to act, if you follow the right course.

[16] What time, what opportunity are you looking for, men of Athens, that is better than the present? When will you do what you must, if not now? Has the man[15] not already seized all of our positions; and if he becomes master of this land too, will we not suffer the most shameful fate of all? Are the people whom we promised readily to preserve if they went to war not now at war? Is he not the enemy? Is he not in possession of our property? Is he not a barbarian? Is he not whatever one could call him? [17] By the gods, after allowing all this and practically helping him arrange it, are we then going to seek out those responsible? For we will not take responsibility ourselves, of that I am sure. In the dangers of war, no one who runs away accuses himself; he accuses the general and the men positioned nearby and everyone else instead. And yet, I presume, they lost the battle because of everyone who ran: the one who accuses the rest could have held his position, and if each man had done so, they would have won.

[18] So it is now. Someone does not propose what is best: let someone else stand up and offer a proposal, instead of accusing him. Another man offers a better proposal: carry it out, and good luck to you. Suppose the proposal is unpleasant: there the speaker is no longer at fault, unless he omits the necessary prayer. Praying, men of Athens, is easy: you just collect everything you want in a few words. But making a choice, when the task is to consider real issues, is no longer that simple: you have to take what is best over what is pleasant, if you cannot have both together.

[19] "If someone has a way for us to leave the theoric fund alone and propose other sources of revenue for the military, is he not the better advisor?" you might say. Absolutely, men of Athens, if that is actually possible. It shocks me, though, if it ever has happened or will happen to

anyone that, after expending what he has on what he does not need, he has a plentiful supply of what he no longer has for what he does need. Now, in my opinion, speeches of that kind are largely founded on each person's wishes. That is why self-deception is the easiest thing of all: everybody believes what he wants to believe, but reality often does not work that way. [20] So, men of Athens, see what the situation allows and how you will be able to go abroad and draw pay. It is not a mark of intelligent or noble men to neglect a wartime operation due to lack of funds and then bear lightly the consequent reproach, nor to take up arms and attack the Corinthians and Megarians[16] but allow Philip to enslave Greek cities because our troops lack supplies.

[21] I have not chosen to say these things pointlessly, in order to make enemies of some of you. I am not so stupid or unfortunate as to wish to make enemies without thinking I was doing some good. Rather, I judge it to be the job of a just citizen to choose the preservation of our affairs over popularity in speaking. In fact, I hear—perhaps you have too—that the speakers in our ancestors' time, whom all those who come up here[17] praise but do not emulate in the least, employed this habit and custom in their policies. I am talking about the renowned Aristeides;[18] Nicias;[19] my own namesake;[20] Pericles.[21]

[22] But since then these politicians have appeared who constantly ask you, "What would you like? What shall I propose? How shall I oblige you?" The interests of the city have been sacrificed for immediate popularity; things like this happen; and all their affairs are in fine shape, while yours are disgraceful. [23] Consider further, men of Athens, how someone might summarize the deeds of your ancestors' time and those of your time. It will be a brief account and one well known to you, for prosperity is possible if you use your own examples, not those of others.

[24] They, who were not flattered or fawned upon by their politicians the way you are now by yours, ruled over the Greeks with their consent for forty-five years.[22] They deposited more than 10,000 talents on the Acropolis.[23] The king who held that region[24] was subject to them, as a barbarian should be subject to Greeks. They fought in person on both land and sea and set up many a fine trophy;[25] and, alone among men, they left behind a reputation for deeds that is more powerful than envy.

[25] That is how they conducted themselves in Greek affairs. Now observe how they handled their affairs within the city, both public and private. In public they decked out for us so many and such beautiful edifices and temples and offerings inside them that they left none of their successors the possibility of surpassing them. And in private they were so modest and so steadfastly devoted to the spirit of the constitution [26] that if any of you actually knows what the house of Aristeides or Miltiades[26] or any of those outstanding men of the day looked like, he sees that it was no more impressive than their neighbor's. You see, they did not conduct the city's business for their own personal advantage; rather, each of them thought that he must increase the commonwealth. Because they administered Greek affairs faithfully, divine affairs piously, and their own affairs equitably, they acquired great prosperity, as you would expect.

[27] That was the way their affairs stood back then, with the men I mentioned as their leaders. And how do our affairs stand now under the direction of these worthy individuals? Is it similar, or even close? They—about the rest I will keep silent, although I have plenty I could say, but I will say this: having come upon such an open field as you all see, with the Spartans in ruins, the Thebans fully occupied, and nobody else qualified to contest first place with us, when we could both enjoy secure possession of what is ours and referee the rights of others, [28] we stand deprived of our own territory; we have spent over 1,500 talents to no good use; the allies we acquired during the war these men have lost in time of peace; and we have trained an enemy of such strength against ourselves. Otherwise let someone come up here and tell me from what source other than ourselves Philip has risen to power.

[29] "But, my friend, if those affairs are in pathetic shape, certainly things in the city itself are doing better now." And what could one mention? The battlements we are plastering? The roads we are repairing? The fountains? The useless nonsense? Take a look at the men who have brought you these policies.[27] Some of them have gone from rags to riches; others from obscurity to fame; some have adorned their private homes more impressively than public edifices. The more the city's situation declines, the more theirs improves.

[30] What really is the cause of all these things, and why really was everything fine then but wrong now? Because in those days the people itself had the courage to act and fight, was master of the politicians, and was itself in charge of dispensing all benefits; each of the others was happy to receive from the people his share of honor, authority, and other benefits. [31] But now it is the opposite. The politicians are in charge of all benefits, and everything is done through them. As for you, the people, you have been hamstrung, deprived of money and allies, and relegated to the role of underling and appendage; you are happy if these men dispense theoric allotments to you or conduct the Boedromia,[28] and, manliest of all, you even feel grateful to them for what belongs to you. And they keep you penned up in this city and lead you to these things and tame you, training you to their hands! [32] Now, in my opinion, it is never possible for those who commit petty and lowly acts to possess a great and vigorous spirit; for just as the practices of men are, so must their spirits be. By Demeter,[29] I would not be surprised if I should incur greater harm at your hands for talking about these things than the men who did them; for you do not always allow free speech on all topics, and in fact I am surprised that it has been allowed now.

[33] If, then, even now you should rid yourselves of these habits and be willing to fight and act in a manner worthy of yourselves, and use your domestic surplus as start-up capital to obtain benefits abroad, then maybe, just maybe, men of Athens, you might acquire an absolute and sizable benefit and get rid of sources of income such as these,[30] which resemble the morsels doctors give their patients. Those neither inject strength nor permit death; likewise, these funds that you now distribute among yourselves are neither large enough to provide sufficient assistance nor small enough to allow you to give them up and do something else; they merely increase the idleness of each one of you.

[34] "So, you're proposing pay for service?" someone will ask.[31] Yes, I am; and also the immediate establishment of one and the same system for everything, men of Athens, so that each man receives his share of public money and provides the city with whatever it might need. Suppose it is possible to be at peace: he is better off staying at home, relieved of the necessity of doing something shameful out of poverty. Suppose that something happens like what has happened now: supported by this

same income, he is ready to serve in person as a soldier, as is right, in defense of his country. Suppose one of you is above military age:[32] what he now receives irregularly without doing any good, he will receive, under an equal arrangement, for overseeing and managing all that must be done.

[35] And in short, without any subtractions or additions except small ones, I have removed the chaos and brought the city into order, by instituting the same arrangement for receiving money, serving in the military, sitting on juries, and doing whatever each man's age allows and the opportunity dictates. Nowhere have I proposed that we should distribute what belongs to those who do their jobs to those who do not, or that we ourselves should sit lazy, idle, and helpless, hearing about the victories of whoever's mercenaries.[33] That is what is happening now. [36] And in no way do I criticize the man who does something necessary on your behalf;[34] rather, I call upon you to do for yourselves that for which you honor others, and not to yield the place of virtue, men of Athens, which your forefathers earned through many glorious dangers and bequeathed to you.

I have pretty much said what I think is beneficial. May you make the choice that will benefit the city and all of you.

# 8

# DEMOSTHENES 5

*On the Peace*

## Introduction

The settlement of the Third Sacred War and the honors bestowed upon Philip by the Delphic Amphictyony (Part Two, Philip and Athens, pp. 75–6) caused bad feeling at Athens. Philip had failed to live up to several promises made by Aeschines and Philocrates earlier in the year (§10), and Athenian sentiments quickly turned against their new ally. The Athenians refused to recognize Philip's membership on the Amphictyonic Council, boycotted the meeting at which he was elected to preside over the Pythian Games, and took in Phocian refugees. Philip and other Amphictyonic states responded with complaints (§§14, 19). Late in 346, Demosthenes delivered his oration *On the Peace*, urging the Assembly to abide by the Peace of Philocrates and avert a war against Philip and the Amphictyonic League.

In the introduction (§§1–3), Demosthenes notes the difficulty of Athens' position and the multiplicity of opinions, and urges the Assembly not to delay action by excessive deliberation. The narration (§§4–12) begins with a statement of false modesty, followed by three instances in which Demosthenes offered the right counsel, in regard to Euboea (§5), Neoptolemus (§§6–8), and the promises of Aeschines and Philocrates (§§9–10).

Demosthenes' proposal (§§13–14) is a simple one: Athens must live up to the terms of the Peace of Philocrates and avoid providing the Amphictyonic Council with an excuse to declare a sacred war. Several proofs (§§14–23) are then offered in support of the proposal: Athens could easily withstand a war against Thebes alone (§§15–16) but not a war against the entire Amphictyony and Philip (§§18–19). The Thebans and Thessalians cooperated with Philip from private

motives but ended up acting in his interests and against their own
(§§20–23). In his conclusion (§§24–25) Demosthenes offers blunt
comparisons with recent events to convince his countrymen to keep
the peace: the Athenians have sacrificed more important interests
without breaking the treaty, and they should not violate it now for
the sake of "the shadow in Delphi."

### On the Peace

[1] I see, men of Athens, that our present business involves considerable unpleasantness and confusion, not only because we have thrown
away many of our interests and there is nothing to gain by giving nice
speeches about them, but also because, by the same token, regarding our
remaining interests, there is not even a single point on which everyone
can agree on what is expedient: some favor this course of action, others
another. [2] Deliberation is by nature unpleasant and difficult, but you
have made it much more difficult, men of Athens. All the rest of
mankind customarily makes use of deliberation before the fact; you do
so after the fact. The result of this is that, for as long as I am aware, he
who criticizes the mistakes you have made is held in high esteem and
considered a good speaker, while your interests and the reasons for your
deliberation slip away from you. [3] Nonetheless, despite this state of
affairs, I think—and I stand here having persuaded myself—that if you
are willing to step away from your shouting and bickering and listen, as
befits those considering such important issues on behalf of the city, I
will be able to make a proposal and offer counsel which will improve
our present situation and preserve the matters under discussion.

[4] I know perfectly well, men of Athens, that speaking in the Assembly about oneself and the speeches one has given always brings considerable profit to those who have the audacity to do it. I, however, consider it
so vulgar and offensive that, even when I see that it is necessary, I nonetheless hesitate. But I think that you will better judge what I am now
going to say if you bear in mind a few of the things I have said in the past.

[5] First of all, men of Athens, when things in Euboea were in disar-
ray and certain individuals were trying to persuade you to render aid to
Plutarchus and undertake an inglorious and expensive war,[1] I was the

first and only one to come forward and speak in opposition, and I was practically torn apart by those who persuaded you to make many great mistakes for the sake of small profits. After a short time had passed, after incurring shame in the bargain and suffering what no people had ever suffered at the hands of those they came to help, you all realized the poor character of those who had convinced you to do this and the superiority of my proposal.

[6] And again, men of Athens, when I noticed Neoptolemus the actor using his profession as a pretext to obtain safe conduct, doing the greatest harm to the city, and managing and supervising communications from you in the interest of Philip,[2] I came forward and told you, motivated by no personal enmity or sycophancy,[3] as subsequent events have made clear. [7] In this case I will not blame those who spoke in Neoptolemus' defense (there was not a single one) but you yourselves: if you were watching tragic actors in the Theater of Dionysus, and not discussing matters of security and affairs of state, you could not have listened to him with such favor or to me with such hostility. [8] Yet by now, I think, you have all realized that, while he claimed to be taking that trip then to enemy territory in order to collect money owed to him there, bring it back here, and undertake liturgies,[4] and while he relied most heavily on the argument that it was terrible to bring charges against people who transferred their assets from there to here, when he could safely do so on account of the peace, he liquidated the visible property[5] he had acquired here and went off to Philip with the proceeds.

[9] These two events, which I predicted, bear witness in favor of the speeches I gave, since I brought them to light correctly and justly, exactly as they were. And third, men of Athens—and after mentioning just this one thing I will immediately proceed to the topic I have come forward to discuss—when we ambassadors came home after receiving the oaths concerning the peace,[6] [10] at that point certain people[7] were promising that Thespiae and Plataea would be rebuilt; that Philip, if he gained control, would save the Phocians and break up the Theban state; and that Oropus would be yours and Euboea would be returned in exchange for Amphipolis.[8] Led on by these deceptive hopes, you abandoned the Phocians, which was neither advantageous nor, perhaps, honorable. It will be clear to you that I did not deceive you or keep

silent in regard to any of these promises: I told you publicly—as I know you recall—that I neither knew of nor expected such developments, and thought that anyone who spoke of them was talking nonsense.

[11] All these things, which I clearly foresaw better than others, men of Athens, I will not attribute to any cleverness or pretense of superiority, nor will I pretend that my judgment and foresight are due to any causes other than those I will tell you, and they are two. The first, men of Athens, is good luck, which I see to be more powerful than all the cleverness and wisdom men possess. [12] Second, I judge and assess our affairs for free: no one could point to any profit attached to my policies and proposals. Thus, that which is advantageous presents itself to me in its correct form, however it appears on the basis of the actual facts. But when you add money to one side or the other, as on a scale, it carries the calculation with it and pulls it down toward its own side; and one who has done this can no longer calculate anything correctly or soundly.

[13] Now, the first thing that I say must be established is this: we must see to it that anyone wishing to outfit the city with allies or a contribution[9] or anything else does so without breaking the existing peace—not to say that the peace is admirable, or even worthy of you. But whatever its character, it would have suited our interests more had the peace never happened than for us to violate it now that it has happened: we have thrown away many assets whose possession would make the war safer and easier for us than it is now.

[14] Second, men of Athens, we must see to it that we do not provoke those men who have assembled and are now claiming to be the Amphictyons[10] to a necessary pretext for declaring a common war against us. If war should flare up again between us and Philip over Amphipolis or some such private claim not shared by the Thessalians or Argives or Thebans, I do not think that any of them would declare war against us, [15] least of all (and please do not shout out before you hear it) the Thebans—not because they are well-disposed toward us, and not because they would not like to gratify Philip, but because they know perfectly well (even if you might call them utterly stupid)[11] that, if war arises between them and you, they will bear all the ill effects while someone

else[12] sits in wait for the benefits. They would not, therefore, abandon themselves to this fate unless the war had a common origin and cause.

[16] And even if we went back to war with the Thebans over Oropus[13] or some other private concern, I think we would suffer no harm: I think that our allies and theirs would send aid if someone invaded our lands but would not help either of us mount an invasion. For, in point of fact, this is how alliances work—those that are worthy of consideration—and the fact of the matter is naturally like this. [17] Each ally's goodwill toward either us or the Thebans does not extend equally to our safety and to our conquest of others: everyone would like us to be safe for their own sake, but no one wants either of us to conquer them and be their masters.

What, then, do I fear, and what do I think we must guard against? The possibility that the war to come may seize upon a common pretext and a common grievance shared by all. [18] If the Argives and Messenians and Megalopolitans and the rest of the Peloponnesians who are similarly minded become hostile because we send an embassy to the Spartans and appear to accept some of their actions; and if the Thebans, who already are hostile, they say, become even more hostile because we harbor their fugitives[14] and display our ill will toward them in every way; [19] and if the Thessalians become hostile because we harbor Phocian refugees;[15] and if Philip becomes hostile because we hinder his admission to the Amphictyony, I fear that all of them, each angry about his own concerns, may bring a common war against us, using the resolutions of the Amphictyons as a pretext. Each of them will then be drawn along beyond what is in their interests, as happened with the Phocians.

[20] You certainly know that, as it turned out, the Thebans, Philip, and the Thessalians did all cooperate, although they did not share individual desires in the least. The Thebans, for their part, were unable to prevent Philip from crossing and taking control of the pass,[16] nor even from showing up last and getting the glory for their efforts. [21] Now the Thebans have made some progress in terms of recovering their land, but in terms of honor and reputation they have performed most shamefully; for if Philip had not crossed the pass, they would have gained nothing. This is not what they wanted; but since they had the desire to take Orchomenus and Coroneia but not the ability, they put up with all of it.

[22] Now, as for Philip, some people no doubt have the audacity to say that he did not want to hand over Orchomenus and Coroneia to the Thebans but was compelled. Well, good luck to them; but I do know that Philip certainly did not care about that issue more than he wanted to seize the passes, get the glory for appearing to bring the war to a decision on his own authority, and conduct the Pythian Games himself.[17] These are the things he longed for most.

[23] The Thessalians wanted neither of these things: they did not want either the Thebans or Philip to become powerful, since they believed it was all directed against them. Their desire was to gain control of the Amphictyonic meeting[18] and matters at Delphi, two significant advantages. They cooperated in the aforementioned actions out of yearning for these things. You will find that each was induced by their own individual concerns to do many things they did not want to do. This, I tell you, this is what we must guard against.

[24] "So we are supposed to carry out these orders[19] out of fear? Are you giving us these orders too?" Far from it. I think we must see to it that we do nothing unworthy of ourselves, that war does not occur, and that we appear to everyone to possess good sense and to plead a just cause. In response to those who think we should boldly endure whatever comes and who do not foresee war, I want to consider the following. We allow the Thebans to occupy Oropus; and if someone were to ask us, bidding us tell the truth, "Why?" we would answer, "To avoid war." [25] Likewise, we have just now ceded Amphipolis to Philip under the terms of the treaty;[20] we allow Cardia to be positioned separate from the rest of the Chersonese;[21] we allow the Carian[22] to seize the islands, Chios, Cos, and Rhodes; and we allow the Byzantines to bring vessels into port,[23] clearly because we believe that the tranquility that results from the peace brings us more benefits than butting heads and bickering over these issues. It would therefore be silly and completely hard-headed of us, who have dealt thus with each of them individually concerning our own and most essential interests, now to go to war with all of them over the shadow in Delphi.[24]

# 9

# DEMOSTHENES 6

*Second Philippic*

## Introduction

In 344, the Athenians sent an embassy to the Peloponnese with the purpose of agitating against Philip. The Macedonian king sent a letter of complaint to Athens, and in response to that complaint Demosthenes delivered his *Second Philippic* before the Athenian Assembly (Part Two, Philip and Athens, p. 77). In this oration, Demosthenes casts Philip as the enemy of Athens, charges him with violating the Peace of Philocrates, and demands its rectification (*epanorthôsis*). Unfortunately, the reply that Demosthenes proposes to give to Philip's envoys (§28) never materializes.

In the introduction (§§1–5), Demosthenes again draws the distinction between speech (at which the Athenians are proficient) and action (in which they are sluggish). In order to rectify the situation, they must choose the correct course of action over the most convenient. The narration (§§6–27) deals with the growing power of Philip and the attendant threat to Athens. Philip's actions following the conclusion of the Peace of Philocrates have favored Thebes, Argos, and Messenia over Athens (§§6–11). Despite Athens' greater naval power and her status as his ally, Philip has chosen to make common cause with Thebes, because he knows that Athens represents the only obstacle to his domination (§§12–17). He realizes that the Athenians are aware of his actions and is therefore resolved to make the first strike; this is why he has made friends of the Thebans and Argives (§§18–19). At this point Demosthenes recaps a speech he recently gave to the Messenians, despite which he believes they will ally with Philip (§§20–26); he hopes that the Athenians will display more intelligence (§27).

At §28, Demosthenes offers to present a proposal but does not do so. Instead, in the proofs that follow (§§28–36), he launches an attack on his rivals. Two groups are to blame for the current state of affairs: those who relayed the promises Philip made in his attempts at peace (§§28–29) and those who supported Philip and opposed Demosthenes following the return of the second embassy of 346 (§§29–30; Part Two, Philip and Athens, p. 75). These men deceived the Athenians into extending the Peace to cover Philip's descendants, and now the situation is deteriorating further (§§31–33). Responsibility for the adverse developments following the Peace lies with Demosthenes' opponents (§§34–36). In his conclusion (§37), the orator prays that the truth of his statements not be proven to the detriment of the Athenian people.

### Second Philippic

[1] Whenever speeches are given, men of Athens, concerning what Philip is doing and how he is violating the peace,[1] I see that the speeches for our cause are always manifestly just and sympathetic,[2] and that everyone who accuses Philip is always deemed to say what needs to be said. But I see virtually none of the necessary actions, or the things that make these speeches worth hearing, being done. [2] Instead, all the city's affairs have reached the point where, the more extensively and clearly one exposes Philip as both transgressing the peace with you and plotting against all the Greeks, the more difficult it becomes to advise what we must do.

[3] The reason for this, men of Athens, is that those seeking unfair gain have to be stopped by deeds and actions, not by words. But, in the first place, we who come up here[3] avoid proposing and advising these things, hesitating to incur your enmity; instead we discuss in detail what Philip is doing, and how terrible it is, and things like that. Second, you who sit here are better equipped than Philip when it comes to speaking in the interest of justice and understanding when someone else does so; but when it comes to stopping him from doing what he is currently engaged in, you are utterly lazy.

[4] The resulting state of affairs is a necessary one, I suppose, and perhaps reasonably so. Each of you does better at the pursuits in which

you spend your time and which you take seriously: Philip at actions, you at words. So if, even now, you are satisfied with pleading the more just cause, that is easily done and requires no additional effort. [5] If, however, we must examine how to rectify the present situation and not let it get even further away from us without our noticing it, and how to avoid being confronted by a power of such magnitude that we cannot raise a hand in resistance, then the same manner of deliberation that we have employed in the past will not do; instead, all of us speakers, and you our listeners, must choose the course that is best and that will save us over the easiest and most pleasant one.

[6] Now, first of all, men of Athens, if anyone remains confident when he sees how powerful Philip is and how much he controls, and thinks that this presents no danger to the city and that all these preparations are not directed at you, I am dumbfounded; and I wish to ask all of you alike to listen to me as I briefly state the reasons that it has occurred to me to expect the opposite and to consider Philip our enemy. Then, if you find that I possess superior foresight, you may follow my advice; but if you favor those who feel confident and have placed their trust in him, you may side with them.

[7] Here is my assessment, men of Athens. What did Philip control immediately after the peace was established? Thermopylae and the affairs in Phocis.[4] What then? How did he make use of these? He deliberately chose to act to the benefit of the Thebans and not to the benefit of our city. Why did he do that? Because, I suppose, he was examining his calculations with an eye to his own aggrandizement and to putting everything under his control, and not at all with an eye to peace or tranquility or any just motive; [8] and he correctly perceived that he could not offer or perform for our city and men of our character anything so significant as to persuade you to abandon any of the other Greeks to him for the sake of your own profit. He saw that you would take justice into account, avoid the dishonor inherent in such an act, foresee all that you ought, and oppose him, if he tried to do anything of the sort, just as you would if you were at war.

[9] As for the Thebans, he believed (as in fact it turned out) that, in exchange for what was accruing to them, they would allow him to do

everything else however he wanted; and not only would they not act against him or stand in his way, but they would even fight at his side if he told them to. And now, having made the same assumption about the Messenians and Argives, he is treating them well. This is the greatest tribute to you, men of Athens: [10] by these actions of his you have been judged to be the only people of all who would not betray the common rights of the Greeks for any profit, nor trade your goodwill toward the Greeks for any favor or benefit.

It is reasonable that he made this assumption about you and a different one about the Argives and Thebans, not only looking at the present but also taking past actions into account. [11] He discovers and hears, I think, that your ancestors, when they could have ruled over the rest of the Greeks provided that they themselves submitted to the Great King, not only refused to put up with that offer when Alexander, the ancestor of these people, came as a herald to discuss the matter, but even chose to abandon their country and submit to whatever suffering resulted.[5] After that they performed the deeds that all men forever love to recount but no one has been able to relate in a worthy manner—for that reason I too will pass them over, and rightly so (for the deeds of those men are greater than anyone could express in words). As for the ancestors of the Thebans and Argives, the former fought alongside the barbarian, and the latter offered no resistance.[6]

[12] Thus Philip knows that both those cities would be happy to profit privately without considering the common good of the Greeks. He believed, then, that if he chose you, he would be selecting people who would be his friends provided that he did what was right; but if he brought them over to his side, he would have accomplices to his own greed. That is why he chooses them instead of you, both then and now. He certainly does not see that they have more triremes[7] than you do, nor has he discovered an inland empire and renounced one on the coast and in the ports. Nor does he fail to recall the statements and promises on the strength of which he got the peace.[8]

[13] But, by Zeus, someone claiming to know all this might say, it is not out of greed or for the reasons I allege that Philip did those things, but because the demands of the Thebans are more just than yours. Of

all possible reasons, though, this is the one he cannot give now. How could the person who commands the Spartans to let go of Messene claim that he handed over Orchomenus and Coroneia to the Thebans because he believed it was just?[9]

[14] But, by Zeus, he was compelled (this is the rest of the argument);[10] and against his judgment, caught in the middle between the cavalry of Thessaly and the hoplites[11] of Thebes, he made these concessions. Fine. So they claim that he is going to hold the Thebans under suspicion, and some of them go around telling stories that he is going to fortify Elatea.[12] [15] Well, he is "going to" do those things, and he will continue "going to" do them, by my judgment; but he is not "going to" join the Messenians and Argives in attacking the Spartans: he is already sending in mercenaries and dispatching money, and he himself is expected any day at the head of a large force.[13] So he is trying to destroy the Spartans, the existing enemies of Thebes, but he is now saving the same Phocians he himself previously annihilated? Who would believe that? [16] I do not think that Philip, either if he had been forced at first to act against his will or if he were now renouncing the Thebans, would constantly oppose their enemies. Rather, based on his present actions, he clearly did those things by choice as well; and based on all his actions, if one views them correctly, he is clearly marshalling all of his intrigues against our city.

[17] And this does occur to him now out of a kind of necessity. Consider this. He wants to rule, and he has come to the understanding that you are his only opponents in this. He has been doing wrong for a long time now, and he himself is most conscious of that fact. It is thanks to your possessions which he occupies that he has a secure hold on all the rest; he believes that, if he were to let Amphipolis and Poteidaea go, he could not even be safe staying at home. [18] He therefore knows both that he is plotting against you and that you are aware of it. Assuming you to be sensible men, he thinks that you have good reason to hate him; and he is in an agitated state, expecting to suffer some harm if you seize the opportunity—unless he beats you to the punch.

[19] That is why he is awake, on stand-by, and fostering certain people against our city: the Thebans and those Peloponnesians who

have the same goals as the Thebans,[14] men whom he thinks will be happy with the present situation due to their greed but will foresee none of the consequences due to their stupidity of character.[15] Yet surely people of even moderate intelligence can discern visible examples. I had occasion to mention these to the Messenians and to the Argives; perhaps it would be better for you to have heard them as well.

[20] "How irritated, men of Messenia," I said, "do you think the Olynthians were to hear it, if anyone said something against Philip in those days when he was letting them have Anthemus, to which all previous kings of Macedon laid claim, and was giving them Poteidaea while expelling the Athenian colonists, and had thus taken upon himself their enmity toward us and granted them the enjoyment of that region?[16] Do you think they expected to suffer as they did, or would have believed it had someone told them? [21] All the same," I said, "having briefly enjoyed possession of foreign territory, they stand deprived by Philip of their own for a long time, sent into ignominious exile, not just defeated but betrayed and sold as slaves by their own people. These excessively close associations with tyrants, you see, are not safe for constitutional governments.[17]

[22] "What about the Thessalians? Do you think," I said, "that when he was expelling their tyrants[18] for them, and again when he was giving them Nicaea and Magnesia,[19] they expected that they would have the decadarchy[20] that has now been established? Or that the man who gave them back the Amphictyonic meeting[21] would appropriate their revenues[22] for himself? Impossible. But these things did in fact happen, and we can all see them. [23] As for you," I said, "you look on as Philip makes gifts and promises; if you really are intelligent, pray that you do not see him when he has already deceived you and led you astray.

"By Zeus," I said, "there are all sorts of things that cities have come up with for their defense and security, such as palisades and walls and ditches and other things of that sort. [24] These are all made by hand and require expenditure. But there is one common trait that the nature of sensible men possesses as an ingrained defense, and which is a benefit and salvation to all, and especially to the masses against tyrants. And what is that? Distrust. Guard this; hold on to this. If you preserve this, no terrible harm will befall you.

[25] "What are you looking for?" I said. "Freedom? Do you not see, then, that even the titles Philip bears are completely foreign to that concept? For every king and tyrant is the enemy of freedom and the opponent of law. Will you not watch out," I said, "that, in your quest to be rid of war,[23] you do not acquire a master?"

[26] They listened to this and shouted that it was correctly spoken, and they also heard many other speeches from the ambassadors both in my presence and again later; nonetheless, it seems, they will not reject Philip's friendship or his promises. [27] Now, it is not so strange if Messenians and certain Peloponnesians are going to do something contrary to what they rationally see is best. But you, who both understand on your own and hear us telling you that you are being plotted against, that you are being surrounded, will, it seems to me, as a consequence of doing nothing at once, have to endure everything before you realize it: so much more powerful is immediate pleasure and ease than what will happen at some point in the future.

[28] Regarding what we must do you will deliberate later among yourselves,[24] if you are sensible; what I will now discuss is how you may vote the necessary response.[25]

Now, it would be just, men of Athens, to call up[26] those who brought the promises on the strength of which you were persuaded to make peace.[27] [29] I myself would never have undertaken to serve as ambassador, nor would you (I know) have stopped fighting, if you thought Philip would do such things after achieving peace; but the statements he made at that time were far different from these actions of his. And it would be just, again, to call up another group. Whom? The people[28] who—when I came back from the second embassy, the one to receive the oaths,[29] with peace already in effect, and, perceiving that the city was being cheated, publicly declared and solemnly protested and refused to let Thermopylae or the Phocians be abandoned—[30] said that I, being a water-drinker,[30] was logically a difficult and unpleasant type of person; and that Philip, if he crossed the pass,[31] would do exactly what you would pray for: he would fortify Thespiae and Plataea, put a stop to the Thebans' hubris,[32] dig a canal through the Chersonese at his own expense,[33] and restore to you Euboea and Oropus in exchange for

Amphipolis.[34] You remember, I know, that all these things were said right here on this platform, although you are not good at recalling those who do you wrong.

[31] And, most shameful of all, in pursuit of your hopes you even voted to extend this same peace to our respective descendants:[35] so completely were you taken in. So why am I telling you this now and saying that you should call up these men? By the gods, I will tell you the truth freely and not conceal it. [32] My purpose is not that, by resorting to abuse, I may give myself an equal opportunity to speak,[36] while yet again providing those who originally butted heads with me with a pretext for getting something else from Philip. Nor is it my purpose to prattle pointlessly. Rather, I think that some day Philip's actions will cause you more grief than they do now. [33] For I see the situation progressing; and I truly hope my guess is wrong, but I am afraid that it is already too close at hand.

When you are no longer permitted to ignore what is going on, when you no longer hear from me or whomever that these things are directed against you, but all of you see it personally and know it well, I think you will be angry and harsh. [34] What truly scares me is that, with the ambassadors maintaining their silence concerning the matters on which they know they have taken bribes, it may result that your anger falls upon those attempting to rectify[37] some part of what those ambassadors have lost. For I see that some people generally release their anger not upon those responsible but upon those closest at hand.[38]

[35] Therefore, while these problems are still in the future and coalescing, and we are listening to each other, I want to remind each of you again—although you know it perfectly well—who it was that persuaded you to abandon the Phocians and Thermopylae,[39] control of which places has given Philip control of the routes into Attica and the Peloponnese and has caused you to deliberate not concerning questions of right or foreign affairs, but affairs in your own land and a war against Attica, a war that will bring pain to each individual if it arrives, and that was born on that very day.[40] [36] For if you had not been led astray then, the city would have no problem now. Philip would certainly never have achieved victory at sea and invaded Attica with his fleet,[41] nor

would he have come marching across Thermopylae and Phocis with his army. Instead, he would either do the right thing and remain quiet, keeping the peace, or else immediately find himself in a war of the sort which compelled him back then[42] to long for peace.

[37] Now, as far as reminding you is concerned, enough has been said. May it never come to pass, all you gods, that my statements be put to the test with extreme severity; for I would never wish anyone, even if he deserves to die, to suffer a penalty that comes along with danger and punishment for us all.

# 10

# HEGESIPPUS = [DEMOSTHENES] 7

*On Halonnesus*

## Introduction

The speech *On Halonnesus*, preserved as number 7 in the corpus of Demosthenes, was written and delivered not by Demosthenes but by Hegesippus, an anti-Macedonian ally of Demosthenes who had acquired the nickname Crobylus ("Topknot": e.g., Aeschines 3 *Against Ctesiphon* 118) from the way he wore his hair. *On Halonnesus* was ascribed to Hegesippus by the ancient critic Libanius on the basis of both style and content (see §§33, 42–43 with notes). Demosthenes shared Hegesippus' position regarding the Halonnesus affair (Aeschines 3 *Against Ctesiphon* 83), but his own speech on the topic does not survive.

Demosthenes' *Second Philippic* had swayed Athenian opinion against Philip; during the ensuing two years the Athenians continued agitating against Macedon despite offers from Philip in 343 and 342 to amend the Peace of Philocrates. The offer of 342, contained in a letter conveyed to Athens by Philip's envoys (§46), included a proposal to give the small northern Aegean island of Halonnesus to Athens (Part Two, Philip and Athens, p. 78). In this speech, Hegesippus rejects the proposal on the grounds of language: Philip offers to "give" (*dounai*) Halonnesus to Athens, whereas, since the island properly belongs to Athens, Philip should offer to "give" it "back" (*apodounai*: §§5–6). In addition, Hegesippus insists (e.g., §18) on the rectification (*epanorthôsis*: Part Two, Philip and Athens, p. 77) of the Peace of Philocrates by means of two major revisions: Amphipolis must be restored to Athenian control (§§26–29); and the peace must be extended and converted into a Common Peace (§§30–31).

In his introduction (§1), Hegesippus reassures the Assembly that Philip will not deter him and his patriotic colleagues from speaking candidly and in the interests of Athens. The mass of the speech (§§2–45) consists of a mixture of narration and proofs that aims to expose Philip's injustices and to urge the Athenians to stand by their proposed amendments to the Peace. Athens should reject the offer of Halonnesus (§§2–8). There is no need for jurisdictional agreements with Macedon (§§9–13). Philip is guilty of bad faith in enforcing the clause in the Peace providing for joint operations against piracy (§§14–17).

Hegesippus then moves on to the topic of *epanorthôsis*. The embassy of Python (Part Two, Philip and Athens, p. 77) offered to review the terms of peace, which Philip now denies (§§18–23). The Peace of Philocrates was illegal, since it contradicted earlier decrees regarding Amphipolis; Hegesippus' proposal to amend the peace was thus legal (§§24–25). Philip's claim to Amphipolis is without merit; the city belongs to Athens (§§26–29). The rest of the Greeks should be included in the peace, and Philip has agreed, but his actions belie his words (§§30–32); the promises of Philip are not to be trusted (§§33–35).

Further allegations against Philip follow. He has violated the peace by seizing territories and by executing a *proxenus* of Athens (§§36–38). He concedes the Chersonese to Athens but misdraws its boundary and interferes in Athenian affairs there (§§39–44). Those Athenians who support Philip are traitors deserving of death (§45).

In his very brief conclusion (§46), Hegesippus promises to compose a response to Philip that will suit the interests of Athens.

### On Halonnesus

[1] Men of Athens, there is no way that the accusations that Philip brings against those who address you about your rights will keep us from advising you on your interests. It would be a terrible thing if letters sent from him were to abolish the freedom of speech on this platform.[1] First, men of Athens, I wish to go through in detail the issues Philip has raised in his letter; after that, the matters the ambassadors[2] discuss we[3] too shall discuss.

[2] Philip begins on the topic of Halonnesus by saying that he gives it to you as his property, but he denies that you have the right to demand it back from him, since it was not yours either when he took it or now that he holds it. He told us similar things when we were on an embassy to him, to the effect that he got possession of the island by ridding it of pirates, and it properly belonged to him. [3] It is not hard to deprive him of this argument, because it is not just. All pirates seize places that belong to someone else and fortify them as bases from which to inflict harm on others. A person who punished and conquered such pirates would certainly not be making a reasonable claim if he were to say that what they held unjustly and was not theirs was now his.

[4] If you agree to this, then, if pirates were to seize some location in Attica or on Lemnos or Imbros or Scyros⁴ and somebody kicked those pirates out, what prevents that location where the pirates were, and which belongs to us, from becoming the property of those who punished the pirates? [5] Now, Philip is not unaware that this cause of his is unjust; he knows it as well as anyone, but he thinks you have been led astray by those individuals who have previously promised to manage affairs here to his liking and are now doing so. And in fact it does not escape him that by either word, whichever one you use, you will have the island, whether you "receive" it or "receive" it "back."⁵

[6] So what difference does it make to him, not to use the right word and "give" it "back" to you, but instead to use the wrong word and "give" it as a gift? His purpose is not to have it accounted as some good service toward you (what a ridiculous service that would be!), but to show all the Greeks that the Athenians are happy to receive maritime lands from the king of Macedon.⁶ This you must not do, men of Athens.

[7] Now, when he says that he is willing to submit these matters to arbitration, all he is doing is mocking you, first by asking Athenians to arbitrate with an upstart from Pella a dispute over islands, whether they are yours or his. When your power, which freed the Greeks, cannot preserve your possessions on the sea, but the jurors to whom you refer the issue, who control the vote, can preserve them for you (unless Philip buys them off), [8] how are you not admitting by doing this that you have renounced all your claims on the mainland? How are you not

demonstrating to all mankind that you will not fight it out with him over a single thing, if, rather than fighting it out for your possessions on the sea (where you say your strength is), you take the dispute to court?

[9] He also says that he has sent men to you to make jurisdictional agreements,[7] and that such agreements will go into effect not when they are ratified in your court, as the law commands, but when they are brought back to him—thus rendering a decision made by you subject to appeal to him. You see, he wants to anticipate you on this point and to establish it as a stipulation in the jurisdictional agreements that you, as the injured party, charge him with none of his previous offenses regarding Poteidaea, but confirm his seizure and ownership as rightful.[8] [10] And yet the Athenians who lived in Poteidaea—although they were not at war with Philip but were his allies, and despite oaths sworn by Philip to the inhabitants of Poteidaea—had their possessions robbed by him. These are the offenses he wants you to sanction on all counts, stating that you file no complaints and do not consider yourselves wronged.

[11] Let the past be sufficient proof to you that Macedonians have no need for jurisdictional agreements with Athenians: neither Amyntas, Philip's father, nor their other kings ever concluded jurisdictional agreements with our city. [12] And yet, in fact, there was more intercourse between our peoples then than now, since Macedonia was dependent on us and paid us tribute,[9] and we used their markets and they ours more then than now, and commercial lawsuits were not heard then, as they are now, on a strict monthly basis,[10] resulting in no need for jurisdictional agreements between peoples so distant from each other.

[13] Nonetheless, even though nothing of the sort existed at the time, there was no use in making jurisdictional agreements either for them to sail from Macedonia to Athens to obtain justice or for us to sail to Macedonia; instead, we used their law there to obtain justice, and they used our law here.[11] So do not fail to realize that the point of these proposed jurisdictional agreements is for you to admit that your claim to Poteidaea is no longer reasonable.

[14] Now, concerning the pirates, he says that it is right for you and him to engage in joint defense against those who commit crimes on the sea.[12] All he is doing by this is calling upon you to recognize his authority

on the sea, to concede that without Philip you are unable to keep up your guard on the sea, [15] and further to grant him *carte blanche* to sail around and anchor at the islands on the pretext of defending them against the pirates, and to corrupt the islanders and raise them in revolt against you. It is not enough that his fugitives have been conveyed to Thasos by your generals;[13] he wants to appropriate the other islands as well, sending along men to sail with your generals and to cooperate in the defense of the sea. And yet there are some who say that he has no need of the sea. [16] So, although he feels no such need, he is outfitting triremes[14] and constructing dockyards, and he is willing to dispatch naval expeditions and commit no small expenditures to maritime ventures, to which he assigns no value!

[17] Do you think, men of Athens, that Philip would ask you to make these concessions to him if he did not feel contempt for you and complete trust in those people here whom he has purposely acquired as friends—people who are not ashamed to live for Philip and not for their own country, and who think that when they take gifts from him, they are taking them home, when in fact they are selling what they have at home?

[18] Now, regarding the rectification of the peace, which was granted to us by the ambassadors he sent, we rectified it to terms that all men agree are just; namely, that each side should have what is its own.[15] Philip asserts that he did not grant this and that his ambassadors made no such statement to you, simply because he has been persuaded by those he treats as friends that you do not remember what was said in the Assembly. [19] But that is the one thing you cannot possibly forget: it was at the same meeting of the Assembly that the ambassadors who came from him spoke to you and the decree was written; thus it is not possible, since the speeches were given right there and the decree was read out immediately afterward, that you voted a resolution that misrepresented the ambassadors. So this letter he has sent accuses not me but you, claiming that you sent back your resolution in reply to something you did not hear.

[20] And as for the ambassadors themselves, whom your decree supposedly misrepresented, when you read out your answer to them and

invited them to enjoy your hospitality,[16] they did not dare to come or to say, "You are misrepresenting us, men of Athens: you say that we said what we did not say"; instead, they took their leave in silence. Now, since Python,[17] who was serving as ambassador then, got a good reception among you with his speech, I want to remind you, men of Athens, of the actual words he spoke: I know you remember them. [21] They were very close to those used by Philip in his present letter: he accused those of us who speak ill of Philip; and he criticized you because, while Philip has set out to treat you well and has chosen to acquire you as friends over all the Greeks, you prevent it by accepting statements from people who treat him to malicious accusations, attempted extortion, and slander. For (Python said) reports like this, when Philip hears that people were speaking ill of him and you were accepting it, change his mind, since he is being openly distrusted by the very people whose benefactor he has chosen to be.

[22] Python therefore urged the speakers in the Assembly not to criticize the peace, for it was not worth it to annul the peace; but, if there was anything in the treaty that was not properly written, he urged you to rectify it, saying that Philip would comply with whatever you decreed. On the other hand, if people persisted in their slanders but made no proposals of their own by which the peace would remain in force and Philip would stop being the object of distrust, he urged you to pay no attention. [23] You listened to this speech and accepted it, and you said that Python's words were just. And just they were. But he gave this speech not with the goal of removing from the peace items that benefited Philip and on whose inclusion he had spent a considerable sum, but because he had received advance instruction from his teachers here, who did not expect anyone to make a proposal contrary to the decree of Philocrates, which lost Amphipolis.[18]

[24] Now I, men of Athens, did not venture to make any illegal proposal; but it was not illegal to make a proposal contrary to the decree of Philocrates, as I will show you. The decree of Philocrates, by which you have lost Amphipolis, contradicted the earlier decrees by which you acquired that area. [25] So then this decree, the decree of Philocrates, was against the law, and it was not possible to make a legal proposal consistent with this illegal decree.[19] But by making a proposal consistent with those earlier decrees, which were legal and preserved your territory,

I made a legal proposal, and I also exposed Philip as deceiving you and wishing not to rectify the peace but to make you distrust those who spoke on your behalf.

[26] Now, all of you know that Philip allowed us to rectify the peace but is now denying it. And he says that Amphipolis belongs to him, since you decreed that it was his when you decreed that he should have what he held.[20] You did pass that decree, but you did not decree that Amphipolis belonged to him: for it is possible to hold what belongs to someone else, and not all who hold hold that which is their own; many have acquired what belongs to another. Thus this sophistry of his is silly.

[27] And he remembers the decree of Philocrates, but he has forgotten the letter he sent to you when he was besieging Amphipolis, in which he agreed that Amphipolis belonged to you: he said that after he captured it by siege he would "give" it "back" to you, since it belonged to you and not to those who held it.[21] [28] As it seems, those who lived in Amphipolis before Philip took it held Athenian land, but now that Philip has taken it, he holds not Athenian land but his own; likewise, he possesses Olynthus and Apollonia and Pallene not as foreign territory but as his own.[22] [29] Does it appear to you that, in all these letters to you, Philip is being careful publicly to say and do what all men agree is just, and not to display utter contempt—a man who says that the place that the Greeks and the Great King of Persia decreed by common consent to belong to you[23] is his and not yours?

[30] Regarding your other amendment to the peace—namely, that the other Greeks who are not parties to the peace should be free and autonomous, and if anyone wages war on them, the parties to the peace should render aid—[31] which you make in the belief that it is just and generous that not only we and our allies and Philip and his should be at peace, while those who are neither our allies nor Philip's should be up for grabs, to be destroyed by more powerful forces, but that they too should enjoy security as a result of your peace, and that we should truly be at peace, laying down our arms—[32] as for this amendment, Philip agrees in his letter, as you can hear, that it is just and he accepts it. But he has deprived the men of Pherae of their city and planted a garrison on their acropolis (to make them autonomous, of course!); he marches

on Ambracia; and as for the three cities in Cassopia[24] —Pandosia, Boucheta, and Elatea, colonies of Elis—after burning their countryside to the ground and forcing his way into the cities, he handed them over to his brother-in-law Alexander[25] to be his slaves. He really wants the Greeks to be free and autonomous, as his actions show!

[33] Now, concerning the promises he continues to make to you, that he will confer great benefits upon you, he claims that I slander and mis-represent him to the Greeks:[26] he says that he never promised you any-thing. This is how shameless he is, the man who wrote in a letter that is now in the Council Hall that, if the peace came about, he would confer enough benefits upon you to muzzle us who spoke against him. He said he would put these in writing forthwith, if he knew that the peace was going to happen, clearly implying that these benefits that we were going to enjoy once the peace came about were at hand and ready. [34] But now that the peace has come about, those benefits which we were sup-posed to enjoy are nowhere to be seen, while the destruction of the Greeks has occurred to an extent that you know. And he promises you in the present letter that, if you trust his friends who plead his case and punish us who slander him to you, he will bring you great benefits. [35] But the nature of the benefits will be as follows: he will not give you back what is yours (for he says it is his);[27] and his gifts will not be lo-cated in the inhabited world (in order to avoid his being slandered to the Greeks), but apparently some other land and some other place will appear where you will be given these gifts.

[36] Now, regarding the places he has seized from your possession during the peace, thereby breaking the treaty and violating the peace, since he has nothing to say and his wrongdoing is clearly exposed, he says he is prepared to submit these matters to arbitration by a fair and impartial court. These are the only things that require no arbitration: the number of days is the deciding factor. For we all know in what month and on what day the peace was concluded. [37] And just as we know that, we also know in what month and on what day Serrheion Teichos and Ergisce and the Sacred Mount were captured.[28] Things done in this manner are not invisible and require no act of judgment; everyone knows which month came first, the one in which the peace was concluded or the one in which these places were taken.

[38] He also says that he has returned all of our prisoners captured during the war. This is the same man who was so eager to win your favor that he executed the man from Carystus, the representative of our city[29]—after you sent three ambassadors to demand his release—and did not even allow the body to be retrieved for burial.

[39] On the topic of the Chersonese,[30] it is worthwhile to examine what he writes to you and also to know what he is doing. He has granted the entire region beyond Agora,[31] as belonging to him and none of your concern, to Apollonides of Cardia[32] to reap its benefits. But the boundary of the Chersonese is not Agora but the altar of Zeus of the Boundaries, located between Pteleum and Leuce Acte (where the Chersonese canal was going to be),[33] [40] as the inscription on the altar of Zeus of the Boundaries shows. Here it is:

> This most beautiful altar was consecrated to the god,
>     placed as the boundary between Leuce and Pteleum,
> by their inhabitants to mark the location. Of the borderland
>     the son of Cronus himself, king of the gods, is mediator.

[41] This area, of an extent which most of you know, he claims as his own; some of it he exploits for himself, some he has given to others as gifts; he makes all your possessions his subjects. And not only does he appropriate the area beyond Agora; he even tells you in the present letter that you must submit to arbitration with the Cardians, who live on this side of Agora[34]—the Cardians, who inhabit your territory[35]—if you have any dispute with them. [42] Well, they do have a dispute with you, and see if the subject is a small one. They claim to inhabit their own territory, not yours; they say that your possessions are foreign holdings, as in a foreign land, while their own are possessions, as in one's own land;[36] and they say that your fellow citizen, Callippus of Paeania,[37] proposed this in a decree.

[43] That they have correct. He did make the proposal; and I brought a lawsuit for an illegal decree[38] against him, but you acquitted him. That is how he has laid your claim to this region open to dispute. But when you put up with arbitrating with the Cardians the question of whether the land is yours or theirs, why will the same right not accrue to the rest of the people of the Chersonese? [44] Further, Philip treats you

with such hubris[39] that he says that, if the Cardians are unwilling to go through arbitration, he will force them—as though you could not force Cardians to do a single thing for you! Well, since you cannot, he says he will force them to do it. Clearly he is bringing you great benefits, is he not?

[45] Now, some people have said that this letter is well written; they deserve your hatred much more than Philip does. For Philip commits all these acts against you in the course of winning glory and great benefits for himself; but all those Athenians who display their goodwill not toward their country but toward Philip are bad men who deserve to die a bad death at your hands—that is, if you carry your brains between your temples and not trampled beneath your heels.

[46] It still remains for me to propose in response to this well-written letter and the ambassadors' speeches an answer which I believe to be just and in your interest.

# 11

# DEMOSTHENES 8

## *On the Chersonese*

**Introduction**

The Athenian presence in the Chersonese peninsula (modern Gallipoli) dated to the reign of the tyrant Peisistratus (Herodotus 6.34–39). The Chersonese owed its importance to its command of the Hellespont, through which merchant fleets transported grain from the Black Sea to Athens.

In 342/1, Philip complained to the Athenians about the actions of their general Diopeithes, who was supporting Athenian cleruchs in the Chersonese and raiding coastal Thrace (§§6, 9; Part Two, Philip and Athens, pp. 79–80). In the resulting Assembly debates, some Athenians advocated assuaging Philip by recalling or monitoring Diopeithes (§§27–28); others urged a declaration of war. In the speech *On the Chersonese*, delivered before the Assembly in the spring of 341 (§18 with note), Demosthenes proposed that Athens support Diopeithes and commit financial and military resources to his aid.

In the introduction (§§1–3), Demosthenes urges his countrymen to put aside personal rivalries and attend to their interests in the Chersonese before it is too late. The narrative (§§4–37) blames Philip, not Diopeithes, for violating the Peace of Philocrates (§§4–8). If Diopeithes' mercenary force is disbanded, Philip will have the advantage and could attack Byzantium and the Chersonese or even closer targets; better to keep him occupied in Thrace (§§9–18). Athens should therefore provide Diopeithes with reinforcements and money (§§19–20). In the current situation, Diopeithes has no choice but to exact "benevolences" (*eunoiai*) from the locals because he receives no financial support from Athens (§§21–27). The problem is not Diopeithes but Philip, and the Athenians must act accordingly (§§28–37).

Demosthenes states his proposals at §§38–47: the Athenians must reverse their current policies (§38), realize that Philip is their enemy and is plotting against them (§§39–45), levy a war-tax and exact contributions from their allies, and support Diopeithes (§§46–47). Next come the proofs (§§48–75) in support of Demosthenes' proposals and against those of his opponents. Athens' current idleness disgraces the city and allows Philip to gain strength (§§48–51). The Athenians need to worry not about their expenditures but about Philip's plans for conquest (§§52–60); Philip's supporters must be rooted out lest Athens suffer the fate of Olynthus and others (§§61–67). Demosthenes takes a brave position by proposing unpopular but beneficial measures (§§68–72). The function of a politician is to advise; the Athenians themselves must act (§§73–75).

In his conclusion (§§76–77), Demosthenes summarizes his proposals. He urges the Assembly to levy a war-tax, to maintain and support Diopeithes' mercenary army, to send ambassadors to agitate against Philip, and to punish politicians who take Macedonian bribes. If the Athenians act immediately, there is hope; if they continue to behave half-heartedly, the city is doomed.


*On the Chersonese*

[1] All your speakers, men of Athens, should not make any speech in pursuit of either enmity or popularity; they should rather disclose what each of them thinks is best, especially when you are deliberating on important public business. Since, however, some of them are motivated to speak partially by rivalry and partially by whatever cause, it is incumbent upon you, the majority, men of Athens, to remove all other factors and to decree and carry out what you think is in the best interests of the city.

[2] Now, our serious concern is with affairs in the Chersonese and with the campaign that Philip has been waging in Thrace for more than ten months now; but most of the speeches have dealt with the actions and intended actions of Diopeithes.[1] As I see it, it is available to you whenever you want to punish anyone whom the laws place under your authority, whether you decide to investigate them straightaway or to

hold off; and it is absolutely unnecessary for me or anyone else to take a hard line on that subject. [3] But as for the possessions that an existing enemy of the city[2] with a sizable force in the Hellespontine region is attempting to seize, and that we will no longer be able to save if we act too late, in regard to these I think it is in our interest to have plans and preparations made as soon as possible, and not to run away from these concerns due to turbulent accusations on other topics.

[4] I am surprised by many of the statements made by the usual speakers in the Assembly; but I was most surprised, men of Athens, by what I recently heard someone say in the Council,[3] to the effect that an advisor should advise us simply either to wage war or to keep the peace. [5] But the fact of the matter is this: if Philip stays quiet, does not hold any of our possessions in violation of the peace, and does not organize all mankind against us, then there is no need for further discussion; we must simply keep the peace, and I see that your side stands ready. If, on the other hand, the oaths we swore and the conditions on which we made peace are there to see, set down in writing, [6] but it is clear that from the beginning—before the departure of Diopeithes and the cleruchs,[4] who now stand accused of having caused the war—Philip wrongfully seized many of our possessions (and here are your decrees of complaint on these issues, which are still in effect),[5] and if it is clear that, during this entire time, he has been constantly seizing the possessions of the other Greeks and barbarians and assembling them for use against us, then what is the meaning of their[6] statement that we must either wage war or keep the peace?

[7] We have no choice in the matter. What we are left with is the most just and necessary of actions, which my opponents pass over on purpose. And what is that? To defend ourselves against the one who waged war on us first. Unless, by Zeus, they respond that, as long as Philip keeps away from Attica and the Peiraeus,[7] he is not wronging the city or making war. [8] Well, if they make your rights depend on that and that is how they define the peace, then everyone can see that what they are saying is not right or bearable or safe for you. Not only that, but these very statements of theirs contradict their accusations against Diopeithes. For why in the world will we give Philip permission to do everything else as long as he keeps away from Attica, when we will not

even allow Diopeithes to come to the aid of the Thracians, or else we will say he is making war?[8]

[9] But, by Zeus, they will respond, while those facts stand exposed, our mercenaries are committing horrendous acts in plundering the region of the Hellespont; Diopeithes commits a crime by diverting ships to shore;[9] and we must not allow him to do it. Fine; so be it; I offer no rebuttal. [10] However, in my opinion, if they are truly going to consider these things from a standpoint of absolute justice, then just as they are seeking to disperse the city's existing force by slandering among you the commander who provides it with pay, they must show that Philip's force will also be disbanded if you are persuaded to do this. Otherwise, observe that all they are doing is putting the city in the same condition that has caused the ruin of all her present interests. [11] For, as you must know, there is absolutely nothing to which Philip owes his conquests more than to his being first on the scene. Having an assembled force around him at all times and knowing in advance what he wants to accomplish, he is suddenly there to attack whomever he decides; but as for us, whenever we learn that something is happening, that is when we are thrown into confusion and make our preparations.[10] [12] Hence, I think, it results that he obtains whatever goal he sets out for with no trouble, while we show up too late, and all the money we spend has been wasted for nothing; we have made a display of our enmity and our willingness to stop him, but by arriving too late we incur the disgrace of our conduct in the bargain.[11]

[13] Also, men of Athens, you must not fail to realize that now too all the rest is just words and pretexts; but the goal of these plots and schemes is that, while you stay at home and the city has no force abroad, Philip may manage everything he wants with absolutely no trouble. Look first of all at what is happening right now. [14] At this very moment he is sitting in Thrace with a large force, and, according to those who are there, he is sending for significant reinforcements from Macedonia and Thessaly. So, if he waits for the etesian winds,[12] then advances on Byzantium and besieges it, first of all, do you think that the Byzantines will stick to the same insanity they display now and not call upon you and ask for your help?[13] [15] I think not: even if there were someone they distrusted more than us, they would let even those people

into their city rather than surrendering it to Philip—that is, unless he caught them first.

Therefore, if we cannot set sail from here[14] and there is no auxiliary force in readiness there, nothing will prevent the Byzantines' destruction. [16] "Right, by Zeus: those people are delusional; they are completely out of their minds." Absolutely; but all the same they ought to be safe, for it is in the city's interest.[15] And actually it is also unclear to us that he will not attack the Chersonese; in fact, if we are to judge from the letter he sent us, he states that he will retaliate against the people in the Chersonese.[16]

[17] Now, if this assembled army[17] remains in existence, it will be able both to render assistance to that region and to inflict some harm on Philip's possessions; but once it is disbanded, what will we do if he attacks the Chersonese? "We'll put Diopeithes on trial, by Zeus." And how is that going to make things better? "Well, we could render aid ourselves,[18] from here." And if we are unable on account of the winds? "Well, by Zeus, he won't reach the Chersonese." And who is going to guarantee that?

[18] Do you see and calculate, men of Athens, the approaching season of the year,[19] for which certain individuals think the Hellespont should be cleared of you and handed over to Philip? What if, when Philip leaves Thrace, he does not approach the Chersonese or Byzantium—consider this possibility, too—but instead shows up at Chalcis and Megara the same way he recently showed up at Oreus?[20] Do you think it would be better to fight him off here and allow the war to come to Attica, or to cook up some trouble for him there? Personally, I prefer the latter.

[19] Knowing and considering these things, we all must not, by Zeus, malign and seek to disband the force that Diopeithes is endeavoring to prepare for the city; rather, we must prepare an additional citizen force, help Diopeithes in providing money, and assist him in other respects as one of our own. [20] For if someone were to ask Philip, "Tell me, would you rather have these soldiers currently under Diopeithes' command—whatever their character (I offer no dispute)—thrive, enjoy a good reputation at Athens, and grow in number with the assistance of the city, or have them scattered and destroyed by certain people's

slanderous accusations?" I think he would choose the latter. So, then, are some of us here doing what Philip would pray to the gods for? Need you look any further for the source of all the city's losses?

[21] Now, I want to conduct a frank examination of the city's current situation and to consider what we are presently doing and how we are handling it. We are unwilling to pay a war-tax[21] or go on campaign ourselves, and unable to keep our hands off public funds.[22] We do not give the allies' contributions[23] to Diopeithes; [22] nor do we approve of what he provides for himself, but we criticize and investigate where it comes from, and what he intends to do, and all that sort of thing. And, even with our current attitude, we are unwilling to take care of our own business: with our words we praise those who give speeches worthy of the city, but with our actions we assist their opponents.

[23] Every time a speaker comes forward, you habitually ask him, "So, what are we to do?" I want to ask you, "So, what are we to say?" For if you will not pay a war-tax, or go on campaign in person, or keep your hands off the public funds, or hand over the allies' contributions, or permit what a person provides for himself, or be willing to take care of your own business, then I do not know what to say. When people grant such licence to those willing to bring slanderous accusations that they even listen to prosecutions before the fact for a person's alleged intended actions, what could one say?

[24] Now, some of you need to understand what the effect of this policy is. I will tell you frankly; in fact, I could do it no other way. All the generals you have ever dispatched on the sea—if this is not the case, I sentence myself to any penalty whatsoever—take funds from the Chians and Erythraeans and whomever they can (I am talking about the inhabitants of Asia).[24] [25] Those with one or two ships take less; those with a larger force take more. And the contributors do not make these payments, small or large, for nothing (they are not that crazy): they are paying for their merchants not to be harmed, their cargoes not to be plundered, their vessels to be escorted, and so on. They say that they are paying "benevolences";[25] that is the name given to this income. [26] And specifically, in the present case, it is patently obvious that all of them will give money to Diopeithes with his army. From what other

source do you think someone who does not receive anything from you and does not have the means on his own to provide pay supports his troops? From the sky? That is not possible; he gets by on what he can collect and demand and borrow.

[27] All that his accusers in the Assembly are doing is announcing to everyone not to give him anything, since he will be made to pay for his intentions, not to mention whatever he has done or accomplished. This is the force of their statements that "he is going to launch a siege" and "he is betraying the Greeks." Do any of these people care about the Greeks who live in Asia? Well, if they do, they are better at caring for others than for their own country. [28] And this is the real meaning of their proposal to dispatch another general to the Hellespont. For if Diopeithes is doing terrible things and forcing vessels into port,[26] a tablet, men of Athens, one little tablet,[27] could put a stop to all of it. And the laws ordain that we impeach[28] such offenders, certainly not, by Zeus, that we monitor them ourselves at such considerable expense and with so many triremes:[29] that would be the height of insanity. [29] To deal with our enemies, whom we cannot seize under the authority of our laws, we must by necessity support soldiers and dispatch triremes and pay war-taxes; but to deal with our own citizens we have the decree, the impeachment, and the *Paralus*.[30] This is how sensible men would proceed; the problems these people are now creating are the products of spiteful and destructive individuals.

[30] Now, the fact that some of them are like this is bad but not so bad. But then you who sit there are already so disposed that, if someone comes up here and tells you that Diopeithes is the cause of all these ills, or Chares,[31] or Aristophon,[32] or whichever citizen you care to name, you immediately agree and shout that he speaks correctly. [31] But if someone comes forward and tells the truth, that "You are speaking nonsense, Athenians. Philip is the cause of all these ills and problems; if he kept quiet, there would be no problem for the city," you cannot dispute the truth of these statements, but, it seems to me, you get angry and reckon as though you were losing something.

[32] The cause of this—and, by the gods, when I am speaking in your best interest, let me have freedom of speech—is that some of your

politicians have made you formidable and harsh in the Assembly but lazy and contemptible in your preparations for war. If someone tells you that the culprit is someone you know you will catch among yourselves, you agree and assent. But if you are told that it is the sort of person you have to punish by overcoming him with armed force and in no other way, then, I think, you do not know what to do, and you get angry at being found out.

[33] The situation ought to be, men of Athens, the opposite of what it is now. All your politicians ought to train you to be mild and generous in the Assembly, for there are decided questions of right involving your-selves and your allies, but to show yourselves formidable and harsh in your preparations for war, for there the contest is against our enemies and opponents. [34] As it is now, though, by courting popularity and currying your favor to excess, they have put you in such a condition that in the Assembly you are soft and flattered, hearing everything with an ear to pleasure, but in the real world of current events you are already at mortal risk.

Come now, by Zeus: if the Greeks should demand from you an ac-counting of the opportunities you have let slip by out of laziness up to the present moment, and if they should ask you, [35] "Men of Athens, do you constantly send us ambassadors and tell us that Philip is plotting against us and all the Greeks, and that we have to watch out for the man, and all that sort of thing?," we would have to say yes and admit it, for that is what we do. "So then, you most pathetic of all people, when the man was gone for ten months, prevented by disease and winter[33] and war[34] from being able to return home, [36] you neither liberated Euboea nor recovered any of your own possessions. But while you remained at home, at your leisure, and healthy (if, that is, they would call people who act in this way "healthy"), he set up two tyrants in Euboea, planting them like forts, one right across from Attica and the other on the Sciathos side.[35] [37] And, rather than ridding yourselves of these problems (if that was all you wanted to do), you let them be? Clearly you have stepped aside for Philip; you have made it obvious that, even if he dies ten deaths, you will not move any more than you already have. Why, then, do you come as envoys and lodge accusations and cause us trouble?" If they say this, how will we reply? What will we say, Athenians? I, for one, don't know.

[38] Now, there are those who think they are putting a speaker to the test when they ask him, "So, what should we do?" To them I will give the most just and true answer: you should not do what you are doing now. Furthermore, I will discuss each individual point in detail, and let them be as willing to act as they are eager to inquire.

[39] First, men of Athens, you must fix it firmly in your minds that Philip is waging war against the city and has broken the peace (and you must stop accusing each other of this) and that he is the adversary and enemy of the entire city and the very ground beneath it—[40] and, I add, of every person in it, including those who think they are in his best graces. If they do not believe me, let them look at Euthycrates and Lasthenes of Olynthus,[36] who appeared to be on the friendliest of terms with him but now, after betraying their city, have been ruined worst of all. There is nothing he makes war on more than our constitution; there is absolutely nothing he plots and investigates more than how he can destroy it.

[41] And, in a way, it is rational for him to do so. He knows perfectly well that, even if he becomes master of everything else, he cannot hold anything securely so long as you live under a democracy; if at any point he suffers one of those slip-ups that often befall a person, all those elements that are currently forced into cooperation will come and seek refuge with you. [42] For you are not naturally well disposed to seek advantage for yourselves and control an empire;[37] you are, however, skilled at preventing others from seizing power and taking power away from those who have it, and in general you are a nuisance to those who aim at empire and ready to rescue all men to freedom. So Philip does not want the prospect of liberation by you to sit waiting for opportunities against him; far from it. And on that point his reasoning is neither poor nor pointless.

[43] So, first of all, you must regard Philip as an irreconcilable enemy of our constitution and our democracy. If you are not convinced of this in your hearts, you will not be willing to make a serious effort in defense of your interests. Second, you must know clearly that all his present machinations and preparations are directed against our city; and wherever someone defends himself against Philip, he defends us too. [44]

Certainly there is no one stupid enough to assume that Philip covets those miserable towns in Thrace (for what else would you call Drongilum, Cabyle, Masteira, and the places he is now seizing?) and is putting up with hard work and winters and the utmost risks for the sake of capturing them, [45] but does not covet the harbors, dockyards, and triremes of Athens, and her silver mines and their significant revenues, but will allow you to keep them, while he spends his winter in the pit of hell for the sake of the millet and emmer in the storage cellars of Thrace. That is not possible; he is engaging in those machinations there, just like all the rest, with the goal of becoming master of things here.

[46] What, then, would sensible men do? Acting with knowledge and resolve, they would throw off this excessive and pernicious laziness; they would pay the war-tax and demand contributions of their allies; and they would see to it and act so that this assembled army[38] stays together, so that, just as Philip has a force at the ready to injure and enslave all the Greeks, so you have one at the ready to save them and bring them aid. [47] You see, none of our necessary goals can ever be achieved by dispatching auxiliary forces;[39] they must be achieved by equipping a force, furnishing it with support, paymasters, and public slaves,[40] and ensuring that the strictest watch may be kept over the funds, with the aforementioned individuals held accountable for the money and the general held accountable for military operations. And if you do this, expressing true resolve, you will compel Philip to wage a just peace and stay in his own country—which would be the best possible result—or else you will fight him on equal footing.

[48] Now, if anyone thinks these proposals require great expense and considerable labor and effort, he is absolutely correct. But if he takes into account what will happen to the city in the future if he does not resolve to do this, he will find that it profits us to do our duty voluntarily. [49] Even if some god guarantees (for no man could qualify to guarantee such an important matter) that, if you stay quiet and abandon everything, Philip will not come for you in the end, it is disgraceful, by Zeus and all the gods, and unworthy of you, of the traditions of the city, and of the deeds of your ancestors to abandon all the other Greeks to slavery for the sake of your own ease. For my part, I would rather be dead than be the one who proposed that; all the same, if someone else makes that

proposal and convinces you, fine, do not defend yourselves, abandon everything.

[50] If, on the other hand, no one supports that idea, and we all know the opposite in advance, that the more places we allow him to control, the more difficult and powerful an enemy we will have to deal with, then how far will we go to dodge the issue? What are we waiting for? When, men of Athens, will we be willing to do what we must? [51] "When it is necessary, by Zeus." Well, the necessity that one would say compels free men is not only already at hand but has long passed us by; and as for the necessity that compels slaves, clearly we must pray that things not come to that. How do these differ? For a free man the strongest compulsion is his sense of shame at the events surrounding him; I know of no compulsion we could mention which is more powerful than that.[41] For a slave, however, it is blows and bodily injury, things which I pray do not occur and are not a fit topic of discussion.

[52] Although I would be happy to discuss all the other issues and to demonstrate how certain individuals are harming you with their policies, I will let the rest go. But I will say this: whenever it falls to you to discuss something regarding Philip, immediately someone stands up and says that keeping the peace is good and supporting a large force is difficult, and that "certain people want to plunder our funds," and so forth. As a result they put you off while leaving him in peace to do whatever he wants. [53] From this it comes about that you remain at leisure and do nothing immediately—for which, I fear, you will one day feel you have paid a high price—while they receive the popularity and the pay[42] for their actions.

In my opinion, though, it is not you who must be persuaded to keep the peace—you sit there already persuaded—but the one who is committing acts of war; if he is persuaded, your side stands ready. [54] What you must view as unpleasant is not how much we spend on our security, but rather what we will suffer if we are unwilling to do so. As for the prospect of our funds being plundered, that is to be prevented by proposing a means of protection that will secure them, not by abandoning our interests. [55] And in fact this is exactly what irritates me, men of Athens: that some of you are pained by the possible plundering of our funds, when you have the power to watch over them and punish any offenders; but it does not pain you that Philip is snatching up all of Greece just like that, one place at a time, and is doing so with you as his goal!

[56] What in the world, then, is the reason, men of Athens, that none of these people[43] ever say that the one who is so openly campaigning, committing injustices, and capturing cities is creating war, but instead they allege that war will be brought about by those who advise you not to tolerate or neglect such actions? I will tell you. [57] It is because they want to turn the anger that you reasonably feel when you suffer some distress due to the war against those who offer the best proposals on your behalf, so that you put those men on trial instead of defending yourselves against Philip, and so that they themselves can prosecute rather than paying the penalty for what they are currently doing. This is what it means when they tell you that certain people here among you want to start a war, and this is what the actual dispute concerns.

[58] However, I know perfectly well that, with no Athenian having yet proposed war, Philip holds many of the city's other possessions and now has sent an auxiliary force to Cardia.[44] Now, if we are willing to pretend that he is not waging war on us, he would be the most foolish man alive to try to prove us wrong. [59] But when he attacks us personally, what are we going to say? For he will say that he is not waging war, just as he was not waging war on Oreus, when his troops were in their territory,[45] nor, before that, on Pherae, when he drove up to their walls,[46] nor, to start it all, on Olynthus, until he was right there in their land with his army.[47] Even then will we say that those urging self-defense are creating war? In that case, all we are left with is slavery, since there is no other option between failing to defend ourselves and not being allowed to live in peace and quiet.

[60] And in fact you are not risking the same things as everyone else: Philip does not want to make the city subject to him but to eradicate it completely. For he knows perfectly well that you will not be willing to be his slaves, nor, even if you become willing, will you know how (for you are accustomed to ruling);[48] you will, however, have the ability to cause him more problems than all the rest of mankind, if you get the opportunity.

[61] This is, therefore, a contest of life and death, and it befits you to realize that and to detest and nail to the board[49] those who have sold themselves to Philip. For it is impossible, impossible, to defeat your enemies outside the city unless you first punish your enemies in the city itself. [62] Why do you think he is currently treating you with hubris[50] (for, as I see it, that is exactly what he is doing)? Why do you think he deceives the others (if nothing else) by treating them well but simply threatens you? For example, by giving numerous gifts to the Thessalians, he seduced them into their present condition of slavery; and no one could count all the gifts he gave earlier to the poor suffering Olynthians—Poteidaea and many others—in deceiving them. [63] Now he is leading the Thebans on, having handed them Boeotia[51] and freed them from a great and difficult war.[52] Thus, after reaping some profit of their own greed, some of the aforementioned peoples have already suffered in ways everyone knows, and the rest will suffer whenever it may befall them.

About the possessions you have been robbed of in the meantime I will say nothing. But in how many ways were you deceived in the very act of making the peace![53] [64] Were you not deceived with regard to the Phocians, Thermopylae, your interests in the Thraceward region—Doriscus, Serrhion, Cersobleptes himself?[54] Does Philip not now hold the city of Cardia and admit it?

Why, then, does he behave that way with the rest and differently with you? Because your city is the only one of all in which immunity is granted for speaking on behalf of the enemy. It is safe for a person to take money[55] and speak in the Assembly, even when you have been robbed of what belongs to you. [65] It would not have been safe to speak in support of Philip in Olynthus if the mass of Olynthians had not benefited as well by enjoying the profits of Poteidaea. It would not have been safe to speak in support of Philip in Thessaly if the mass of Thessalians had derived no benefit from Philip's expelling their tyrants and returning the Amphictyonic meeting to them;[56] nor would it have been safe in Thebes before he returned Boeotia to them and destroyed the Phocians. [66] But in Athens, although Philip not only has robbed you of Amphipolis and the territory of Cardia but is also equipping Euboea for use as a stronghold against you and now advancing on Byzantium, it is safe to speak in support of Philip.

And, as a consequence, some of these people[57] have quickly gone from rags to riches, from anonymity and obscurity to honor and fame, while you, quite the opposite, have gone from honor to obscurity and from plenty to poverty. You see, I believe that a city's wealth is found in her allies and their trust and goodwill, and you are poor in all those assets. [67] And, because you neglect those things and let them go, he is prosperous and powerful and feared by all Greeks and barbarians, while you are left lonely and lowly, resplendent in your abundance of merchandise but laughable when it comes to the preparations you should have made. I see that some of the speakers do not take for themselves the advice which they give to you: they say you must keep quiet even if someone does you wrong, while they themselves cannot keep quiet in the Assembly even with no one wronging them.

[68] And then whoever happens to come up here[58] says, "Well, you are not willing to make a proposal or take a risk; you are cowardly and soft." Well, I am not rash, loathsome, and shameless, and I pray I do not become so; but in fact I consider myself braver than the great majority of your reckless politicians. [69] You see, men of Athens, the man who disregards the city's interests and judges, confiscates, bribes, and prosecutes does not act out of any bravery: his boldness is risk-free, because he holds as a guarantee of his safety the ability to give speeches and conduct politics to your liking. But the man who often opposes your will in your own best interest and never speaks to gain popularity but always proposes what is best, who chooses the sort of policy in which Fortune controls more than the calculations of men[59] but offers himself as responsible to you for both—[70] this is the man who is brave. And this is the sort of man who is a truly useful citizen, not those who have lost the city's greatest possessions for the sake of a day's popularity.

So far am I from emulating those men or considering them worthy citizens of the city that, if someone were to ask me, "Tell me, what good have you done for our city?," although, men of Athens, I could list my trierarchies and choregies[60] and payments of war-tax and ransomings of prisoners-of-war and other such acts of generosity, I would mention none of those things, [71] but instead the fact that I pursue none of the sort of policies mentioned above. Perhaps, like others, I could prosecute and court favor and confiscate and do all the other things my adversaries do, but I have never placed myself in any of those positions. Nor have I been motivated by either profit or personal honor; rather, I consistently offer proposals that cause my reputation among you to sink below many others', but that would increase your power, if you listen to me. I hope it does not arouse envy to say so.

[72] Nor, it seems to me, is it the mark of a just citizen to seek out the sort of policies by which I will straightaway become the first man among you, while you come in last of all. Rather, the city must grow hand-in-hand with the policies of its good citizens; and everyone must always make the best proposal, not the easiest. For nature will follow the easiest course on its own; the good citizen has to lead his fellows along the best course with instructive speeches.

[73] You know, I have previously heard some sort of comment to the effect that I do always say what is best, but what comes from me is nothing but words, and the city needs deeds and action. I will tell you my position on this, concealing nothing. I think that a person who advises you has no job other than to say what is best; and I believe I can easily demonstrate that this is the case. [74] As I am sure you know, the renowned Timotheus once gave a speech in the Assembly,[61] telling you that you had to send aid and save the Euboeans, when the Thebans were trying to enslave them. And in his speech he said something like this: "Tell me," he said, "you have the Thebans on an island, and you are deliberating how you will handle them and what you should do? Will you not fill the sea with triremes,[62] men of Athens? Will you not stand up right now and march to the Peiraeus? Will you not launch the ships?"

[75] This, then, is what Timotheus said, and you did it; as a result of both these things, the deed got done. Now, if he had made the finest proposal he could—as he did—but you had been too lazy and taken none of his advice, would the city have obtained any of the results it did? Impossible. The same applies to whatever I propose now: you must seek the actions from yourselves, and the knowledgeable proposal of what is best from the man who comes up here.

[76] I want to state my proposal in summary form and then step down. I say that we must levy a war-tax. We must keep our existing force[63] together, making corrections if anything seems not to be in good

shape, not disbanding the whole thing because of whatever faults someone may point out. We must dispatch ambassadors in all directions to instruct, admonish, and exact funds. Along with all these things, we must
everywhere punish and detest those who accept bribes to influence affairs, so that those reasonable men who behave with justice may be
deemed by everyone else and by themselves to have made the right decision. [77] If you handle your affairs in this way and stop neglecting
them all, perhaps, perhaps even now they may still improve. But if you
continue to sit there, taking things seriously enough to shout and express approval, but shrinking away when it becomes necessary to do
something, then I can see no speech that will be able to save the city
without your doing your duty.

# 12

# DEMOSTHENES 9

## *Third Philippic*

**Introduction**

Demosthenes delivered the *Third Philippic* before the Athenian Assembly in the late spring or summer of 341, not long after the speech *On the Chersonese*. Between the delivery of these two speeches, the prospect of a Macedonian campaign against Byzantium (8.14) had become a reality (§34); Philip would commence his siege in the summer of 340.

The introduction to the *Third Philippic* (§§1–5) dwells on the customary theme of Athenian idleness and Macedonian opportunism. The narrative (§§6–46) begins with the assertion that Philip is at war with Athens, contrary to the arguments of the Athenian peace party (§§6–8). Philip will never declare war, but his actions violate the Peace of Philocrates and pose a threat to the security of Greece (§§9–20). Philip's crimes are greater than those committed by Athens, Sparta, or Thebes during their successive hegemonies (§§21–35); the Greeks are deterred from resisting Philip by mutual mistrust and a tendency toward corruption (§§36–46).

Next come the proofs (§§47–69). Philip is more dangerous than the Spartans were (§§47–50). The Athenians must confront him away from Attica, relying on guerrilla tactics and avoiding pitched battles (§§51–52). Before proceeding abroad, however, the Athenians must punish Philip's agents at home, learning from the examples provided by Olynthus, Eretria, and Oreus (§§53–69). Demosthenes' proposal (§§70–75) calls for the mobilization of soldiers, triremes, and money; the dispatch of ambassadors to stir up opposition to

Macedon; and monetary support for Diopeithes in the Chersonese (cf. Demosthenes 8).

In his conclusion (§76) Demosthenes expresses confidence in his proposal and prays that whatever course the Assembly chooses may prove beneficial.

**Note on the text.** Two versions of the text of the *Third Philippic* have been transmitted to us by the manuscripts. In the translation that follows I have placed in italics those parts present in the longer version but not in the shorter.

### Third Philippic

[1] Many speeches are given, men of Athens, at almost every Assembly meeting concerning the injustices Philip has been committing since he concluded the peace,[1] not just against you but against the others as well. And everyone, I know, would say—even if they would not actually do it—that we must speak and act so that Philip will cease his hubris[2] and pay the penalty for it. I see, however, that all our affairs have been gradually neglected, to the point where—I am afraid to utter an ill-omened statement, true though it may be—if everyone who came forward wanted to propose, and you wanted to approve, measures that would result in the most pathetic state of affairs possible, I think you could do no worse than your current condition.

[2] Now, perhaps there are many reasons for these things, and it is not due to one or two causes that the situation has come to this. But if you examine it correctly, you will find that it is especially due to those who choose to court popularity rather than proposing what is best. Some of these people, men of Athens, in protecting those areas in which their reputation and power lie, exhibit no forethought for the future, *and they therefore think that you should not either.*[3] Others, by bringing slanderous accusations against those in charge of public affairs, are only acting so that the city will punish itself and be occupied with that, while Philip will have the ability to say and do whatever he wants.

[3] Such political behavior, customary as it is for you, is the cause of your troubles. I call upon you, men of Athens, if I tell some part of the

truth with frankness, not to become angry with me because of it. Look at it like this. In other contexts, you think that freedom of speech should be so common to everyone in the city that you have given it to foreigners and slaves; you could see slaves in great number among us saying what they want with greater impunity than citizens enjoy in some other cities. But you have completely eliminated free speech from public deliberation. [4] It then results that in the Assembly you are soft and flattered, hearing everything with an ear to pleasure, while in the real world of current events you are already at mortal risk.[4] Well, if this is your attitude even now, I do not know what to say. If, on the other hand, you are willing to hear what is in your interest without flattery, I am ready to tell you. For, in fact, even if our affairs are in entirely pitiful shape and many of them have been abandoned, nonetheless it is still possible to rectify them all, if you are willing to do what you must.

[5] And what I am about to say may be incredible, but it is true: what was worst about our past is best for our future. And what is that? The fact that our affairs are in bad shape when you have taken none of the necessary steps, great or small. You see, if you had done everything you ought to and things were in this condition, there would be no hope for improvement.[5] As it is, though, Philip has conquered your laziness and negligence, but he has not conquered the city. You have not been beaten; you have not even moved.

[6] *So, if we were all in agreement that Philip is at war with the city and in violation of the peace, then the speaker who came forward would only have to propose and advise the safest and easiest way to resist him. But since some people are of such a strange attitude that, although Philip is capturing cities and occupying many of your possessions and wronging all mankind, they put up with certain individuals[6] saying repeatedly in the Assembly that it is some of us[7] who are creating the war, necessity dictates that we be on our guard and correct this: [7] for the fear is that a person who proposes and advises resistance may incur responsibility for having brought about the war. For my part, first of all, I state and define the issue as follows; namely, whether it is up to us to decide whether we should be at peace or at war.*

[8] Now, if it is possible for the city to be at peace, and if it is up to us—to start from there—then I say that we must be at peace; and I call

upon him who takes that position to make a proposal, put it into effect, and not cheat us. But if someone else, with his weapons in his hands and a considerable force around him, throws the word "peace" in your face while himself performing acts of war, what is left for you except to defend yourselves? Say you are at peace, if you like, as he does; I have no problem with that. [9] But if someone understands as peace a situation which allows Philip to seize everything else and then come for us, first of all, he is out of his mind, and secondly, he is talking about a peace obeyed by you in regard to Philip, not one obeyed by Philip in regard to you. This is what Philip is buying with all the money he spends:[8] the ability to make war on you without your making war on him.

[10] If we are actually going to wait until he admits to making war on us, we are the stupidest of all men. For even if he marches on Attica itself and the Peiraeus, he will not say that—if, that is, we are to judge from his conduct toward the others. [11] To give one example, he told the Olynthians, when he was forty stades[9] away from their city, that one of two things must happen: either they must cease to inhabit Olynthus or he must cease to inhabit Macedonia.[10] All the previous time, whenever someone accused him of any such behavior, he would wax indignant and send ambassadors to respond on his behalf. To give another example, he went to visit the Phocians, as if visiting allies, and he had Phocian ambassadors escorting him on his trip; and here in Athens the masses contended that his passage[11] would not profit the Thebans.

[12] And, as a matter of fact, just the other day he went to Thessaly as a friend and ally and seized Pherae, which he still holds. And most recently he claimed to have sent his soldiers to visit the poor suffering Oreites[12] out of goodwill: he had heard that they were ill and suffering civil strife, and it was the duty of true allies and friends to be present at such times of crisis. [13] So, given his choice to deceive those people— who would have inflicted no harm but might have taken precautions to avoid suffering any—rather than declaring his intent and using force, do you suppose that he will make war on you by open declaration, and do so while you are still willingly deceived? [14] That is not possible: he would be the stupidest of all men, if you, the injured party, issued no complaint against him, instead accusing your own people, but he resolved

your internal strife and dissension and announced that he was turning it against himself! He would also be taking out of his employees' mouths the words that they use to put you off, telling you that Philip, for his part, is not at war with the city.

[15] Is there, in the name of Zeus, any sensible person who would judge whether someone is at war or at peace with him based on words rather than actions? Certainly not. Well, from the beginning, as soon as the peace went into effect—with Diopeithes not yet serving as general and the men currently in the Chersonese not yet sent out[13]—Philip was capturing Serrhium and Doriscus and was expelling from Serrheion Teichos and the Sacred Mount[14] the soldiers stationed there by your general.[15] [16] And what was he doing when he did this? He had taken the oath of peace.[16] And let no one say, "What does that mean? Why does the city care?" Whether these matters are insignificant, or none of your concern, is a separate issue; piety and justice carry the same weight whether the transgression is great or small. So tell me, when he dispatches mercenaries and admits to sending aid to the Chersonese, which the Great King and all the Greeks have acknowledged as yours,[17] and when he writes as much in his letter,[18] what is he doing?

[17] He says that he is not making war; I, however, am far from agreeing that he is abiding by the peace with you when he commits these acts. Rather, I assert that, in making an attempt on Megara,[19] establishing tyranny on Euboea,[20] and now advancing on Thrace[21] and intriguing in Peloponnesian affairs,[22] and in using his army to do all that he does, he is violating the peace and making war on you—unless you are going to say that men directing siege engines are waging peace until they have already brought them up to your walls. But you will not say that, for he who acts and plots for my capture makes war on me, even before he fires a missile or shoots an arrow.

[18] Now, what would put you at risk, if something were to happen? The Hellespont in the hands of another;[23] Megara and Euboea under the control of your enemy; the Peloponnesians siding with Philip. Am I, then, supposed to tell you that the man aiming this siege engine at your city is waging peace? [19] Not by a long shot. By my definition, he has been at war with us since the day he destroyed the Phocians. As for

you, if you resist him immediately, I say you will have come to your senses; but if you leave him alone, you will be unable to resist him when you do want to. My position is so far from that of your other advisors, men of Athens, that I think now you should not be investigating the Chersonese or Byzantium [20] but coming to their defense and watching over them to see that they suffer no harm *and sending our soldiers who are there now*[24] *everything they ask for.* Further, you must deliberate concerning all the Greeks with the understanding that they are in a situation of grave danger. And I want to tell you why I am so afraid for our situation, so that, if I am reasoning correctly, you may share in my assessment and exercise some care for yourselves, even if you are not willing to do so for the others; but if you decide that I am speaking nonsense and have gone insane, you need not pay attention to me, as though I were in my right mind, either now or ever again.

[21] Philip's original rise to greatness from insignificant and lowly beginnings; and the Greeks' mutually distrustful and divisive attitudes; and the fact that it was much more unexpected for him to grow so powerful from what he once was than, now that he has already seized so much, for him to place the rest under his dominion as well; and all such topics, which I could discuss in detail, I will pass over. [22] This I will say, though. I see that all mankind, taking their lead from you, has conceded to him the thing over which all previous Greek wars have been fought. And what is that? The right to do whatever he wants, to mutilate the Greeks and strip them bare one by one, just like that, and to attack and enslave their cities. [23] Now, you were the leaders of Greece for seventy-three years,[25] and the Spartans were her leaders for twenty-nine years;[26] even the Thebans possessed some strength during those most recent times after the battle of Leuctra.[27] Even so, neither you nor the Thebans nor the Spartans were ever, men of Athens, conceded by the Greeks the right to do whatever you wanted; far from it. [24] Instead, for one thing, since you—or, I should say, those Athenians back then—appeared to some people to behave immoderately, everyone considered it necessary—even those with no complaints against the Athenians—to go to war with Athens along with the injured parties.[28] And again, after the Spartans had risen to empire and arrived at the same supremacy you had enjoyed, when they attempted to extend their

power and tried to alter established institutions beyond moderation,[29] everyone became embroiled in war, even those with no complaints against the Spartans.

[25] Why do we need to discuss the rest? We ourselves and the Spartans, despite having no mutual wrongs to cite at the outset, nonetheless found it necessary to go to war due to the wrongs we witnessed others suffering. And further, all the faults committed by the Spartans during their thirty years, and by our ancestors during their seventy years, are fewer, men of Athens, than the offenses Philip has committed against the Greeks in the less than thirteen years he has been on top[30]—to put it better, their offenses do not even constitute a fraction of his.

[26] *This is easy to demonstrate in a few words.* I pass over Olynthus and Methone and Apollonia and thirty-two cities in the Thraceward region,[31] all of which he has eradicated so savagely that a traveler there cannot easily tell whether they were ever inhabited. I will also remain silent concerning the destruction of the Phocian people, great as it was. But what about Thessaly: how is it doing? Has he not taken away their constitutions and cities and established tetrarchies,[32] so that they are enslaved not just city by city but tribe by tribe as well? [27] Are the cities of Euboea not already ruled by tyrants, and that on an island next to Thebes and Athens?[33] Does he not write explicitly in his letters, "I am at peace with those who are willing to listen to me?" Does he not write these things but fail to live up to them with his actions? Instead, he goes after the Hellespont;[34] earlier he attacked Ambracia;[35] in the Peloponnese he holds Elis, a city of such importance;[36] and just recently he launched a plot against Megara.[37] Neither Greece nor barbarian country can contain the man's greed.

[28] And although all of us Greeks see and hear of these developments, we do not send ambassadors to each other regarding them and express our indignation: we are in such poor shape and so undermined, city by city, that up to this very day we have been unable to do a single beneficial or necessary thing. We cannot unite or form any partnership of aid and friendship. [29] Instead, as the man grows more powerful, we overlook it; each of us, it seems to me, has decided to profit in the interval

while someone else is ruined, rather than investigating or acting for the salvation of Greece. I say this because everyone is aware that Philip is just like the recurrence or onset of a fever or some other illness that reaches even the person who currently appears to be quite far away.

[30] And you all know that, as for everything the Greeks suffered at the Spartans' hands or at ours, at least they were wronged by legitimate sons of Greece. You could interpret it in the same way as if a legitimate son born to great wealth managed something poorly and incorrectly: for that individual action he deserves criticism and prosecution, but you cannot say that he lacked the standing, as relative or heir, to act.[38] [31] If, however, a slave or supposititious child[39] ruined and spoiled what did not belong to him, Heracles! how much more terrible and infuriating everyone would say it was. But this is not their attitude concerning Philip and his present actions, even though he is not a Greek or related to the Greeks at all, or even a barbarian from a place respectable to mention, but a pest from Macedonia, a place where in the past you could not even buy a decent slave.

[32] And yet what act of the utmost hubris does he leave undone? In addition to his destruction of cities, does he not conduct the Pythian Games, the common competition of the Greeks, even sending his slaves to run the games in his absence?[40] *Does he control Thermopylae and the approaches to Greece, occupying those places with garrisons and mercenaries?*[41] *Does he also possess the right to consult the god first—a right not even shared by all the Greeks—having shoved aside us, the Thessalians, the Dorians, and the rest of the Amphictyons?*[42] [33] Does he write to the Thessalians regarding the manner in which they are to govern themselves? Does he dispatch mercenaries, some to Porthmus to expel the Eretrian democrats, others to Oreus to install Philistides as tyrant?[43] The Greeks see these things but put up with them nonetheless; they seem to me, at least, to watch as they would watch a hailstorm: everyone prays that it does not fall on him, but no one tries to prevent it.

[34] And it is not only his hubristic acts against Greece as a whole which meet with no resistance, but even his crimes against each individual—for this is the utmost limit. Has he not attacked Ambracia and Leucas, property of the Corinthians? Has he not sworn to hand

over Naupactus, property of the Achaeans, to the Aetolians?[44] Has he not taken away Echinus, property of the Thebans,[45] and is he not now proceeding against the Byzantines, his own allies?[46] [35] As for our possessions, I omit the rest, but does he not hold Cardia, the greatest city of the Chersonese?[47] And all of us who suffer this treatment delay and display our cowardice and cast glances at our neighbors, distrusting each other instead of the one who is mistreating us all. And yet, when he treats all of us with such brutality, what do you think he is going to do when he becomes master of each of us individually?

[36] What, then, is the cause of this? For it is not without reason and just cause that the Greeks were so readily disposed to freedom then or to slavery now. There was something then—there was, men of Athens—in the minds of the masses that is not present now, which conquered the wealth of the Persians, led Greece on the path of freedom, and met no defeat in battle on sea or land, whose loss now has spoiled everything and turned the entire situation upside down. [37] And what was it? *Nothing complicated or ingenious; simply that* people who took money from those desiring to rule or corrupt Greece were universally detested, and a conviction of receiving bribes was a very unpleasant prospect: they punished such offenders with the harshest penalty. [38] Thus the opportunity for any given action, which Fortune often provides even to the negligent at the expense of the attentive, could not be bought from the politicians or the generals; nor could their concord with each other, their distrust for tyrants and barbarians, or, in general, anything of the sort.

[39] Now, however, all these have been sold away like merchandise in the agora;[48] and the things which have been imported in their place have left Greece ruined and destroyed. What are these? Envy, if someone has received something; mockery, if he admits it; *pardon for those who are convicted;* hostility, if someone criticizes them; and everything else attached to bribery. [40] You see, as far as triremes[49] are concerned, and the sheer amount of men and money, and the abundance of other materiel, and all other criteria by which one might judge cities powerful, everyone possesses these in far greater number and magnitude now than their predecessors did. But these assets are made useless, ineffective, and worthless by those who offer them for sale.

[41] Certainly you all see that this is the state of things now, and you need no further testimony from me. That the opposite situation obtained in prior times I will show you, not in my own words, but by reciting a document of your ancestors which they inscribed on a bronze pillar and set up on the Acropolis, *not for their own use (since even without this document they possessed the necessary attitude), but so that you might have an example to remind you how seriously you ought to treat such matters.* [42] *So, what does the document say?* It reads, "Arthmius son of Pythonax of Zeleia shall be an outlaw and a public enemy of the Athenian people and of their allies, himself and his descendants." Next is written the reason for which this occurred: "because he brought the gold from the Medes to the Peloponnese."[50]

That is the document. [43] Consider, now, by the gods, what the intent of those Athenians back then was in doing this, or what their decision entailed. Because a citizen of Zeleia, Arthmius, a slave[51] of the Great King (Zeleia is in Asia) brought gold to the Peloponnese—not to Athens—in the service of his master, they registered him and his descendants as public enemies of the Athenians and their allies, and outlaws. [44] This was not what one would call outlawry in the ordinary sense; for what was it to a Zeleite if he was not going to share the rights of Athenian citizens? *But this is not what it means.* Rather, it is written in the homicide laws, concerning individuals in whose cases homicide trials are not granted, *but whose killings are sanctioned*: "and let him die an outlaw." The meaning is this: he who kills a person in this category is free of pollution.[52]

[45] They therefore considered the safety of all the Greeks to be their concern: they would not have cared if someone tried to buy and corrupt people in the Peloponnese unless this were their understanding. And they chastised and punished those whom they detected so severely that they even put their names on a pillar. It resulted from this, with good reason, that the Greeks were formidable to the barbarian, not the barbarian to the Greeks. But such is not the case now, for you do not possess the same attitude toward these or other matters.

What is your attitude? [46] *You know it yourselves; why do I have to accuse you on all counts? And all the rest of the Greeks are in a similar condition and no better than you. This is why I declare that the present situation requires considerable effort and good planning. What do I mean?* Do you bid me tell you? And will you not get angry?

[47] Now then, there is a silly argument advanced by those who want to reassure the city that goes like this: "Philip is not yet as powerful as the Spartans once were when they ruled over all the sea and land, with the Great King as their ally, and nothing could withstand them; and our city resisted them nonetheless and was not eradicated."[53] But in my opinion, although great progress has been made in practically all areas and nothing now is similar to what it was then, no greater revolution and advance has occurred than in the art of war. [48] First of all, I hear that in those days the Spartans and everyone else would invade and ravage the land for four or five months—during the campaigning season proper[54]—with armies of citizen hoplites, and would then withdraw and return home. They were so old-fashioned—or, rather, such good citizens—that nothing was bought from anyone with money; instead they fought a customary and open kind of war.

[49] Now, however, you must see that traitors have caused most losses and nothing gets decided by pitched battle; you hear that Philip marches wherever he pleases not because he leads a phalanx of hoplites, but because he has attached to himself light infantry, cavalry, archers, mercenaries, that sort of army.[55] [50] And, on top of that, whenever he attacks a city suffering from internal illness,[56] and no one comes out to defend their land due to distrust, he positions his engines of war and lays siege. I say nothing of summer and winter, how there is no difference between them and no specified off-season during which he lets up.[57]

[51] Assuming, then, that we all know these things and take them into consideration, we must not admit the war into our land, nor twist our necks looking at the simplicity of the previous war against the Spartans; rather, with our policies and preparations we must establish our defense as far away as possible, seeing to it that Philip does not budge from his home and that we by no means fight it out at close range.[58] [52] For, when it comes to war, we have many natural advantages—if, men of Athens, we are willing to do what we must—including the nature of his

country, much of which we can plunder and ravage, and countless other factors. For a pitched battle, however, he is better trained than we are.

[53] You must not only recognize these things and resist him with military operations; in addition, with your reasoning and judgment you must detest those who plead his case in the Assembly, keeping in mind that it is not possible to conquer the enemies of the city until you punish their underlings in the city itself.[59] [54] Which, by Zeus and the other gods, you will not be able to do. You have sunk to such depths of idiocy or insanity or I don't know what to call it (it has often occurred to me to fear this too, that some supernatural power is driving our affairs) that, for the sake of reproach or envy or humor or whatever motive you happen to act upon, you demand speeches from hirelings, some of whom do not even deny their status, and you laugh when they insult people. [55] Awful though this is, it gets still worse: you have allowed these people to pursue their policies in greater safety than the politicians who speak for you! And yet look at how many disasters have been facilitated by your willingness to listen to this sort of people. I will state facts with which you will all be familiar.

[56] Of those active in politics at Olynthus there were some who belonged to Philip and served him in everything, and others who served the best interest of their city and acted to prevent the enslavement of their fellow citizens. Which side brought their country to ruin? Which side betrayed the cavalry, by whose betrayal Olynthus was lost? Philip's supporters, who, while the city still existed, maliciously prosecuted and slandered those who made the best proposals such that the people of Olynthus were even persuaded to banish Apollonides.[60]

[57] And it is not just among the Olynthians and nowhere else that this habit has caused all sorts of trouble. In Eretria, when they had rid themselves of Plutarchus and his mercenaries, and the people held the city and Porthmus,[61] some wanted to put their affairs in your hands, while others wanted to put them in Philip's. For the most part the poor unfortunate Eretrians preferred to listen to the latter party, and in the end they were persuaded to expel the men who spoke in their interests. [58] And in consequence their ally Philip sent them Hipponicus and a thousand mercenaries, tore down the walls of Porthmus, and installed

three tyrants: Hipparchus, Automedon, and Cleitarchus.⁶² Since then he has already expelled them from their country twice when they wanted to save themselves, *sending once the mercenaries under Eurylochus, and again those under Parmenion.*⁶³

[59] Why do we need to discuss the majority of cases? At Oreus,⁶⁴ though, Philistides⁶⁵ worked for Philip, as did Menippus and Socrates and Thoas and Agapaeus, who are now in charge of the city (and everyone knew it); but a person by the name of Euphraeus, who once lived here among us,⁶⁶ was working to keep the Oreites free and slaves to no one. [60] The other ways in which this man was treated with hubris and abused by the people would make a long story; but a year before the capture of Oreus he denounced Philistides and his associates as traitors, having detected what they were doing. A large band of men, with Philip as their chorus-master⁶⁷ and chairman, dragged Euphraeus off to prison on a charge of stirring up the city.

[61] Seeing this, the people of Oreus, instead of coming to his aid and nailing them to the board,⁶⁸ showed no anger at them and declared him deserving of his punishment and celebrated. After that, they⁶⁹ had all the freedom they wanted to work for their city's capture, and they arranged to effect it; any of the masses who noticed was terrified into silence, remembering what had happened to Euphraeus. So miserable was their condition that no one dared utter a sound in the face of such disaster approaching until the enemy was assaulting their walls in full battle order. At that point, some tried to defend their city, others worked to betray it.

[62] With their city captured in such a shameful and dishonorable manner, the traitors rule as tyrants; as for their previous saviors, who had been ready to do anything whatsoever to Euphraeus, some they banished, others they executed. The esteemed Euphraeus killed himself, bearing witness in deed that he had taken a stand against Philip on behalf of his fellow citizens from just and pure motives.

[63] What, then, is the reason, you are probably wondering, that the Olynthians and Eretrians and Oreites were more friendly to Philip's defenders than to their own? It is the same reason that obtains among you. Those who speak in your best interests sometimes cannot offer a

popular proposal, even if they want to, because they have to see to the preservation of our affairs; while the other group collaborates with Philip in the very acts by which it gains popularity. [64] The former urged the payment of war-taxes; the latter said it was unnecessary. The former urged war and distrust; the latter urged peace, until they were caught in the trap. All the other instances occurred, I think, in the same way (so as not to describe them individually): one group proposed what would make itself popular; the other proposed what would save their city. Mostly, in the end, the masses submitted not so much for their own pleasure or out of ignorance; they gave in because they thought all was lost.

[65] I fear, by Zeus and Apollo, that you will suffer the same fate, when you count it all up and realize that there is nothing you can do. May our situation never come to that, men of Athens; it is better to die ten thousand deaths than to do anything to flatter Philip *and sacrifice any of the men who defend your interests.* What a fine return the Oreites have received for entrusting themselves to Philip's friends and rejecting Euphraeus! [66] What a fine return the people of Eretria have received for driving out your ambassadors[70] and placing themselves in Cleitarchus' hands: they are slaves, whipped and slaughtered. How nobly Philip spared the Olynthians, who elected Lasthenes hipparch and banished Apollonides![71]

[67] It is stupidity and cowardice to entertain such hopes, and to take bad advice and be unwilling to do anything that you should, instead listening to those who speak on behalf of the enemy and thinking that you inhabit a city of such magnitude that no disaster will befall you regardless of what happens. [68] And it would surely be a disgrace to say at some later point, "Who could have thought this would happen? By Zeus, we should have done this and that and not done the other thing." The Olynthians could mention many things now which, if they had foreseen them at the time, would have prevented their destruction. So could the Oreites; so could the Phocians; so could each of the peoples that have been brought to ruin. [69] But what good does it do them? While the ship is still safe, be it large or small, that is the time for the sailor and the helmsman and each man down the line to show his zeal and see to it that no one either intentionally or unintentionally capsizes the vessel; but when the sea overwhelms it, the effort is pointless.[72]

[70] As for us, then, men of Athens, while we are still safe, possessing the greatest city, the most resources, the finest reputation, what are we to do? Someone has probably been sitting here wanting to ask this for a while now. I will tell you, by Zeus, and I will also draft a proposal, so that you may approve it, if you like. First of all, we ourselves[73] must see to our defense and make preparations, I mean with triremes and money and soldiers; for certainly, even if everyone else submits to slavery, we must fight for freedom.

[71] Having made all these preparations ourselves, and having made them conspicuous, then let us summon the rest to join us; let us dispatch ambassadors to give these instructions *in every direction: I mean to the Peloponnese, to Rhodes, to Chios, to the Great King (for it is not foreign to his interests to keep Philip from conquering everything),*[74] so that, if you convince them, you will have partners in the dangers and the expenses, if necessary, and if not, you will at least impose delays on the situation.[75] [72] Since the war is against a man and not against the might of a united city, this is not a useless undertaking; nor were last year's embassies sent around the Peloponnese to lodge accusations, when I and that excellent man Polyeuctus there and Hegesippus[76] and the rest of the ambassadors circulated and caused Philip to hold his position rather than attacking Ambracia or setting out against the Peloponnese.

[73] Now, I am not proposing that we summon the others when we ourselves are unwilling to take a single necessary step on our own behalf. It would be silly for us to claim to care about other people's interests when we abandon our own, and to neglect the present but make others fear for the future. This is not what I mean; rather, I say that we must send money to the men in the Chersonese[77] and do whatever else they call for. We must prepare ourselves, and we must convoke, assemble, instruct, and admonish the rest of the Greeks; this is the duty of a city with as great a reputation as you possess. [74] And if you think the Chalcidians or the Megarians will save Greece while you run away from the problem, you are not thinking correctly: each of them will be happy if they can save themselves. This has to be done by you; this is the prize your ancestors won and bequeathed to you through many grave dangers. [75] But if each of you is going to sit there searching for what he wants and figuring out how he himself can avoid doing anything, in the

first place, he will never find anyone to do it for him; and secondly, I fear that we will be compelled to do all the things we do not want to do at the same time.

[76] This is what I have to say; this is what I propose. I think that even now, if these measures are put into effect, our situation can still be rectified. But if someone has a better proposal than this, let him speak and advise us. And whatever you decide, I pray to all the gods that it be to your benefit.

# 13

# PHILIP = [DEMOSTHENES] 12

*Letter of Philip*

## Introduction

In the summer of 340, as he was advancing toward Perinthus and Byzantium, Philip sent the Athenians a letter, which survives as speech 12 in the corpus of Demosthenes (Part Two, Philip and Athens, p. 80). When Philip composed the letter, he had already reached the Hellespont (§16). He does not mention Perinthus; either he had not yet arrived or he felt no need to mention it to the Athenians.

After an opening salutation, Philip states his reason for sending the letter (§1). The body of the letter (§§2–23) contains numerous complaints against Athens. Philip cites the mistreatment of heralds and the conduct of Diopeithes (§§2–4); the activities of Callias (§5); Athenian negotiations with Persia (§§6–7); attempted interference with Philip's activities in Thrace (§§8–10); Athens' refusal to submit to arbitration regarding Cardia (§§11); the ongoing wrangling over Halonnesus (§§12–15); and the hostility of Athenian cleruchs in the Chersonese (§16).

Philip urges the Athenians to negotiate rather than fight; he accuses Athenian politicians of fostering hostilities but refuses to bribe them into cooperation (§§17–20). He then justifies his claim to Amphipolis (§§20–23). In conclusion, Philip accuses the Athenians of aggression and announces his intention to defend himself (§§23).

**Note on authorship.** Scholarly opinion on the authenticity of this letter is divided. While some believe it was written by Philip himself or by one of his officials, others, citing historical inconsistencies (§9 with note), consider it a later forgery. In either case, the letter presents an accurate representation of Macedonian claims and interests in 340.

*Letter of Philip*

[1] Philip to the Council and people of Athens, greetings.[1]

Since I have repeatedly dispatched envoys in order that we might abide by our oaths and agreements,[2] but you have paid no attention, I thought I should send you a letter concerning the reasons I consider myself wronged. Do not be taken aback by the length of the letter; my charges are numerous, and it is necessary to be completely clear about all of them.

[2] First, when Nicias the herald was kidnapped from my country, you not only failed to inflict the appropriate punishment on the criminals, but you even imprisoned the victim for ten months; as for the letters he was carrying from me, you read them out on the platform.[3] Then, when the Thasians harbored the Byzantines' triremes, as well as any pirates who so desired, you thought nothing of it, although the treaty[4] explicitly states that those committing such acts are to be our enemies.

[3] In addition, around that same time, Diopeithes invaded the country, reduced the people of Crobyle and Tiristasis[5] to utter slavery, and sacked the neighboring part of Thrace. Finally he sank to such lawlessness that he arrested Amphilochus, who had come as an ambassador on the matter of the prisoners-of-war, put him to the most extreme tortures, and then released him for a ransom of nine talents.[6] And he did this with the approval of your Assembly. [4] And yet crimes against heralds and ambassadors are considered impious by everyone else and especially by you:[7] at least, when the Megarians slew Anthemocritus,[8] your Assembly went so far as to bar them from the Mysteries[9] and set up a statue in front of the gates as a memorial to the crime. Since you expressed such hatred for the perpetrators when you were the victims of these acts, how is it not bizarre for you now to commit them openly yourselves?

[5] And further, Callias,[10] the general you sent, seized all the inhabited cities on the Gulf of Pagasae, which were bound by oath to you and by alliance to me; and he sold into slavery all those sailing for Macedonia, judging them to be enemies. And for that you praised him in your decrees! I therefore have no idea what more novel development will occur if you admit that you are at war with me, since, when we were in

open disagreement, you dispatched pirates, sold into slavery those sailing for my country, aided my adversaries, and ravaged my land.

[6] Apart from that, you have sunk to such depths of insanity and hostility that you have even dispatched envoys to the Persian[11] to persuade him to make war on me. This is the most surprising thing. For before he captured Egypt and Phoenicia,[12] you decreed that, if he altered the *status quo*, you would call upon me as well as all the other Greeks to attack him. [7] Now, however, your hatred of me is so excessive that you are negotiating with him concerning a defensive alliance. Yet, in antiquity, your forefathers (as I hear) censured the Peisistratids for leading the Persian against the Greeks;[13] but you feel no shame at doing the same things you continue to charge the tyrants with.

[8] On top of everything else, you even order me in writing in your decrees to allow Teres and Cersobleptes[14] to rule Thrace, stating that they are Athenian citizens. But I know that these men are not included with you in the peace treaty, not listed on the pillars,[15] and not Athenian citizens. However, Teres has campaigned with me against you; and Cersobleptes was eager to swear the oaths to my ambassadors in private but was thwarted by your generals, who declared him an enemy of the Athenians.[16] [9] How, then, is it fair or just for you to label him an enemy of your city when it suits your interests, but to declare the same man a citizen when you want to trump up accusations against me? How is it fair or just that when Sitalces, to whom you had granted citizenship, was killed, you immediately established friendship with his killer, but you undertake a war against us for Cersobleptes' sake?[17] And you do so with the clear knowledge that no recipient of such gifts gives a single thought to your laws and decrees.

[10] All the same—if I am to pass over all the rest and speak concisely—you granted citizenship to Evagoras of Cyprus and Dionysius of Syracuse[18] and their descendants. So if you convince those who expelled each of them[19] to return power to the men they banished, then take back from me as much of Thrace as Teres and Cersobleptes ruled. But if you see fit to bring no charges against their conquerors but continue to bother me, how would I not be justified in defending myself against you?

[11] On these topics I still have a number of rightful claims to make, but I choose to omit them. I do, however, state that I am coming to the aid of the Cardians.[20] I became their ally before the peace; and you are unwilling to submit to judgment, although I have asked you many times, and they not a few. Therefore, how would I not be the lowest of all men if I deserted my allies and showed more respect for you, who harass me in every way, than for those who remain at all times my steadfast friends?

[12] And further—if I should not omit this too—you have become so arrogant that, while in the past you used to charge me only with the offenses mentioned above, most recently, when the Peparethians[21] complained of awful treatment, you ordered your general to exact a penalty from me on their behalf. I showed more leniency in their punishment than they deserved: they seized Halonnesus in time of peace and refused to return either the island or its garrison,[22] although I repeatedly sent letters on those topics. [13] And even though you had accurate knowledge of the situation, you took into consideration none of the Peparethians' crimes against me, but only their punishment. And yet I did not seize the island either from them or from you, but from the pirate Sostratus. So, if you claim that you gave it to Sostratus, you admit to dispatching pirates; if, on the other hand, he controlled it against your will, what outrage have you suffered in my taking it and making the region safe for sailors?

[14] And, when I tried to exhibit such considerable care for your city and give you the island, your politicians would not allow you to "take" it but counseled you to "take" it "back,"[23] so that I would either submit to orders and admit that I was in possession of foreign territory or, if I did not surrender the place, I would fall under the suspicion of the masses. Realizing this, I challenged you to submit the dispute to judgment, so that, if Halonnesus were awarded to me, I could "give" the place to you, but, if it were adjudged to you, I could then "give" it "back" to your people.

[15] I made this request repeatedly, but you paid no attention, and the Peparethians seized the island. So what should I have done? Should I not have punished those who had broken their oaths? Should I not have brought vengeance upon the perpetrators of such arrogant violence?

And further, if the island belonged to the Peparethians, what business was it of the Athenians' to demand it back? And if it was yours, how are you not furious at them for seizing what did not belong to them?

[16] Our enmity has progressed to such a degree that, when I wanted to cross into the Hellespont with my fleet,[24] I was forced to send it across the Chersonese under the protection of my army: your cleruchs, in accordance with the decree of Polycrates, were at war with me; you had taken a vote to that effect; and your general[25] was inciting the Byzantines and announcing to everyone that you ordered him to make war if he got the opportunity. Despite such mistreatment, I kept away from your city's triremes and territory, although I was equipped to take most or all of them; and I have continued to challenge you to submit to judgment concerning our reciprocal accusations. [17] And yet consider whether it is nobler to decide the question by weapons or by words, to be our own referees or to persuade someone else to do it. Take into account, too, how inconsistent it is for Athenians to force Thasians and Maronites to have the Stryme affair decided by words,[26] but themselves not to resolve their dispute with me in the same manner—especially when you recognize that you will lose nothing if you are defeated, but if you win, you will acquire places now under my control.

[18] But the most unreasonable thing of all, I think, is this. I sent ambassadors from my entire alliance to be witnesses, and I am willing to conclude a just agreement with you concerning the Greeks; but you refused to listen to my ambassadors' statements on the subject, when you could have either removed from danger those harboring some unpleasant suspicion against me or openly exposed me as the lowest of all men. [19] This offer benefited the people, but it did not profit the politicians. The experts on your government say that for your politicians peace is war and war is peace. Whether they cooperate with your generals or trump up charges against them, they always get something from them; and further, by insulting your most distinguished citizens and the most reputable foreigners on the platform, they get themselves a reputation among the masses for being men of the people.

[20] Now, by making a very small payment, I could easily put a stop to their slanders and make them sing my praises. But I would be ashamed

if I openly bought your goodwill from the people who, in addition to everything else, have reached such a level of audacity that they even endeavor to dispute with me the possession of Amphipolis, to which I believe my claim is considerably more just than my rivals'.[27] [21] For if Amphipolis belongs to the people who originally conquered it, how is my possession of it not rightful? My ancestor Alexander was the first to occupy the place, and he dedicated a golden statue at Delphi as first-fruits from the Persian prisoners-of-war he took there.[28] And if someone disputes this and demands that Amphipolis belong to those who later became its masters, that right is mine as well; for I conquered by siege the people who drove you out and honored the Spartans as their founders, and I took the place.[29]

[22] Now, all of us inhabit our cities either because our ancestors bequeathed them to us or because we won control of them in war. But you neither took Amphipolis first nor possess it now, and you stayed in the region for the shortest time; yet you lay claim to the city, and you do so despite providing your own strongest assurances in support of my position. I repeatedly discuss Amphipolis in my letters, and you have recognized my right to possess it, by concluding the peace when I was in possession of the city, and then an alliance on the same terms.[30] [23] And further, how could any ownership be more secure than my owner-ship of Amphipolis, which was originally seized by my ancestors, then became mine again in war, and was conceded to me a third time by you, who habitually dispute even things which are none of your business?

These are my charges. And since you started it, and since, thanks to my discretion, you are now launching further assaults on my interests and injuring me to the best of your ability, I shall defend myself, with justice on my side, and, with the gods as my witnesses, I shall handle my business with you.

# PART THREE
## ATHENS UNDER ALEXANDER

### Sources

For affairs at Athens during the reign of Alexander the Great (336–323) we depend heavily on oratory and epigraphy. Among the speeches in the corpus of Demosthenes, orations 17 (*On the Treaty with Alexander*: spurious), and 18 (*On the Crown*) are of particular importance. Aeschines 3, *Against Ctesiphon*, is the prosecution speech to which Demosthenes' *On the Crown* responds. Most of the preserved speeches of three other orators, Hypereides, Lycurgus, and Deinarchus, were delivered in Athens during this period. Other useful literary sources include Arrian's *Anabasis of Alexander*; books 17 and 18 of Diodorus' *Library of History*; and Plutarch's *Lives* of Demosthenes, Phocion, and Alexander.

We also possess a large number of Athenian inscriptions on stone from Alexander's reign. Laws and decrees datable to a specific year have been collected and edited systematically (but not translated) by C. J. Schwenk, *Athens in the Age of Alexander* (Chicago 1985). Some of the more important inscriptions are included by M. N. Tod in the section of his *Greek Historical Inscriptions* covering Alexander's reign (nos. 183–205), and a number of these are translated by P. Harding, *From the Peloponnesian War to the Battle of Ipsus* (Cambridge 1985), including the renewal of the League of Corinth (Tod, no. 183 = Harding, no. 102) and the ephebic oath (Tod, no. 204 = Harding, no. 109).

### Accession of Alexander, 336

Upon the assassination of Philip, his twenty-year-old son Alexander III (the Great) succeeded to the Macedonian throne. The death of

Philip revived Greek hopes of independence from Macedon. At Athens, Demosthenes celebrated by donning a garland of flowers, and the Assembly decreed that a gold crown be awarded posthumously to Philip's assassin, a Macedonian nobleman named Pausanias. The Athenians sent clandestine communications to Attalus, one of Philip's generals, and rose in revolt together with the Thebans and others.

Alexander responded quickly and decisively, marching on Thebes at the head of the Macedonian army. On his arrival, the Thebans surrendered and the Athenians apologized; soon thereafter the League of Corinth met and elected Alexander *Hêgemôn* (leader) of the League in his father's place. Learning of Attalus' intrigues with the Athenians, Alexander had him killed; as Macedonian custom dictated in cases of treason, all Attalus' male blood relatives shared his sentence (Q. Curtius Rufus 8.6.28).

### Revolt in Greece, 335

Believing Greece secure, Alexander headed north, where he defeated the Triballi and the Illyrians. Meanwhile, false reports of Alexander's death on campaign, together with a subvention of 300 talents from the Great King of Persia, Darius III Codomannus, had encouraged the Greeks to rebel once again under the leadership of Thebes and Athens. The Thebans assaulted the Macedonian garrison in their citadel, the Cadmeia; in response Alexander rushed south and invested Thebes. After waiting three days for the Thebans to surrender, on the fourth day he stormed and captured the city. As punishment, the League of Corinth ordered that Thebes be razed to the ground and her surviving inhabitants sold into slavery. Alexander executed the sentence, leaving only the house of the poet Pindar standing in a display of respect.

Witnessing the destruction of Thebes and reasonably believing that they would be next, the Athenians sent ten ambassadors to Alexander with a letter of apology and congratulations. Alexander responded by ordering the surrender of rebel leaders including Demosthenes, Hypereides, and Lycurgus. Citing a fable about sheep surrendering their watchdogs to the wolf (Plutarch, *Demosthenes* 23), Demosthenes convinced the Assembly to dispatch a second embassy to ask Alexander to reconsider. Alexander proved receptive and drastically reduced his demand to the banishment of the general Charidemus. Athens thus escaped disaster.

## Administration of Lycurgus

From 335 to Alexander's death in 323, Athens enjoyed peace and increased prosperity. For the latter the Athenians were largely indebted to Lycurgus, who administered the state treasury from 336 to his death in 324. Lycurgus increased revenues considerably, instituted a public building program, and renovated and expanded the Athenian military. He is also sometimes credited with the reorganization of the ephebic system, which took place in 336: thenceforth the ephebes, Athenian men in their first two years of adulthood, underwent compulsory military training and guarded the borders of Attica (*Ath. Pol.* 42.2–5). A surviving fourth-century inscription (Tod, no. 204 = Harding, no. 109) contains the oath sworn by all ephebes.

### *Eisangelia* (Impeachment)

The age of Lycurgus saw the increased use and broadened scope of the legal procedure called *eisangelia* (usually rendered in English as "impeachment"). Defendants charged under the *eisangelia* statute underwent a preliminary hearing, usually before the Assembly; their cases were then referred to a jury-court (*dikastêrion*) for trial (General Introduction, pp. 5–6). The *eisangelia* procedure was originally intended primarily for the prosecution of magistrates in office and aimed at acts of treason against the state, such as subverting the democracy, betraying Athenian interests, and receiving bribes (see the law quoted by Hypereides 4.7–8).

By the 330s, *eisangelia* was being abused: under color of the subversion-of-democracy clause, prosecutors brought impeachments for relatively petty offenses such as seduction (Hypereides 1), overcharging for flute-girls, fraudulent deme registration, and misrepresentation of a dream (Hypereides 4.1–3). Lycurgus was especially active in prosecutions by *eisangelia*: he spoke in some trials himself (e.g., Lycurgus 1 *Against Leocrates*; Hypereides 4.12) and offered his services as logographer in others (such as the Lycophron case: Lycurgus fr. X–XI Conomis *1 –2 Against Lycophron*; cf. Hypereides 1.3).[1]

Those Athenians who protested the abuse of *eisangelia* found their champion in the orator and politician Hypereides, who defended at least several of the men prosecuted by Lycurgus. By the end of the 330s, a remedy was in place to check malicious prosecution by *eisangelia*: a fine of 1,000 drachmas (General Introduction, p. 10) was levied against any prosecutor in an *eisangelia* who received less than twenty percent of the jury's votes.[2]

## *Crown* Case, 330

The final showdown in the long and bitter rivalry between Demosthenes and Aeschines took place in 330, when Aeschines prosecuted Demosthenes' associate Ctesiphon on a *graphê paranomôn* (General Introduction, p. 8). In 336, Ctesiphon had carried a decree in the Council of 500 awarding a gold crown to Demosthenes for his public services. Six years later, Aeschines brought Ctesiphon to court. In his speech *Against Ctesiphon* (oration 3), Aeschines not only specifically attacks the legality of Ctesiphon's decree but launches an all-out assault on the political career of his arch-enemy Demosthenes. Demosthenes responded with his celebrated oration *On the Crown* (oration 18), a masterpiece of oratory that vindicated his record, overwhelming the legal merits of Aeschines' case. The acquittal of Ctesiphon and triumph of Demosthenes drove Aeschines into a self-imposed exile on Rhodes, where he founded a school of rhetoric.

## Tensions between Alexander and the Greeks, 324

In 324, Alexander's actions alienated many of his Greek allies, including Athens. From his headquarters at Susa he issued two directives. The Exiles Decree, announced at the Olympic games of 324, ordered all Greek cities to repatriate their exiles except for temple-robbers, homicides, and Thebans (Hypereides 5 col. 18; Diodorus 17.109.1, 18.8.2–5). The Athenians objected to the Exiles Decree since it threatened their possession of Samos, which was occupied by Athenian cleruchs. Some surviving inscriptions attest to compliance with the decree by various Greek states, including Mytilene (Tod, no. 201 = Harding, no. 113) and Tegea (Tod, no. 202 = Harding, no. 122).

The second issue concerned the deification of Alexander. Alexander claimed descent from Achilles and Heracles, and his pretensions to divinity had been encouraged by the oracle of Zeus Ammon at Siwah in Libya, which had addressed him in the winter of 332/1 as the son of Zeus (Plutarch, *Alexander* 27). Already worshiped as a god, or the son of a god, in the East, in 324 Alexander ordered the Greeks to follow suit. Many cities complied, sending ambassadors to Alexander bedecked with garlands as though on a holy mission (Arrian, *Anabasis of Alexander* 7.23.2). At Athens, Demades brought the issue before the Assembly, for which he was fined ten talents after Alexander's death; Demosthenes sarcastically proclaimed, "Let him be the son of Zeus, and of Poseidon too, if he wants" (Hypereides 5 col. 31).

### Harpalus Affair, 324–323

In the summer of the same year, a scandal was touched off at Athens by the arrival of Alexander's fugitive treasurer Harpalus, who had absconded with the enormous sum of 5,000 talents. The Athenians granted Harpalus asylum and deposited the 700 talents he brought with him on the Acropolis for safe-keeping. By the fall, with Macedonian officials pressing Athens for his extradition, Harpalus had fled to Crete, where he met his death; his money remained on the Acropolis, or so the Athenians thought. However, when they inventoried the funds on the Acropolis, they discovered only 350 talents remaining (Hypereides 5 col. 10).

Immediately accusations flew, with prominent Athenians suspected of using Harpalus' money for bribes. The Council of the Areopagus was entrusted with the investigation; its report, issued early in 323 after six months of inquiry (Deinarchus 1 *Against Demosthenes* 45), concluded that Demosthenes, Demades, and others had received funds from Harpalus. Ten special prosecutors, including Hypereides, were appointed to try the accused before a jury of 1,500. Demosthenes, charged with appropriating twenty talents, was convicted and fined fifty talents; unable to pay, he was imprisoned but managed to escape into exile. Substantial parts of the speech Hypereides delivered at Demosthenes' trial (oration 5, *Against Demosthenes*) survive. Deinarchus, a logographer of Corinthian birth, composed speeches delivered by another prosecutor against Demosthenes (oration 1), Aristogeiton (oration 2), Philocles (oration 3), and others.

### Death of Alexander and Aftermath, 323–322

On June 13, 323, after a brief illness, Alexander the Great died at Babylon. Alexander's demise inspired the Greeks to fight for their freedom from Macedonian rule one last time. At Athens, Hypereides, who had never abandoned his hawkish position toward Macedon, and Demosthenes, who was recalled from exile, incited the Assembly to war. A brief and unsuccessful uprising, labeled the Hellenic War by the insurgents and the Lamian War by modern historians, lasted roughly a year, from summer 323 to summer 322, when it was crushed by Antipater. Antipater dissolved the rebel alliance and granted no recognition to the League of Corinth; the fragile illusion of alliance between Macedon and the Greek states that had existed since 338 gave way to the harsh reality of Macedonian overlordship.

In the aftermath of the revolt, orders were issued for the arrest of anti-Macedonian agitators, including Demosthenes and Hypereides. Demosthenes' captors hunted him down in the Argolid, where he took poison concealed in a pen (Plutarch, *Demosthenes* 29). Hypereides was apprehended, haled before Antipater, and tortured, but (according to one story) swallowed his own tongue to avoid divulging state secrets ([Plutarch], *Lives of the Ten Orators* 849b). Thus the great age of Attic oratory came to an end.

# 14

# HYPEREIDES 1

*For Lycophron*

## Introduction

Hypereides wrote this speech for delivery by Lycophron, an Athenian prosecuted by *eisangelia* (Part Three, Athens under Alexander, pp. 189–90) for seducing the wife of a fellow citizen. Lycophron delivered the speech before a jury-court (*dikastêrion*: General Introduction, pp. 5–6). The lead prosecutor was one Ariston; Lycurgus (§3; Part Three, Athens under Alexander, pp. 189–90) assisted by composing two speeches for the prosecution, of which small fragments survive (Lycurgus fr. X–XI Conomis). The verdict in the case is unknown.

The name of Lycophron's alleged lover is also not known; she had been married twice and was the sister of the renowned Olympic athlete Dioxippus (§§5–6). The career of Dioxippus helps us to narrow down the probable date of the speech: a fragment of another speech written for Lycophron's defense, probably also by Hypereides (*Oxyrhynchus Papyri* no. 1607, fr. 13; see §20 with note) reads, "…that [when he was about to marry?] his sister to Charippus, Dioxippus left town for Olympia to win a crown for the city." Dioxippus won the Olympic pancration in 336, before joining Alexander's expedition to Asia (presumably in 334: for his exploits there see Diodorus 17.100–101). Therefore, if the common editorial supplement to the Oxyrhynchus fragment is correct, the wedding of Dioxippus' sister to Charippus can be placed in 336; since Lycophron subsequently spent three years as hipparch on Lemnos, his trial will have taken place in 333 at the earliest.

A lower limit for the trial can also be established. Lycophron asserts that Ariston chose to prosecute by *eisangelia* because it was risk-free (§12). By 330 (Demosthenes 18 *On the Crown* 250), however, *eisangelia* prosecutors faced a fine of 1,000 drachmas if they failed to garner one-fifth of the jury's votes (cf. Part Three, Athens under Alexander, p. 190). Thus the trial of Lycophron occurred between 333 and 330.

From what we can reconstruct of the introduction to this speech (fr. 1–3), Lycophron gave instructions to his jury and quoted the impeachment law. The bulk of the surviving speech consists of a blend of narration and proofs (fr. 4–§18). The last significant fragment (fr. 4) mentions the death of the woman's first husband and the subsequent birth of a child. The continuous part of the oration begins with an attack on Ariston for sycophancy (§§1–2). Lycophron then employs an argument from probability to disprove the prosecution's allegations regarding his behavior at Charippus' wedding (§§3–7). He attempts to win sympathy by emphasizing the advantages enjoyed by prosecutors (§§8–11). He then lodges a procedural objection: rather than bringing an improper *eisangelia* for seduction, Ariston should have availed himself of an existing legal remedy (§§12–13). A lifetime of good behavior, both at Athens and on Lemnos, renders the prosecution's charge improbable (§§14–18). In his conclusion (§§19–20), Lycophron asks the jury's permission to call his advocates (*synêgoroi*: General Introduction, p. 6), and then summons Theophilus to the platform.

### For Lycophron

*Fragment 1*

> ...each man both [in private][1] and in public, and then in the law and the oath[2] which commands you to listen equally to the prosecution and the defense, and...

*Fragment 2*

> ...conduct their prosecution, thus you allow me as well to defend myself in the manner I have chosen and however I am able. And let none of you confront me in the middle of my speech and ask, "Why are you telling us this?" Nor must you add anything of your own to the prosecution, but rather to the defense...

*Fragment 3*

Nor does the law grant whomever wishes the power to assist in the prosecution against the accused while prohibiting assistance to the defense. But, so that I do not use up a lot of words before getting to the issue, I will proceed to my actual defense. I pray to the gods to come to my aid and deliver me safe from the present trial; as for you, men of the jury, I ask this favor: first...

...either betrayal of dockyards or arson of government buildings or seizure of the Acropolis...[3]

*Fragment 4*

...Euphemus[4]...first...when that man died...-ros of Phlya[5]...from[6] him...and they called upon...that the woman...he left his wife pregnant by him, which was not against the law. Now, if they supposed that these affairs occurred as Ariston writes in the impeachment, they certainly should not have prevented the closest relatives from ejecting Euphemus, but allowed it. As it is, however, in so doing they have borne witness by their own action that the accusation against me is false. In addition, how is it not strange that, if something had happened to the child[7] during its birth or even later, they would be relying on this will,[8] in which...

...Euphemus...he prevented...furnishing...depositions...

*Unnumbered Fragments*

...for he cannot deny his own hand.

...to be sluggish...

[1]...He had Ariston's slaves in his works. And he himself testified to this before you[9] in court, when he was on trial against Archestratides. [2] This is what this man Ariston does: he goes around issuing summonses to all mankind; whoever does not give him money he puts on trial and prosecutes, and whoever is willing to pay he lets go, and gives the money to Theomnestus. Theomnestus takes the money and buys slaves; he furnishes Ariston with provisions as one would give pirates,

and he pays him one obol[10] per slave per day, so that Ariston may be an eternal sycophant.[11]

[3] It is fitting, men of the jury, to examine the issue from another angle too; namely, from the initial accusations they brought straightaway before the Assembly.[12] My family sent me a letter describing the impeachment and the accusations they brought against me in the Assembly when they handed in the impeachment. Among these accusations it was written that Lycurgus says, claiming to have heard it from the family, that I accompanied the procession when Charippus was marrying the woman, and urged her not to have sex with Charippus but to guard herself carefully.

[4] Now, what I told my friends and family immediately upon my arrival I will now tell you as well: if these allegations are true, I will admit to having committed all the rest of the acts listed in the impeachment. But I think everyone can easily see that they are false. For who in the city is so senseless as to believe these statements? [5] First of all, men of the jury, there had to be a muleteer and an usher accompanying the team of horses pulling the bride's carriage. Then there had to be slaves accompanying her in the procession, and Dioxippus:[13] he escorted her because she was being given in marriage as a widow. So then, was I so out of my mind that, with so many other people accompanying the procession, and Dioxippus and Euphraeus, his sparring-partner, who are by common consent the strongest men in Greece, [6] I did not hesitate to say such words of a free woman where everyone could hear, nor was I afraid that I would be throttled to death on the spot? For who would have put up with hearing such things about his own sister as these men accuse me of saying, and would not have killed the man who said them?

[7] And, to top it all off, as I said a little earlier,[14] was Charippus so stupid (as it seems) that although, as they claim, the woman had previously declared that she had pledged herself to me, when he then heard me urging her to abide by the oaths she had sworn, he married the woman? Do you think that lunatic Orestes would have done this, or Margites, the biggest idiot of all?[15]

[8] Now I think, men of the jury, that in trials prosecutors have many advantages over defendants. Because the trial is risk-free for them, they say whatever they want and make false allegations with ease, while the

men on trial, out of fear, forget to say much, even about their own actions. [9] Second, since prosecutors get to speak first, they not only state their rightful arguments on the issue but cook up fraudulent abuse against their defendants and distract them from their defense. Thus for the defendants one of two things results: either they defend themselves against the irrelevant slanders and fail in their defense on the issue; or, by failing to recall the prosecution's accusations, they leave the jurors with the impression that what has been said is true.

[10] And, in addition, prosecutors slander in advance those who are scheduled to help the defendants,[16] and they distort the defense of the man who is actually on trial. This is what my adversary Ariston here made an effort to do in his prosecution, refusing to allow me the benefit of those mounting the platform[17] for me to assist in my defense. And why shouldn't they defend me? Is it not right for friends and family to help men on trial? Is there any more democratic institution in the city than the assistance that those who know how to speak render to citizens in danger who do not know how? [11] But you, Ariston, have not only made your speech about my advocates; you even arrange my defense and pass the order to the jurors as to what they should listen to, how they should bid me defend myself, and what they should not allow me to say. How is this right, that you have conducted your prosecution however you wanted, but, having advance knowledge of the just responses I have to your lies, you snatch my defense out from under me?

[12] Also, you accuse me in the impeachment of subverting the democracy by transgressing the laws; but you yourself have taken a flying leap over all the laws and handed in an impeachment for charges for which there are existing public lawsuits before the *thesmothetae* provided by law.[18] Your goals were, first, to go to trial without risk;[19] and second, to be able to write in your impeachment tragedies of the sort you have now composed: you blame me for making numerous women grow old in their houses without husbands, and for making many others cohabit with unsuitable men in contravention of the laws. [13] Now, you cannot name any other woman in the city to whom I am responsible for these misfortunes; and, as for the one over whom you have brought this prosecution, did you think it was fitting for her to be betrothed to and cohabit with Charippus, one of your fellow citizens, or to grow old in her house

unbetrothed—a woman who was betrothed straightaway, with Euphemus contributing a talent of silver to her dowry, obviously not out of
immorality but out of decency?[20]

[14] So then, men of the jury, my adversary can say whatever he
wants and make his false allegations; in my opinion, though, you should
reach a verdict on me not from the slanders of my prosecutor, but by
scrutinizing the entire life I have lived. For it is impossible for anyone in
the city to be either immoral or decent without you the people noticing
it; the passage of time is the most accurate witness to each individual's
character, [15] especially regarding accusations such as this one. In the
case of offenses that can be committed at any time during a person's life,
one must investigate starting with the actual charge brought against the
accused. With seduction, though, a man cannot start at the age of fifty;
either he has been that way for a long time—and let my adversaries
show this—or it is likely that the accusation is false.

[16] As for me, men of the jury, in spending my entire life with you
in the city I have never been the object of any accusation of immorality;
no charge has arisen concerning me in connection with any citizen; I
have not been a defendant in a lawsuit, nor have I prosecuted anyone.
Rather, the whole time I have continually raised horses in an ambitious
fashion, going beyond my ability and exceeding my means.[21] I have
been crowned by the entire cavalry for bravery, and also by my colleagues in office.[22] [17] For you, men of the jury,[23] voted me first phylarch,[24] then hipparch for Lemnos;[25] there I was the only hipparch ever
to hold office for two years, and I remained there for the additional
third year, not wishing to exact pay for the cavalry recklessly from citizens in a needy condition. [18] And during that time no one there
brought a charge against me either private or public; I was, however,
awarded three crowns by the people at Hephaestia and three more by the
people at Myrine.[26] These things should prove to you for this trial that
the accusations against me are false. It is not possible for one who is immoral in Athens to be good on Lemnos; nor did you regard me as such
when you dispatched me there, placing two of your cities in my trust.

[19] You have heard, men of the jury, pretty much all I had to say in my
own defense. But since the prosecutor, who is not inexperienced in

speaking and accustomed to frequent litigation, called as advocates men who would help him wrongfully destroy a citizen, I too ask and beseech you to command me, as well, to call to the platform those who will speak for me in such an important trial, and to listen with goodwill if any of my family or friends is able to help me, [20] your fellow citizen. I am a private individual unaccustomed to public speaking, but I am on trial and risking not just death—for that is the least of concerns to those who gauge things correctly—but being cast over the borders and not even receiving burial in my homeland after I die.[27] So if you so command, men of the jury, I will call someone to help me. Please come up here, Theophilus,[28] and say what you have to say; the jurors command you.

# 15

# HYPEREIDES 4

*For Euxenippus*

## Introduction

Hypereides delivered this speech as *synêgoros* (advocate: General Introduction, p. 5) for Euxenippus, who was tried by *eisangelia* (Part Three, Athens under Alexander, p. 189) in a jury-court at some point between 330 and 324. The prosecutor, Polyeuctus, accused Euxenippus of falsely reporting to the Assembly the contents of a dream he had while incubating in the Temple of Amphiaraus at Oropus (§§14–15). Lycurgus served as an advocate for the prosecution (§12), as he had in the Lycophron case (Hypereides 1.3). The outcome of the trial is unknown.

In the introduction (§§1–3), Hypereides laments the abuse of the impeachment procedure in recent times, asserting that Euxenippus' actions are not covered by the impeachment law. The bulk of the speech which follows (§§4–39) consists largely of proofs, with occasional narration thrown in. The jurors should examine the impeachment law, and they will find that it is aimed at politicians, not at ordinary citizens like Euxenippus (§§4–10). Polyeuctus is a hypocrite: he wishes to refuse Euxenippus the right to call advocates but has a history of doing so himself (§§11–13). Then follows an account of the dispute over land in Oropus, a decree moved by Polyeuctus, and Euxenippus' dream (§§14–18). Next, Hypereides responds to Polyeuctus' accusation that Euxenippus is a Macedonian sympathizer, with particular attention to the actions of Olympias, mother of Alexander the Great (§§19–26). Polyeuctus should leave private citizens alone and impeach politicians, as Hypereides himself has done (§§27–30). He should stop slandering Euxenippus, realizing that the Athenian people naturally sympathize with targets of sycophancy, which threatens the welfare of the city (§§31–37). Polyeuctus' prosecution of Euxenippus by *eisangelia* is not only procedurally improper but aimed at the wrong man (§§38–39).

In his conclusion (§§40–41) Hypereides urges the jurors to ignore the speeches they have heard and to base their votes on the text of Polyeuctus' impeachment, the impeachment law, and the oath they have sworn. He then directs Euxenippus to ask the jury's permission to call additional advocates and to bring his children up to the platform.

*For Euxenippus*

[1] Well, for my part, men of the jury, as I was just saying to the people sitting next to me, I am amazed that you are not already sick of these sorts of impeachments. In the past, the people impeached in your court were Timomachus[1] and Leosthenes[2] and Callistratus[3] and Philon of Anaea[4] and Theotimus who lost Sestos[5] and others like them. Some of these men were accused of betraying ships, others of betraying cities belonging to Athens, and one[6] because, as a politician, he proposed what was not best for the people. [2] Of these five men not one awaited his trial: they fled the city, as did many other men under impeachment; it was rare to see a man being tried by impeachment having obeyed the summons to court. That is how serious and notorious the offenses were that gave rise to impeachments back then.

[3] But now what is going on in the city is completely ridiculous. Diognides and Antidorus the metic[7] are impeached for hiring out flute-girls for more than the law ordains;[8] Agasicles from the Peiraeus, because he was registered in Halimous;[9] and Euxenippus for the dreams he says he had. None of these accusations has any connection to the impeachment law. [4] Furthermore, men of the jury, in public trials jurors should not submit to listening to the prosecution's case in detail before they examine the actual chief issue of the trial and the rejoinder,[10] to see whether it is lawful or not. It is not, by Zeus, as Polyeuctus said in his prosecution, when he claimed that defendants should not rely on the impeachment law, which ordains that impeachments be brought against politicians themselves, for proposing what is not best for the people, not against all Athenians.

[5] Now, I would not mention anything before this, nor do I think any other topic requires more discussion than this one; namely, how to ensure that, in a democracy, the laws are in control, and impeachments and other trials go to court in accordance with the laws. This is why, for all the offenses that exist in the city, you have passed separate laws concerning each one. [6] Someone commits impiety regarding sacred affairs: there are public lawsuits for impiety before the king archon.[11] He is indecent toward his parents: the archon presides over that.[12] Someone in the city drafts an illegal proposal: there is the council of the *thesmothetae*.[13] He commits acts that call for summary arrest: the office of the Eleven is in place.[14] In the same way for all the other offenses you have assigned laws and officials and the proper courts to each individually.

[7] For what offenses, then, do you think impeachments ought to occur? You already wrote this in detail in the law, so that no one would fail to know. "If someone," it says, "subverts the Athenian people"—and this makes sense, men of the jury: such a charge allows no exemption or adjournment, but must come before the jury as quickly as possible—[8] "or assembles at any place with the purpose of subverting the Athenian people, or assembles a faction; or if anyone betrays a city or ships or an army on land or sea, or, as a politician, does not propose what is best for the Athenian people, taking money." You wrote the first clauses of the law to cover all citizens (since those offenses could be committed by anyone), but the final clause of the law to cover the politicians themselves, who have the power to draft decrees. [9] You would be crazy to write this law in any way other than you did—if, when the politicians reap the honors and benefits of public speaking, you transferred the risks of these ventures onto private citizens.

But regardless, Polyeuctus is such a brave man that, while prosecuting an impeachment, he said that defendants should not make use of the impeachment law. [10] All other prosecutors, when they think that in their earlier speech they have to snatch the defendants' arguments out from under them,[15] order the jurors to refuse to listen to defendants if they speak outside the law, but to challenge their statements and order the reading of the law. But you[16] do the opposite: you think you should snatch away from Euxenippus' defense his refuge in the laws. [11] And, in addition, you assert that no one should come to his aid or serve as his advocate;[17] you order the jurors to refuse to listen to those who mount the platform.[18] And yet what finer or more democratic institution is there in the city than this—and there are many other fine ones—that, when a private citizen is subjected to the danger of a trial and is unable to offer his own defense, any willing citizen can mount the platform and come to his aid, and can inform the jurors about the case in just terms? [12] Well, by Zeus, you yourself have never made use of such a thing! But when you were defending yourself on trial against Alexander of Oion,[19] you requested ten advocates from the tribe Aegeis, of whom I was one, selected by you; and from the other Athenians too you called men into court to assist you.

Why should I mention the other cases? How have you conducted this very trial? Did you not bring as many accusations as you wished? Did you not call Lycurgus as your fellow prosecutor, a man inferior to no one in the city at public speaking and considered moderate and reasonable by these men?[20] [13] So, then, you can call men to assist you when you are the defendant and put your fellow accusers on the platform when you are the prosecutor—you, who not only have the ability to speak on your own behalf but are even capable of causing problems for an entire city—but Euxenippus, as a private citizen and a rather elderly one at that, cannot receive assistance from his friends and relatives, or else they will be slandered by you?

[14] "By Zeus, yes, for his actions are terrible and merit death," as you say in your prosecution. Now look, men of the jury, and examine each of the facts one by one. The Assembly assigned Euxenippus, as one of three, to incubate in the temple.[21] He went to sleep and says he had a dream, which he reported to the Assembly. If you[22] assumed that was true, and that he reported to the Assembly exactly what he saw in his sleep, then what is his offense in reporting to the Athenians what the god ordered him? [15] If, on the other hand, as you say now, you believed he had misrepresented the god and had made a false report to the Assembly to curry favor with certain people, you should not have drafted a decree in response to the dream; rather, as the man who spoke before me said,[23] you should have sent to Delphi to ascertain the truth from the god.[24] But that is not what you did; you composed an independent decree against two tribes[25] that not only was extremely unjust but

also contradicted itself. That is why you were convicted of proposing an illegal decree, not because of Euxenippus.

[16] Let us examine it in the following manner. The tribes, in groups of two, divided up the mountains in Oropus[26] by grant of the Assembly. The mountain in question fell by lot to Acamantis and Hippothoöntis. You proposed that these tribes give the mountain back to Amphiaraus, along with the value of what they had sold,[27] on the ground that the Boundary Commissioners, the Fifty, had previously reserved the mountain for the god and marked it off, and the two tribes were in possession of something that did not belong to them. [17] A little below in the same decree you propose that the other eight tribes provide the difference and pay it to the two tribes, so that they do not come up short. Now, if you were taking away from the two tribes the mountain which belonged to them, how do you not deserve an angry response? If, on the other hand, they held the mountain when it belonged not to them but to the god, why did you propose that the other tribes pay them money in addition? They would have been happy to give back what belonged to the god and not pay a monetary fine besides.

[18] Upon examination in the jury-court, these measures were found to be incorrectly drafted, and the jurors convicted you.[28] So, then, if you had been acquitted, this man would not have misrepresented the god; but since it happened that you got convicted, Euxenippus must be destroyed? And you, who drafted a decree of this sort, were fined twenty-five drachmas, but the man who incubated in the temple on the people's order must not even be buried in Attica?[29]

[19] "Yes; for it was a terrible thing he did in the matter of the bowl, allowing Olympias to dedicate it at the statue of Hygieia."[30] You assume that, by bringing in her name as your provision for this trial and by falsely accusing Euxenippus of flattery, you will arouse the jurors' hatred and anger against him. What you ought to be doing, my good man, is not seeking to cause harm to a fellow citizen by invoking the names of Olympias and Alexander. [20] Instead, when they write letters to the Athenian people that are neither just nor proper, that is when you should stand up and respond on the city's behalf, plead your case against their ambassadors, and travel to the common council of the Greeks[31] in order

to come to the aid of your country. But there you have never stood up or said a word about them; here, however, you hate Olympias in order to destroy Euxenippus, and you call him a toady of her and the Macedonians.

[21] Now, if you can prove that he has ever been to Macedonia, or welcomed any of those people into his home, or dealt with, or even run into, anyone from there, or had any sort of conversation whatsoever concerning these matters at a shop or in the agora[32] or anywhere else, and did not mind his own business with decency and moderation like any other citizen, then let the jurors do with him whatever they please. [22] For if these accusations of yours were true, you would not be the only one to know; everyone else in the city would know, just as they know about all the others who speak or act on the Macedonians' behalf. Not only the individuals involved, but the rest of the Athenians too, and even the children coming home from school, know which politicians serve the Macedonians for pay, and which others host those arriving from Macedonia and welcome them and meet them on the road when they come to town. And nowhere will you see Euxenippus counted alongside any one of these people. [23] But you do not prosecute or put on trial any of those whom everyone knows to be doing these things; no, you accuse Euxenippus of flattery, a man whose life does not admit the charge. And yet, if you had any sense in regard to this bowl that has been dedicated,[33] you would not have accused Euxenippus nor said another word about it here: it doesn't fit. Why not? Please listen, men of the jury, to the account that I am about to give you.

[24] Olympias has lodged complaints concerning events at Dodona[34] that are not just. Accordingly, twice already in the Assembly, before you and the rest of the Athenians and in response to her ambassadors, I have exposed her for making improper complaints against the city. Zeus of Dodona commanded you in his oracular response to adorn the statue of Dione.[35] [25] You made her face as beautiful as possible, along with all its accoutrements; you prepared a lot of valuable decoration for the goddess;[36] and you sent a delegation and a sacrifice at great expense and adorned the statue of Dione in a manner worthy of both yourselves and the goddess. This was the subject of the complaints against you that came from Olympias in her letters; she said that the region of Molossia, where the sanctuary is, belonged to her,[37] and therefore we had no business

altering a single thing there. [26] Well, then, if you vote that the affair with the bowl amounted to an offense, in a way we condemn ourselves for acting incorrectly there; if, however, we put it in the past and let it be, we will have deprived her of her tragic accusations. For it is certainly not the case that Olympias can adorn Athenian sanctuaries while we cannot do the same at Dodona, and at the god's command at that.

[27] It seems to me, though, Polyeuctus, that there is nothing from which you could not create a prosecution. Yet, since you have chosen to be active in politics, and, by Zeus, you have the ability, you should not be prosecuting private citizens and indulging your youthful bravado at their expense. Rather, if one of the politicians does wrong, you should prosecute him, and if a general acts unjustly, you should impeach him. These are the people who have the power to harm the city—those of them who so choose—not Euxenippus or any one of these jurors.

[28] And it is not that I think you should act in this manner while I myself have conducted my political life some other way. Never in my life have I prosecuted a private citizen, though I have in the past assisted some to the best of my ability.[38] Whom, then, have I prosecuted and put on trial? Aristophon of Azenia, who has become a very powerful man in the state; he was acquitted by a margin of two votes in this court.[39] Diopeithes of Sphettus, who was considered the most formidable man in the city.[40] Philocrates of Hagnous, who conducted his political life with the highest degree of audacity and insolence.[41] I impeached him for his services to Philip to the detriment of the city and convicted him in court; and I drafted the impeachment in just form and as the law commands: "as a politician, he proposed what was not best for the Athenian people, taking money and gifts from the opponents of the people." [30] And I was not content to render the impeachment in that form, but I added below: "These things he proposed which were not best for the people, having taken money"—then I wrote his decree underneath. And again, "These things he proposed which were not best for the people, having taken money," and I appended the decree. I wrote this five or six times, because I thought I had to make the trial and the prosecution just.

But, as for the measures you claim Euxenippus proposed that were not best for the people, you had nothing to write in your impeachment;

you are prosecuting a private citizen as though he were a politician. [31] And, after making a brief statement about the rejoinder,[42] you have come bringing other slanderous accusations against him, saying that he tried to marry his daughter to Philocles and undertook Demotion's arbitration,[43] and making other accusations of that sort. Your purpose was that, if the defense should ignore the impeachment and respond to your irrelevant accusations, the jurors would confront them and ask, "Why are you telling us this?"; on the other hand, if they took no account of these accusations, the trial would go worse for them, since that part of the accusations that gets no response is left to the anger of the jurors.[44]

[32] And the most terrible of all the things you have said in your speech—and you thought your motive for saying it would remain undetected, though it did not—is your repeated casual comment that Euxenippus is rich, and again later, that he has accumulated great wealth by wrongful means. It obviously has nothing to do with this trial whether he has acquired many assets or few; but the speaker's malice and his assumption about the jurors are unjust—namely, that they would deliver a verdict on any ground other than the issue itself, and whether the man on trial is doing you wrong or not.

[33] You seem to me, Polyeuctus—you and those who think like you—to have poor knowledge of the fact that there is no people, no monarch, no nation in the world more magnanimous than the people of Athens: when their fellow citizens are victimized by sycophants,[45] either individually or in groups, they do not desert them but come to their aid. [34] First, when Teisis of Agryle registered as public property the property of Euthycrates, which was worth more than sixty talents,[46] and promised after that to register the property of Philippus and Nausicles, alleging that they had become rich from unregistered mines,[47] so far were these people[48] from accepting any such statement or coveting the possessions of others that they straightaway disenfranchised the one who had attempted the malicious accusation of these men by not giving him a fifth of their votes.[49]

[35] And, if you like, there is what the jurors did just recently, last month—how does that not deserve great praise? Lysander had denounced

the mine of Epicrates of Pallene as having been sunk inside the bound-aries[50]—a mine that was already in operation for three years, and in which practically the richest men in the city held shares. Lysander was promising to confiscate 300 talents for the city: that, he said, was the amount of their profit from the mine. [36] Nonetheless the jurors, look-ing not to the prosecutor's promises but to justice, found that the mine was Epicrates'; with one and the same vote they made the shareholders' estates secure and ensured the future operation of the mine. And in consequence the sinking of new mines, previously abandoned out of fear, is now active, and the city's revenues from those sources are again increasing, revenues that certain politicians spoiled by deceiving the people and collecting tribute from the contractors.

[37] The good citizen, men of the jury, is not the one who makes a small contribution while doing great harm to the commonwealth, nor the one who provides immediate funding from an unjust source and thereby eliminates the city's income from a just source, but rather the one who is concerned with what is beneficial to the city's future, with the concord of the citizens, and with your reputation. Some people pay no heed to these things; they take away revenues from the contractors and claim they are providing them, when in fact they are producing poverty in the city. For when it is a frightful prospect to acquire and save, who will want to take the risk?

[38] Well, maybe it is not easy to prevent these people from doing this. But you, men of the jury, just as you have rescued many other citizens unjustly put on trial, so too help Euxenippus and do not overlook him for a worthless case and an impeachment of this sort—not only is he not covered by it, but the impeachment itself has been brought in con-travention of the laws, and, in addition, it has been rendered void in a way by the prosecutor himself. [39] You see, Polyeuctus has impeached Euxenippus for "proposing what was not best for the Athenian people, taking money and gifts from the opponents of the Athenian people." Now, if he were alleging that there were people from outside the city from whom Euxenippus had taken these bribes to collaborate with them, then he would be able to say that, since those individuals cannot be punished, their servants here must pay the penalty. As it is, however, he says that the people from whom Euxenippus received the gifts were

Athenians. So then, with the opponents of the people in the city, you do not punish them but instead cause problems for Euxenippus?

[40] After saying a little more about the vote you are about to cast, I will step down. When you are about to vote, men of the jury, order the clerk to read out to you the impeachment, the impeachment law, and the heliastic oath.[51] Take away all of our speeches, and, judging from the impeachment and the laws, cast whatever vote you decide is just and true to your oath.

[41] Well, Euxenippus, I have given you all the help I could. What remains is to ask the jury to call your friends and put your children on the platform.[52]

# 16

# HYPEREIDES 5

*Against Demosthenes*

## Introduction

Hypereides delivered this speech at Demosthenes' trial stemming from the Harpalus affair (Part Three, Athens under Alexander, pp. 191–192). Demosthenes stood accused of receiving twenty talents of gold from Harpalus (col. 2, 10). The papyrus containing the sole surviving copy of this oration is extremely fragmentary. Significant parts of the text survive, but it is riddled throughout by lacunae (holes), both small and large. Accordingly, Hypereides 5 is not divided into standard sections as are the other speeches in this collection; instead it is cited by the papyrus column numbers.

Fragment 1 (cols. 1–2), containing the very beginning of the speech, comes from the introduction, in which Hypereides addresses the jury and mentions a decree moved by Demosthenes assigning the investigation of the Harpalus affair to the Council of the Areopagus. In fragments 2 through 8 Hypereides combines narration with proofs in attacking Demosthenes. The Council of the Areopagus has conducted its investigation properly but is maligned by Demosthenes (cols. 3–7). Next comes the narration of Harpalus' arrival in Attica and Demosthenes' response, including the arrest of Harpalus and the inventory of his funds (cols. 8–12). Demosthenes took a bribe from Harpalus but claims that he lent the money to the theoric fund (cols. 12–13). Bribery threatens the security of cities (cols. 14–15). Demosthenes has a history of Macedonian partisanship; the arrest of Harpalus harmed Athenian interests (cols. 16–19).

Hypereides next attacks Demosthenes' friends (col. 20) and anticipates an appeal from Demosthenes based on their mutual friendship (col. 21). Older politicians should keep their juniors in line, not vice versa (col. 22). Politicians and generals who take bribes commit a more serious offense than private citizens who embezzle do (cols. 24–26). In the aftermath of Chaeroneia, the Athenians consulted their political leaders rather than punishing them, appointing Lycurgus to head the treasury (cols. 28–29). The politicians should therefore be grateful to the people; Demosthenes, however, has acted against their interests and served Macedon (cols. 30–32). The defendants have convicted themselves; the jury must punish them or else accept complicity in their guilt (cols. 34–35).

The conclusion to the speech probably begins in column 38. The Assembly, the Council of the Areopagus, and the special prosecutors have all done their jobs; now the jury must do theirs (col. 38). In order to avoid ill repute and vindicate their city, they must convict the defendants, paying no heed to their tears (cols. 39–40). The papyrus breaks off shortly before the end of the speech.

On the conviction and sentencing of Demosthenes, and the subsequent deaths of Demosthenes and Hypereides, see Part Three, Athens under Alexander, pp. 191–192.

### Against Demosthenes

### Fragment 1

[col. 1] Well, for my part, men of the jury, as I was just saying to the people sitting next to me, I am amazed at this state of affairs:[1] if indeed, by Zeus, Demosthenes is the only person in the city not subject to the laws that order that whatever agreements someone makes to his own detriment are binding, or to the decrees of the Assembly, in accordance with which you have sworn to cast your votes, and which were composed not by any of Demosthenes' enemies but by the man himself: at his urging the Assembly decreed…not willingly causing his own destruction…

And yet, [col. 2] men of the jury, I assume that justice is clearly with us and against Demosthenes. For, just as in private cases many matters are decided through challenges,[2] so too this matter has been decided. Consider it like this, men of the jury. The Assembly accused you, Demosthenes, of having taken twenty talents[3] against the constitution and the laws. You denied taking it, and you wrote up a challenge in a decree and brought it before the Assembly, entrusting the matter of the accusation against you to the Council of the Areopagus[4]...

*Fragment 2*

[col. 3]...and you maliciously accuse the Council, issuing challenges and asking in these challenges where you got the gold from, and who gave it to you, and where. Maybe you will conclude by asking what you used the gold for after you got it, as though you were demanding a bank statement from the Council! I, on the contrary, [col. 4] would be happy to learn from you why the Council of the Areopagus...unjustly...

*Fragment 3*

[col. 5]...justly...the reports. This is not so; rather, it will be clear that they have handled the affair in the most democratic manner of all. They reported the offenders, and not willingly at that, but under repeated compulsion by the Assembly. And they did not give themselves the power to punish the offenders, but assigned that authority to you. Demosthenes, however, not only thinks that in regard to his [col. 6] own trial he must lead you astray by slandering the report; he is also seeking to obstruct all the city's other cases.[5] You must now take this under consideration, paying careful attention, and you must not be deceived by the defendant's argument. The Council drafted all these reports concerning Harpalus' money in similar form, and drafted the same reports against all the accused. It did not add to any report why it was reporting each man; it merely summed up in writing how much gold each one took, and stated that he should therefore owe so much. Or is Demosthenes going to have more influence among you [col. 7] than the report against him? Not...report...he took...all the rest too: for certainly this is not going to apply only to Demosthenes but not to the others.

In point of fact, your verdict deals not with twenty talents but with 300, and not with one crime but with all of them. For your insanity, Demosthenes, now takes the lead on behalf of all the offenders in regard to both danger and shamelessness. As far as I am concerned, your conviction by the Council to whom you entrusted yourself is sufficient proof to the jury that you took the gold. [col. 8] But as to why you took it, and for what reasons, the whole city…as if…I shall make clear.

When Harpalus came to Attica, men of the jury, and at the same time the men sent by Philoxenus[6] demanding his surrender were brought before the Assembly, at that time Demosthenes stepped up and went through a long speech in which he stated that it was not good for the city to surrender Harpalus to Philoxenus' ambassadors, nor should Alexander be left with any grounds for accusation against the people on Harpalus' account, [col. 9] but the safest course for the city was to safeguard the money and the man, and to deposit on the Acropolis the next day all the money with which Harpalus had arrived in Attica. Harpalus, he said, should immediately disclose the amount of the money—not, it seems, so that Demosthenes might ascertain the amount itself, but so that he would know from how large a sum he should exact his payment. And, sitting down there under the incision where he usually sits,[7] he ordered Mnesitheus the dancer to ask Harpalus the total amount of the money to be deposited on the Acropolis. And Harpalus answered, 700 [col. 10] talents…

…he himself having stated before you in the Assembly that that was the sum total of the money, when 350 talents were deposited instead of 700, he gave no account of the twenty talents he had taken…after stating in the Assembly that there were 700 talents, now you deposit half that amount, and… [col. 11] that…had been deposited…on the Acropolis…these affairs…they were judging the…Harpalus would not have bought the…and the city would not be the object of slanderous accusations. But of all these things, Demosthenes,…is…gold…for…that… [col. 12] he took…staters.[8] But you, who established by decree the guard over his[9] body, and then neither corrected its deficiencies nor prosecuted the responsible parties when it was disbanded, obviously managed this crisis for free? And Harpalus paid gold to the lesser politicians, masters only of clamor and shouting, but you, who preside over all affairs of state, he passed over? Who is going to believe that?

Such is the extent, men of the jury, of Demosthenes' scorn for this affair—or rather, if I am to speak freely, for you and the laws—that at first, it seems, [col. 13] he admitted having received the money, but said that he used it all up on you, advancing a loan to the theoric fund.[10]

And Cnosion and the rest of his friends went around saying that his accusers would force the man to put out in the open what he did not want to, and to say that he had lent the money in advance to the people for the financial administration of the state. Since those of you who heard this were much angrier at the statements made against you the people—as if it were not enough for him to take bribes for personal gain, but he also thought he had to infect the people...

[col. 14]...stating and alleging that the Council[11] wanted to destroy him[12] as a favor to Alexander, as if you were not all aware that no one destroys a man who can be bought; rather, it is the man who can be neither persuaded nor corrupted by money whom people seek by all means to remove. There is, it seems, a danger that you, Demosthenes, cannot be entreated or persuaded to take bribes, or [col. 15] that someone may think that only everyday affairs are ruined by the defendants' venal conduct. For it is no secret that all those who plot against Greek affairs gain control of the small cities by force of arms and the large ones by buying their powerful citizens; nor that Philip became as powerful as he did by sending money from the beginning to the Peloponnese and Thessaly and the rest of Greece, and...those in positions of power and leadership in the cities...

*Fragment 4*

[col. 16]...you trade in maritime funds[13] and issue loans; and, having purchased a house...you do not live in the Peiraeus but lie offshore outside the city. A true leader of the people, however, should be the savior of his country...you tell amazing stories [col. 17] and think it is not obvious to all that, while you claimed to speak on behalf of the people, you were clearly making speeches for Alexander? I think that everyone realized even beforehand that this was what you were doing in regard to the Thebans and all the rest, and that you appropriated for your own personal use money donated from Asia for these purposes,[14] and spent most of it...

...So suddenly did Harpalus [col. 18] fall upon Greece that no one saw him coming. And he found the affairs of the Peloponnese and the rest of Greece in this condition due to the advent of Nicanor and the instructions he came bearing from Alexander regarding the exiles[15] and the...of the general assemblies of the Achaeans, Arcadians, and Boeotians...

[col. 19] This is what you have caused by your decree, by arresting Harpalus. And you have made all the other Greeks send envoys to Alexander, since they have nowhere else to turn; and as for the satraps,[16] who would have come willingly in person to join this force with all the money and soldiers each of them had, not only have you prevented all of them from revolting against Alexander by arresting Harpalus, but also...each of them...

## Fragment 5

[col. 20]...dispatched by Demosthenes, and with Olympias Callias of Chalcis, the brother of Taurosthenes;[17] for Demosthenes wrote the decree making these men Athenian citizens, and he associates with them most of all. And no wonder: since, as I see it, he never stays in the same place, it makes sense that he has acquired friends from the Euripus.[18]

So then, are you going to have the gall to talk to me presently about friendship?... [col. 21] You are the one who dissolved our friendship, when you took gold against the interests of your country and switched sides. You made yourself the object of ridicule, and you brought shame to those who in the past pursued any of the same policies as you.[19] We could have been the most illustrious men among the people and spent the rest of our lives accompanied by good reputations, but you upset it all, and you feel no shame now, a man of your age, being prosecuted by boys[20] for accepting bribes. And yet the opposite should be the case: the younger politicians should receive their education from you, and if they do something overly rash, [col. 22] they should be censured and punished. But in reality the converse holds true: the young are bringing those over sixty to their senses. This is why, men of the jury, you would be justified in being angry at Demosthenes: he has acquired both a considerable reputation and significant wealth thanks to you, but now, on the threshold of old age,[21] he shows no concern for his country. Now, you used to be ashamed at the...before those Greeks who were present, when you convicted certain people, if...such leaders of the people and generals and guardians of affairs...

[Col. 23 contains only small fragments of words.]

*Fragment 6*

[col. 24] For it is not as terrible for someone to take money as it is to take it from where he should not; and the private citizens who took the gold are not guilty of the same offense as the politicians and generals. Why not? Because Harpalus gave the gold to the private citizens to safeguard, while the generals and politicians took it to influence policy. Now, the laws command that ordinary offenders pay back a simple fine,[22] but those who take bribes pay tenfold. So, just as the fine can be levied according to the law upon these…, so too…from you…against them….

For, just as I said in the Assembly, men of the jury, you willingly allow the generals and the [col. 25] politicians to make significant profits: it is not the laws that have granted them the power to do this, but your gentle nature and generosity. The one thing you watch out for is that their gain must occur on your account, not at your expense. By my reckoning, Demosthenes and Demades[23] have received more than sixty talents each from their actual decrees and proxeny grants[24] in the city, apart from the money from the Great King[25] and from Alexander. As neither this income nor that suffices for them, but now they have taken bribes on the security of the very body of the city,[26] how is it not fitting to punish them? If one of you private citizens, [col. 26] in the conduct of some office, makes a mistake out of ignorance or inexperience, he will be overpowered in court by the defendants' rhetoric and either executed or exiled from his country; will the defendants themselves, having committed such terrible crimes against the city, receive no punishment? Because Conon of Paeania took the theoric allotment for his son who was abroad, for the sake of five drachmas, and despite throwing himself on your mercy, he was fined a talent in court with these men as his prosecutors.[27] And because Aristomachus, after becoming president of the Academy,[28] moved a spade from the wrestling-ground to his own garden, which was nearby, used it, and…

[Col. 27 contains only small fragments of words.]

*Fragment 7*

[col. 28]…[29] in the time that followed, the Assembly did not allow us to come before it or engage in discussion; on the contrary, it even used us as advisors and advocates...and the next...it elected him steward of its entire financial administration,[30] assuming that we owed him gratitude, which was in fact right. And, in addition, when we were later put on trial many times as a result of those affairs and [col. 29] of the war itself, these men[31] never convicted us but saved us from everything; and that is the greatest and most trustworthy sign of the people's goodwill. And to propose, Demosthenes,...that you were convicted of your own accord by the decree,[32] they did not make...

[col. 30]...the people, although deprived by Fortune of its own crown, acted so as not to deprive us of the crown it had bestowed. So, since this is how the people treated us, should we not serve it by all just means and, if necessary, die for it? I think we should. But you...against the people...services. For they...not to benefit other people's country, but their own; nor... [col. 31]...and you have continually displayed...and your speaking ability. And when you believed that the Council was going to report those in possession of the gold,[33] you became hostile and stirred up the city in order to knock the search off course; but when the Council postponed its report, stating that the investigation was not yet complete, at that point in the Assembly you consented that Alexander should be the son of Zeus, and of Poseidon too, if he wished,[34] and...

[col. 32]...he wanted...to set up a statue of king Alexander, the invincible god...of Olympia...he reported to the people...

*Fragment 8*

[Col. 33 contains only small fragments of words.]

[col. 34] of the charges, and made a proclamation concerning them. But, instead of giving back what they had taken and being rid of the affair, they proposed penalties and investigations against themselves! When those who from the beginning committed crimes and took bribes are granted immunity but do not pay back the gold, what are we supposed to do? Let them go unpunished? It is disgraceful, men of the jury, to put the safety of the city at risk because of charges leveled against individuals. You cannot acquit the defendants unless you are willing also to accept responsibility for their crimes....

[col. 35]...Men of the jury, do not place these men's greed above your own safety; and do not make war for the sake of dishonorable profits, but for more worthy reasons [col. 36] and a change for the better...

*Fragment 9*

[col. 37]...on their behalf...we made the peace...

[col. 38]...accrue to it[35] from each of us; and it ordered us, the elected prosecutors, to prosecute and expose in court those who had received the money and taken bribes against the interests of their country. It assigned the Council of the Areopagus to report the recipients, and the Council disclosed their identity to the Assembly; the punishment of the offenders it assigned to you...

[col. 39] of the Areopagus. Now, if your vote does not follow law and justice, this, men of the jury, is what you will be left with. That is why all of you must...the safety of the city and the rest of the prosperity you enjoy in this land, both all of you together and each of you individually, and looking upon the tombs of your ancestors, punish the offenders on behalf of the entire city, and...neither imploring speeches nor...those who have taken [col. 40] bribes against the interests of their country and the laws. Pay no attention to the tears of Hagnonides;[36] take into account the fact that for a person who has suffered misfortune...

...but he would have no right to cry, just like pirates who cry on the wheel[37] when they could have avoided boarding ship. So too for Demosthenes: what proper reason will he have to cry, when he could have avoided taking...

*Unplaced Fragments*[38]

...not up to the allotted time...

But you call the younger men to assist you, whom you used to treat with hubris[39] and revile, calling them lushes?[40]

If somebody drank his wine a little too strong, it used to bother you...

...cowardly...

# Notes

## General Introduction

1. [Demosthenes] is read "pseudo-Demosthenes."
2. See, e.g., Aristophanes, *Clouds* (produced in 423) and *Wasps* (produced in 422).
3. For the text of the heliastic oath see Demosthenes 24 *Against Timocrates* 149–151; A. R. W. Harrison, *The Law of Athens*[2] (Indianapolis and London 1998) 2.48.
4. In classical Athens the word did not have the connotation of "flatterer, toady" that it does today.

## Part One: The Thirty Tyrants

1. General Introduction, p. 7.
2. Disarming the populace was a standard tactic employed by Greek tyrants to ensure the stability of their rule. Peisistratus had done so—temporarily—upon seizing power at Athens for the third (and final) time in 546/5 (*Ath. Pol.* 15.3–5).
3. This board of Ten, which succeeded the Thirty, is not to be confused with the Ten who governed the Peiraeus (above, p. 16).

## 1. Lysias 12

1. Throughout his speech Lysias refers repeatedly to "the defendants," as though all of the Thirty were on trial.
2. Two of the Thirty Tyrants.
3. General Introduction, p. 7.
4. That is, with the new oligarchic constitution enacted by the Thirty (Part One, The Thirty Tyrants, pp. 15–17).
5. General Introduction, p. 10.
6. The Cyzicene stater, a coin from Cyzicus in Asia Minor, was struck from electrum (an alloy of gold and silver) and worth something more than the daric. The daric was a gold coin struck by the Persian king Darius I; the standard exchange rate at Athens was about twenty drachmas to the daric.
7. Two more of the Thirty.
8. An otherwise unknown individual.
9. Probably one in the front and one in the back; these are not identical with the three doors Lysias has to pass through to escape (§16).
10. That is, into the city of Athens. The previous action of the speech has taken place in the Peiraeus.
11. Possibly located off the southwest corner of the agora.
12. As wealthy residents (although not citizens) of Athens, Lysias and his family were liable to perform liturgies, such as the maintenance of a chorus at dramatic festivals. The war-tax (*eisphora*) was a property tax levied several times during the Peloponnesian War in order to provide revenues for a flagging state treasury (General Introduction, pp. 8–9).
13. Athenian brides were dowered by their male relatives. By seizing their victims' assets, the Thirty prevented the payment of dowries and thus obstructed a number of weddings.
14. i.e., the Thirty.
15. Lysias is referring to the battle of Arginusae (406). The Athenians defeated the Spartans, then opted to pursue the fleeing Spartan navy before recovering their own dead and shipwrecked sailors. A storm sprang up, preventing the retrieval and resulting in the drowning of the shipwrecked men and the loss of all the bodies. The six Arginusae generals (out of eight in command) who returned to Athens were tried and executed (Xenophon, *Hellenica* 1.6.25–1.7.35).
16. The battle of Aegospotami (405), a terrible and humiliating loss for the Athenians (actually fought on land), which all but ensured Athens' imminent defeat in the Peloponnesian War (Xenophon, *Hellenica* 2.1.18–32).
17. The Thirty did put at least some of their victims on trial before the Council of 500, which served as their kangaroo court (see Lysias 13.36–38).
18. The trierarchy was a liturgy in which a wealthy Athenian (the trierarch) funded (and sometimes captained) a trireme in the Athenian navy (General Introduction, p. 9).

19. The Thirty confiscated the weapons of the majority of Athenians (Part One, The Thirty Tyrants, p. 18).

20. In 411, a group of oligarchs called the Four Hundred seized control of Athens for four months. On the rule of the Four Hundred and the Intermediate Regime which followed, see Thucydides book 8; *Ath. Pol.* 29–32.

21. Athenian forces were encamped on Samos at the time.

22. At this point witnesses came forward to make oral statements; these are generally not preserved in our manuscripts.

23. Aegospotami (above, §36 with note).

24. The title "ephors" (*ephoroi*, literally "overseers") was borrowed from Sparta, which elected annually five magistrates called ephors. The *hetairoi* ("comrades") were members of the oligarchic political clubs (*hetaireiai*).

25. A law ascribed to Solon outlawed tyranny, prescribing either death or loss of citizen rights upon conviction: *Ath. Pol.* 16.10; Andocides 1 *On the Mysteries* 97.

26. The Council of 500 (General Introduction, p. 8).

27. "Impeachment" translates the Greek *eisangelia*. In Athens this was a technical term for a type of lawsuit, originally for offenses amounting to treason (Part Three, Athens under Alexander, pp. 189–90). The Thirty used this procedure against many of their targets.

28. Two men who served as informers under the Thirty. Batrachus (whose name means "Frog") was sufficiently infamous to be mentioned elsewhere ([Lysias] 6 *Against Andocides* 45). Aeschylides is otherwise unattested.

29. Part One, The Thirty Tyrants, p. 19.

30. Cf. Lysias 13.44; Part One, The Thirty Tyrants, p. 19.

31. Lysias thus glosses over the battle of Munychia (Part One, The Thirty Tyrants, p. 19). "The troubles" (*hai tarachai*) is an impressively neutral way to describe these events; Lysias does his best to avoid alienating the former oligarchs on his jury (cf. below, §§92–94).

32. Here the two sides are the democrats (= the "men of the Peiraeus") and the oligarchs (= the "men of the city"); in the previous paragraph they are the moderate oligarchs under Theramenes (in which group Eratosthenes is claiming membership) and the extreme oligarchs under Critias.

33. These are the Ten who succeeded the Thirty (Part One, The Thirty Tyrants, pp. 19–20).

34. The Spartans were famed for their piety and adherence to religious observance. For example, military assistance requested by Athens before the battle of Marathon (490) was delayed until the end of the festival of Apollo Karneios (Herodotus 6.106–107; cf. 7.206).

35. Themistocles masterminded the plan to rebuild Athens' city walls following the defeat of the Persians in 479, and he also oversaw the fortification of the Peiraeus: see Thucydides 1.90–93.

36. Above, §42.

37. Theramenes' father was Hagnon (Xenophon, *Hellenica* 2.3.30). The Commissioners (*probouloi*) were a board of ten established in 413 to take over some of the functions of the Council of 500; in 411

they were incorporated into the Four Hundred (Thucydides 8.1; *Ath. Pol.* 29.2).

38. Peisander played a leading role in establishing the regime of the Four Hundred. Tergiversations such as the one described here earned Theramenes the nickname "the Buskin" (*ho kothornos*: Xenophon, *Hellenica* 2.3.47): a buskin was a shoe worn by actors that fit either foot.

39. Thucydides (8.68) describes Antiphon as the mind behind the Revolution of 411. A few fragments of Antiphon's defense survive (see M. Gagarin and D. M. MacDowell, *Antiphon and Andocides* [Austin 1998] 90–92); Thucydides praises the speech as the finest defense he had ever heard in a death-penalty case. Archeptolemus served with Antiphon as an envoy to Sparta under the Four Hundred ([Plutarch], *Lives of the Ten Orators* 832f–834a).

40. The Spartans.

41. Philochares and Miltiades are unknown; presumably they were either officers under Lysander or prominent Athenian oligarchs.

42. Above, §43.

43. The Council of 500. With this version of Theramenes' defense contrast Xenophon, *Hellenica* 2.3.35–56.

44. Lysias may have had in mind the phrase "the ancestral constitution" (*hê patrios politeia*: see *Ath. Pol.* 34.3).

45. Under the Thirty; see above, §36 with note.

46. *Ta chrêmata ta phanera*, "visible property," is probably a variant on *phanera ousia*, a flexible term that designates buildings and land, and sometimes farm animals, slaves, and furniture. Otherwise it may mean "all their property that can be found," as opposed to that which the Thirty have hidden or taken to Eleusis (Part One, The Thirty Tyrants, pp. 19–20).

47. In this section Lysias refers generally to the supporters of Eratosthenes; in §86 he specifically addresses Eratosthenes' advocates (*synêgoroi*: General Introduction, p. 5), and in §87 Eratosthenes' witnesses.

48. Cf. the description of Polemarchus' funeral, §18.

49. Cf. Lysias' description of the trial of the generals and taxiarchs (13.36–38).

50. Athenian juries voted by secret ballot. See Lysias 13.37 with note.

51. By drinking hemlock (cf. §17).

52. Sparta had barred her allies from harboring Athenian refugees, but some refused to obey: see Part One, The Thirty Tyrants, pp. 18–19.

53. General Introduction, pp. 12–13.

54. That is, they would default on small loans, and, with no family to bail them out, would be enslaved by their creditors.

55. Cf. Lysias 13.93.

## 2. Lysias 13

1. Dionysodorus was the speaker's sister's husband (§40).

2. The speaker has no particular god in mind. Cf. Demosthenes 4.7.

3. At the battle of Aegospotami (cf. Lysias 12.36, 16.4).

4. Taxiarchs were tribal hoplite commanders.

5. Cleophon, called "the lyremaker" by his enemies (*Ath. Pol.* 28.3; Ando-cides 1 *On the Mysteries* 146; Aeschines 2 *On the False Embassy* 76), was the leading demagogue in Athens at the end of the Peloponnesian War.

6. The Long Walls were two parallel walls connecting Athens with the Peiraeus. 1 stade = approximately 1/9–1/8 mile; thus 10 stades = $1\frac{1}{4}$ miles, or a little less.

7. Cf. the portrayal of Theramenes in Lysias 12, especially §§62–78.

8. Candidacy examinations (*dokimasiai*) were required of all incoming Athenian officials, including generals (as here) and members of the Council of 500 (see Lysias 16 with introduction). Those who failed were prevented from taking office.

9. In other words, Cleophon was charged with deserting his post (probably by a *graphê lipotaxiou*). Conviction on this charge normally resulted in the loss of citizen rights (*atimia*); perhaps during the Peloponnesian War the penalty was increased to death.

10. According to Lysias 30 *Against Nicomachus* 11, the members of the Council of 500 were added to Cleophon's jury.

11. Strombichides, who was one of the generals, is also named as a prominent friend of democracy in Lysias 30 *Against Nicomachus* 14.

12. This is the second meeting of the Assembly to debate peace; the first (§8) had occurred several months earlier.

13. Allegations of foreign and/or servile status are a standard tactic of character assassination in Athenian speeches (see General Introduction, p. 7). In the famous Crown case of 330, Aeschines called Demosthenes' mother a Scythian (3 *Against Ctesiphon* 172); Demosthenes retaliated by calling Aeschines' father a slave and his mother a hobgoblin (18 *On the Crown* 129–130).

14. Elaphostictus means "marked (tattooed or branded) with a stag." Presumably he was a slave (or freedman) who bore such a distinguishing mark. By providing this patronymic, Lysias emphasizes Theocritus' lowly origins.

15. The agora (central marketplace) of the Peiraeus, not that of Athens.

16. These two are otherwise unknown.

17. A hill in the Peiraeus, site of a temple of the goddess Artemis where Agoratus and the others sought sanctuary.

18. A decree passed in the archonship of Scamandrius (the year is unknown) prohibited the torture of Athenian citizens: see Andocides 1 *On the Mysteries* 43.

19. Because (according to the speaker) Agoratus is not an Athenian citizen.

20. On the importance of the phrase "in the act" see the Introduction and below, §§85–87.

21. The Theater of Dionysus on Munychia: cf. Thucydides 8.93.

22. See Part One, The Thirty Tyrants, pp. 15–16.

23. The Council of 500 consisted of 10 tribal contingents of 50 councillors. Each tribe's councillors served as the Executive Committee (*prytaneis*) of the Council for one-tenth of the year; the Executive Committee presumably occupied the front rows of seats in the Council House (*bouleutêrion*).

24. Normally Athenian courts used a secret ballot, with the votes being cast into urns. Cf. Lysias 12.91.
25. For the fates of the men of Salamis and Eleusis cf. Lysias 12.52; Part One, The Thirty Tyrants, p. 19.
26. The implication is that these girls had no one to provide their dowries; cf. Lysias 12.21.
27. Not all, actually, but those who were not on the list of 3,000: Part One, The Thirty Tyrants, p. 18; Xenophon, *Hellenica* 2.4.1.
28. Their places of origin (Curium is a city on the southern coast of Cyprus) signal that both men, like Agoratus (according to the speaker), did not have Athenian citizenship.
29. Amphitrope is Hagnodorus' (and Menestratus') deme.
30. See §32.
31. In the late fifth and fourth centuries, the two standard methods of capital punishment at Athens were (1) *apotympanismos*, in which the condemned was nailed to a board and left to die (as here; cf. Demosthenes 8.61, 9.61); and (2) poisoning by hemlock (as in the case of Polemarchus in Lysias 12, and, more famously, Socrates: Plato, *Phaedo* 117a–118a).
32. §§23ff. Cholleidae is Aristophanes' deme.
33. General Introduction, p. 9.
34. General Introduction, pp. 6–7.
35. To discourage sycophancy, any prosecutor in a public lawsuit (*graphê*) who failed to win 20% of the jurors' votes incurred a fine of 1,000 drachmas. On Athenian currency see General Introduction, p. 10.
36. Not necessarily. The homicide legislation of Draco decreed that certain individuals could lawfully kill a seducer caught in the act (Demosthenes 23 *Against Aristocrates* 53). However, Lysias 1 *On the Killing of Eratosthenes* is the only known case where this actually occurred. Numerous other remedies against the seducer existed, including summary arrest (*apagôgê*); a public lawsuit for seduction (*graphê moicheias*); extortion of ransom; and (most infamously) the insertion of a large radish into the anus, possibly combined with depilation of the genitalia by means of hot ash (Aristophanes, *Clouds* 1083–1084).
37. In 415 or 414, during the disastrous Sicilian expedition; Lamachus was one of the commanding generals.
38. See above, §56.
39. Clothes-stealing, together with certain other offenses including theft, seduction, and homicide, was subject to summary arrest (*apagôgê*: General Introduction, p. 5) if the offender was caught in the act. Such offenders were brought before the Eleven (the Athenian magistrates in charge of the prison); if they confessed, they were executed, but if they disputed the charge, they were tried in a jury-court (*Ath. Pol.* 52.1).
40. The Four Hundred ruled Athens briefly in 411 (Lysias 12.42 with note); Phrynichus was one of their ringleaders. With Lysias' version of the assassination of Phrynichus cf. Thucydides 8.92; Lycurgus 1 *Against Leocrates* 112.
41. According to Lysias 7 *On the Olive Tree* 4, Apollodorus received as a gift from the Athenian people a farm that had belonged to Peisander, another leader of the Four Hundred.

42. A preserved Athenian decree and rider of 410/09 (*IG* I³ 102 = Tod, no. 86 = Meiggs-Lewis, no. 85 = Fornara, no. 155) confers honors upon the assassins of Phrynichus. Its primary beneficiary is Thrasybulus of Calydon, who receives Athenian citizenship and other benefits. The decree then goes on to list additional "benefactors," including Agoratus, who receive the right to own real property in Attica (a right usually reserved to Athenian citizens), but not citizenship.
43. The deme in which Agoratus claimed membership.
44. On these events see Part One, The Thirty Tyrants, pp. 18–19.
45. One of the leaders of the exiled democrats. In 399 Anytus was one of Socrates' prosecutors (Plato, *Apology of Socrates* 18b3).
46. The taxiarch was the commander of his tribe's contingent of hoplites (above, §7). Presumably Agoratus tried to take his place among the men of the tribe Erechtheïs, to which the deme Anagyrous belonged.
47. The oligarchs ("men of the city") and democrats ("men of the Peiraeus"). Part One, The Thirty Tyrants, pp. 20–21.
48. Another leader of the democratic opposition.
49. The Greek idiom corresponding to "go to hell" in English.
50. The statute of limitations (*prothesmia*) for most offenses under Athenian law mandated prosecution within five years. This statement by the speaker probably indicates that Agoratus' prosecution occurred more than five years after the death of Dionysodorus; i.e., after 399 (Introduction, p. 41).
51. Greek *ep' autophôrôi*. This originally meant "in the act of theft," but its meaning was broadened to designate being caught in any act, including not just theft but also homicide, oath-breaking, and seduction. Compare the analogous English term "red-handed," which originally meant "with blood on one's hands" but now has a much broader use.
52. Greek *apagôgê*: this word designates both the process of summary arrest employed against Agoratus (Introduction, p. 42; General Introduction, p. 5) and the document authorizing the arrest.
53. That is, first before the Council of 500, then before the Assembly.
54. Part One, The Thirty Tyrants, pp. 20–21; Introduction, p. 42.
55. Abuse of parents was the subject of a public lawsuit (the *graphê*, or *eisangelia, kakôseôs goneôn*: Hypereides 4.6; *Ath. Pol.* 56.6; Isaeus 11 *On the Estate of Hagnias passim*). Lysias states that Agoratus has abused both his birth father (providing no evidence for the accusation) and his "adoptive father," the people of Athens (by depriving it of its staunch defenders).
56. Cf. the similar argument at Lysias 12.100.


# 3. Lysias 16

1. See General Introduction, p. 4.
2. The members of the Council of 500, before whom this speech was delivered (Introduction, p. 8).
3. The battle of Aegospotami (Lysias 12.36 with note; 13.5).
4. Satyrus I (r. 433/2–393/2) was a Thracian ruler friendly to Athens; his kingdom, Pontus, was located in the modern Crimea.

5. Part One, The Thirty Tyrants, p. 19.
6. Rolls of men called up for military service were posted on whitewashed wooden boards.
7. A phylarch commanded the cavalry of his tribe; a taxiarch (below, §16) commanded his tribe's infantry.
8. Cavalrymen received from the state an allotment of money to purchase equipment, which is catalogued in detail by Xenophon, *On Horsemanship* 12.1–12.
9. After the restoration of the democracy, commissioners (*syndikoi*) were appointed to oversee the repayment of funds to the state.
10. For Athenian currency see General Introduction, p. 10. An Athenian bride was expected to bring a dowry with her when she married (cf. Lysias 12.21, 13.45); the dowry was provided by her *kyrios* (guardian: the closest male relative, usually her father, or, as here, a brother). Thirty minae was a substantial dowry.
11. For the problems that dividing an estate could bring, cf. Isaeus 9 *On the Estate of Astyphilus* 17: there two brothers, Thudippus and Euthycrates, argue over the partition of their lands, and Thudippus mortally wounds Euthycrates.
12. In 395, at the beginning of the Corinthian War (395–387/6).
13. General Introduction, p. 10.
14. In spring or summer 394, during the second campaigning year of the Corinthian War (cf. §13).
15. Hoplite warfare was considerably more dangerous for those stationed in the front rows of the phalanx. To be stationed in the first rank was a mark of honor; cf. Tyrtaeus fr. 10 West, lines 1–2: "It is a fine thing for a good man to fall in the front ranks and die fighting in defense of his country."
16. Presumably Thrasybulus of the deme Steiria, the hero of Phyle (Part One, The Thirty Tyrants, p. 19). The speaker's unflattering characterization of Thrasybulus and the tense of the verb "has rebuked" imply that Thrasybulus (d. 389/8: Xenophon, *Hellenica* 4.8.30) was still alive when Mantitheus gave this speech.
17. Agesilaus II, king of Sparta (r. 400 to 359).
18. Commander of his tribe's hoplites (above, §6 with note).
19. Spartan men wore their hair long, as did rich young Athenian men who wished to emulate them. Athenians with more democratic sentiments found this offensive (Aristophanes, *Clouds* 14; *Birds* 1281).

## Part Two: Philip and Athens

1. On Hecatombaeon 6 by the Athenian calendar; see General Introduction, p. 10.
2. Most famous as the site of the battle between the Greeks under the command of King Leonidas of Sparta and Xerxes' invading Persians in August 480 (Herodotus 7.175–239).

3. For the earlier incarnation of this alliance, concluded in 357, see *IG* II² 126 = Tod, no. 151 = Harding, no. 64.
4. On triremes see General Introduction, pp. 11–12. Peltasts were light infantry, named after the small crescent-shaped shields (*peltai*) they carried.
5. On impeachment (*eisangelia*) see General Introduction, p. 5; Part Three, Athens under Alexander, pp. 189–90.
6. This strategy had paid off for the Spartans several times, first in 404 when Lysander used it to force an end to the Peloponnesian War (Xenophon, *Hellenica* 2.2.1–2).

# 4. Demosthenes 4

1. On the internal division of speeches see General Introduction, p. 4.
2. General Introduction, pp. 11–12.
3. Demosthenes refers either to the Corinthian War (395–387/6) or to the more recent hostilities that took place between the foundation of the Second Athenian Confederacy (378/7) and the battle of Leuctra (371).
4. General Introduction, pp. 12–13.
5. Philip.
6. Athens.
7. Demosthenes has in mind particularly the Illyrians and Paeonians (Part Two, Philip and Athens, p. 70).
8. General Introduction, pp. 8–9.
9. Demosthenes has no particular god in mind. Cf. Lysias 13.1.
10. Rumors of Philip's illness or death circulated in Greece following his Thracian campaign of 352 (Part Two, Philip and Athens, p. 72).
11. Part Two, Philip and Athens, p. 69.
12. General Introduction, pp. 11–12.
13. As opposed to hiring mercenary soldiers.
14. The Athenian cavalry at this time numbered approximately 1,000 (Demosthenes 14 *On the Symmories* 13).
15. Demosthenes is referring to Philip's operations of 352–351: see Part Two, Philip and Athens, p. 72.
16. The Athenians mounted a successful expedition to Euboea under Timotheus son of Conon in 357. In 395, Haliartus was the site of one of the opening battles of the Corinthian War; the Athenians, in coalition with Thebes, Argos, and Corinth, defeated the Spartans under King Lysander (cf. Lysias 16.13). At Thermopylae in 352 the Phocians, Spartans, Athenians, and others checked Philip's advance into central Greece (Part Two, Philip and Athens, p. 71).
17. Troops promised on paper (that is, in letters to commanders such as Diopeithes: Part Two, Philip and Athens, pp. 79–80; Demosthenes 8.17) but not delivered.
18. i.e., consist of Athenian citizens (see the details below).

19. This is not implied by what precedes: during the Second Athenian Confederacy Athens often sent out undersupplied, or entirely unsupplied, expeditions. Cf. Demosthenes 8.21.
20. i.e., to obey and follow its general(s) (§19).
21. Athenian men were liable to military service from the ages of 18 to 60 (General Introduction, p. 11) and were called up by age-groups.
22. i.e., for combat, as opposed to, and for the protection of, triremes used as transports (§16).
23. i.e., a guerrilla war.
24. During the Corinthian War (395–387/6). Iphicrates revolutionized the art of war by his use of light infantry called peltasts (Part Two, Philip and Athens, p. 73 with note); in 390 Iphicrates and his peltasts ambushed and annihilated a Spartan *mora* (regiment) of 600 men (Xenophon, *Hellenica* 4.5.11–17). Chabrias succeeded Iphicrates in command at Corinth.
25. In 356 the Athenian general Chares had supported Artabazus, satrap of Hellespontine Phrygia, in his revolt against Artaxerxes III Ochus (Part Two, Philip and Athens, pp. 70–71).
26. Taxiarchs were tribal commanders of infantry, phylarchs tribal commanders of cavalry, and hipparchs staff commanders of cavalry.
27. Greek *hieropoioi*: a board of men who oversaw temples, sacrifices, religious processions, etc.
28. In other words, as figureheads suitable for public display. The agora was the central marketplace of a Greek city; Athens' agora was located just north of the Areopagus and northwest of the Acropolis.
29. Lycophron, the speaker of Hypereides 1, served as hipparch on Lemnos (Hypereides 1.17).
30. A Macedonian who assisted the Athenian general Timotheus in the seizure of Poteidaea in 364 and was honored as a benefactor of Athens in 362. Demosthenes is offended that a Macedonian (however friendly) commands Athenian forces abroad without (apparently) having been voted to the position by the Athenian Assembly.
31. As opposed to rations plus pay; apart from a food allowance, the troops are to support themselves with war booty (see §29 below).
32. Actually ninety-two talents, as is clear from the itemized budget below. On Athenian money see General Introduction, p. 10.
33. Above, §22 with note.
34. This, like most documents in the manuscripts of the Attic orators, has not been preserved.
35. Demosthenes and his partisans.
36. North winds that blow in the Aegean in the summer and early fall.
37. So as to blockade the ports and prevent commerce.
38. These islands were inhabited by Athenian cleruchs.
39. Cape Geraestus is the southern promontory of Euboea. Philip intercepted grain transports bound for Athens and exacted a fee for their safe passage.
40. The *Paralus*, one of two Athenian state vessels (the other was the *Salaminia*). This occurred in spring 352.
41. Festivals held in Attica in honor of Athena and Dionysus, respectively.

42. Philip captured these cities in 354, 352, and 356 respectively. They are given in chronological order in Demosthenes 1.9, 12–13; see Part Two, Philip and Athens, pp. 69–72.
43. The chorus-leader (*chorêgos*) financed a comic or tragic chorus, depending on the festival (General Introduction, p. 9).
44. The gymnasiarch superintended athletic competitions, such as torch-races, at festivals.
45. The trierarchy was a liturgy in which the wealthiest men in Athens financed the city's warships (General Introduction, p. 9). A man who did not wish to discharge an appointed liturgy could claim that another man was wealthier than he and challenge him to an exchange of property (*antidosis*). The challenged party was compelled either to accept the liturgy or to exchange the entirety of his estate for that of his challenger. Claiming (comparative) poverty in order to avoid a liturgy is an example of the "pretended incapacity" Demosthenes decries in §37 (and above, §7).
46. Metics were free foreign residents of Attica. Independent slaves (Greek *chôris oikountes*, literally "those living separately") were slaves living apart from their masters and generating their own income (General Introduction, p. 7).
47. Again (as in §29), the text of the document is not preserved.
48. i.e., without soldiers: cf. Demosthenes 3.5.
49. The *bêma* (General Introduction, p. 8).
50. Every Athenian official was subject to a review of conduct (*euthynai*) at the end of his term (cf. Chapter 1, the Introduction to Lysias 12, p. 23).
51. Kidnappers and clothes-stealers were liable to *apagôgê* and to an automatic death sentence if they confessed (see, in Chapter 2, the Introduction to Lysias 13; Lysias 13.68 with note).
52. i.e., the federations of Boeotia and Arcadia.
53. The Great King of Persia, Artaxerxes III Ochus (r. 358–338).

# 5. Demosthenes 1

1. In the Chalcidice.
2. Explained below at §§8–9.
3. Philip. Cf. Demosthenes 4.3.
4. According to the scholiast, Philip executed the former and slaughtered the latter as they sought sanctuary in a temple.
5. General Introduction, pp. 8–9.
6. As opposed to dispatching mercenaries.
7. In 357.
8. The *bêma* (General Introduction, p. 8). Hierax and Stratocles were leading Amphipolitan opponents of Macedon.
9. Philip captured Amphipolis later in 357 (Part Two, Philip and Athens, p. 69).
10. Cf. Demosthenes 4.35.

11. Above, §6 with note.
12. In the fall of 352 (Demosthenes 4.10 with note, 3.5; Chapter 6, Philip and Athens, p. 72).
13. King of the Molossi of Epirus (Hypereides 4.25 with note) and paternal uncle of Philip's wife Olympias.
14. Cf. Demosthenes 4.42.
15. The member cities of the Chalcidic League (Introduction, p. 97).
16. General Introduction, pp. 11–12.
17. A carefully oblique reference to the theoric fund (Part Two, Philip and Athens, p. 72).
18. In other words, Demosthenes wants to connect receipt of the theoric grant with the performance of military service, thus effectively converting the theoric grant into military pay.
19. On the *eisphora* (war-tax) see General Introduction, pp. 8–9. Demosthenes here proposes extending the war-tax to all Athenians; this would naturally make the alternative (redirecting the theoric fund) more attractive to the majority.
20. On Philip's seizure of Pagasae see §13; on the Thessalian response see Demosthenes 2.7, 11.
21. i.e., the kings of Paeonia and Illyria. Cf. Shakespeare, *Hamlet* 1.1.15, where "the Dane" is the king of Denmark.
22. Athenian orators never tired of harping on the bad reputation of the Thebans, which they earned by medizing in 480 and confirmed (in Athenian eyes) during their hegemony of Greece (371 to 362): cf. Demosthenes 18 *On the Crown* 18, 98; 20 *Against Leptines* 109; Aeschines 3 *Against Ctesiphon* 133; Isocrates 5 *Philippus* 53–54. When the *First Olynthiac* was delivered, Thebes was allied with Philip in the Third Sacred War.
23. While Athenian men were liable to military service from the ages of 18 to 60 (General Introduction, p. 11), the oldest age-groups were not usually called up for foreign service. Demosthenes is here addressing the younger men in the Assembly.
24. Demosthenes refers to the review of conduct in office (*euthynai*), which all outgoing Athenian officials had to undergo (Chapter 1, Introduction to Lysias 12, p. 23).

# 6. Demosthenes 2

1. In 357: Philip promised to restore Amphipolis to Athens in exchange for Pydna (Part Two, Philip and Athens, p. 69).
2. On Magnesia see Demosthenes 1.13, 1.22. The "Phocian war" is the Third Sacred War (Part Two, Philip and Athens, pp. 71 ff).
3. Cf. Demosthenes 1.6.
4. In 364 Perdiccas III (Philip's predecessor) and Timotheus campaigned with success against the Chalcidic League. On the capture of Poteidaea see Demosthenes 1.9, 12; Part Two, Philip and Athens, pp. 69–70. For

Philip's intervention in Thessaly see Demosthenes 1.12–13; Part Two, Philip and Athens, p. 71.

5. The Foot Companions (*pezetairoi*) were a Macedonian regiment that served as the king's bodyguard.

6. Greek *kordakismous*, literally "(acts of) dancing the *kordax*." The *kordax* was a dance performed by comic choruses but not respectable in other circumstances (see Aristophanes, *Clouds* 540).

7. With these stock accusations of Macedonian debauchery cf. Theopompus *FGrHist* 115 F 81, 225.

8. Demosthenes elsewhere (9.50; cf. [Demosthenes] 11 *Response to Philip's Letter* 17) remarks that the crucial difference between Philip and the Greeks is that Philip campaigns year-round rather than respecting the Greek campaigning season (which stretched roughly from April to October: General Introduction, p. 12).

9. See Demosthenes 4.3 with note.

10. General Introduction, pp. 8–9.

11. This contradicts Demosthenes 1.23.

12. i.e., with citizen forces, as opposed to (or in addition to) hiring mercenaries; cf. Demosthenes 4.21, 1.20.

13. Lampsacus and Sigeum were located on the coast of Asia Minor, at the northeast and southwest ends of the Hellespont respectively; they were probably seized by Chares in 356. On the ransacking of ships cf. Demosthenes 8.24–25.

14. Greek *erizein kai diestanai*; perhaps an intentional allusion to Homer, *Iliad* 1.6 *diastêtên erisante*.

15. General Introduction, p. 9.

16. In this extended metaphor Demosthenes divides the Assembly into two symmories, each with a leader (*hêgemôn*, the title given to the richest man in a symmory) and a general (the equivalent of the *epimelêtês*, "superintendent"). The Three Hundred are the 300 wealthiest men in Athens, who had to pay the entire amount due from their symmories to the treasury and subsequently reimburse themselves by collecting payments from the other members (see Demosthenes 37 *Against Pantaenetus* 37; [Demosthenes] 42 *Against Phaenippus* 25; Isaeus 6 *On the Estate of Philoctemon* 60).

17. Cf. Demosthenes 4.21.

# 7. Demosthenes 3

1. November 352 (Part Two, Philip and Athens, p. 72). For the Athenian calendar see General Introduction, p. 10.

2. i.e., with citizens; cf. Demosthenes 4.21, 1.20, 2.27.

3. General Introduction, pp. 11–12, 8–9, 10.

4. The first three months of 351/0.

5. The Eleusinian Mysteries, rites in honor of Demeter and her daughter Persephone celebrated yearly at Eleusis in the month of Boedromion.

6. In other words, without the citizen soldiers originally decreed.

7. Cf. Demosthenes 1.13.
8. Demosthenes quotes this phrase either from a decree or from the treaty between Athens and the Chalcidic League.
9. Cf. Demosthenes 1.7.
10. Olynthus.
11. Cf. Demosthenes 1.25–26.
12. In the current situation, sanctions threatened any speaker who proposed (as Demosthenes does here) diverting the theoric fund to other uses (Part Two, Philip and Athens, p. 72).
13. Eubulus and his supporters.
14. General Introduction, pp. 12–13; on Philip's hubris cf. e.g., Demosthenes 4.3.
15. Philip. Cf. Demosthenes 4.3, 1.3.
16. The scholiast explains that the Corinthians had neglected to invite the Athenians to the Isthmian Games; the Athenians processed to the festival with an armed escort and compelled the Corinthians to admit them. The most recent campaign against the "damned Megarians" took place in 350/49 ([Demosthenes] 13 *On Organization* 32, with Androtion *FGrHist* 324 F 30 and Philochorus *FGrHist* 328 F 155; for the epithet cf. Demosthenes 23 *Against Aristocrates* 212). The scholiast appears to allude to the same incident.
17. To the *bêma* (General Introduction, p. 8).
18. Aristeides, nicknamed "the Just," was a prominent Athenian politician in the early fifth century. He was ostracized in 483/2 and conducted the original tribute assessment for the Delian League in 478/7 ([Aristotle], *Constitution of the Athenians* 22.7, 23.5).
19. A prominent Athenian general during the Archidamian War. Together with the Spartan king Pleistoanax, he played a pivotal role in bringing about the peace that bears his name (421). He was one of the commanders of the doomed Sicilian expedition (415–413) and was executed by the victorious Sicilians in 413.
20. Demosthenes son of Alcisthenes, an Athenian general during the Archidamian War. His most famous exploit was the seizure of Pylos and (with Cleon) Sphacteria in 425. Sent to Sicily in 413 to reinforce the Athenians under Nicias, he was executed by the Sicilians after surrendering.
21. The leading figure in Athenian politics from the mid-fifth century to his death in 429. The most important of his domestic reforms were the institution of payment for jury service and a law (451/0) restricting Athenian citizenship to the children of two Athenian citizen parents. Elected general for fifteen consecutive years up to his death, Pericles championed a defensive strategy in the Archidamian War.
22. From the foundation of the Delian League (478) to the beginning of the Archidamian War (431). Demosthenes rounds the figure down to 45; Thucydides rounds up to 50 (1.118.2), and the portion of Thucydides' *Histories* that covers this period (1.89–118) is commonly called the *Pentecontaetia* ("Fifty Years"). Cf. Demosthenes 9.23.
23. The treasury of Athens was maintained in the opisthodomos of the Parthenon. Thucydides (2.13) gives a maximum figure of 10,200 talents

(9,700 talents in coin plus 500 talents of uncoined precious metal); Diodorus (12.40.2) and Isocrates (8 *On the Peace* 69) round to an even 10,000 talents.

24. Macedonia; the kings in question are Alexander I Philhellen (r. ca. 498–452) and Perdiccas II (r. ca. 452–413), who were at times friendly, but hardly "subject," to Athens.

25. After a battle, the side claiming victory (sometimes both) would set up a trophy (Greek *tropaion*), usually in the form of a set of enemy armor.

26. The Athenian general who devised the winning strategy at the battle of Marathon (490).

27. Eubulus and his supporters.

28. A festival of Apollo Boedromios celebrated in (and namesake of) the month Boedromion.

29. The Greek goddess of agriculture. It is probably not coincidental that Demosthenes swears an oath by this divinity immediately after comparing his countrymen to farm animals.

30. The theoric disbursements mentioned in §31.

31. Cf. Demosthenes 1.19.

32. Over the age of 60 (General Introduction, p. 11).

33. Presumably a reference to Chares or Charidemus (Introduction, p. 113; Part Two, Philip and Athens, p. 73).

34. The mercenary commander of §35.

# 8. Demosthenes 5

1. On the Euboean revolt of 348 see Part Two, Philip and Athens, pp. 73–74.

2. Cf. Demosthenes 4.18. To pursue his craft, Neoptolemus was allowed free passage between Athens and Macedonia. He and his fellow actor Aristodemus traveled to Macedonia, then returned to Athens and spoke in support of Philip (Demosthenes 6.28 with note; 19 *On the False Embassy* 12, 315).

3. General Introduction, pp. 6–7.

4. General Introduction, pp. 9–10.

5. Greek *phanera ousia*: see Lysias 12.83 with note.

6. The reference is to the second Athenian embassy to Philip in 346 (Part Two, Philip and Athens, p. 75).

7. In particular, Aeschines and Philocrates. Cf. Demosthenes 6.30; 19 *On the False Embassy* 112.

8. These promises fall into three categories. (1) The humiliation of Thebes. Thespiae and Plataea had been destroyed by Thebes in 372 (Xenophon, *Hellenica* 6.3.1; Diodorus 15.86); the reestablishment of these towns would break (or at least challenge) Thebes' hegemony over southern Boeotia. "Breaking up the Theban state" (cf. Demosthenes 4.48) means dissolving the Theban-led Boeotian League into its constituent towns. Oropus, on the Boeotian-Attic border, had been a bone of contention

between Thebes and Athens for years. (2) The return of Euboea to Athenian control in exchange for Athenian recognition of Philip's possession of Amphipolis, which he had held since 357 (Part Two, Philip and Athens, p. 69). (3) The preservation of Phocis. The Phocian seizure of Delphi was the *casus belli* of the Third Sacred War (355–346). At the conclusion of the Peace of Philocrates, the Athenians were concerned with preserving Phocis as a buffer to the north. At the end of the war, however, the towns of Phocis were dissolved into villages, the Phocians were disarmed, an indemnity of sixty talents *per annum* was levied on them, and their votes on the Amphictyonic Council were transferred to Philip (Part Two, Philip and Athens, pp. 75–76).

9. Members of the Second Athenian Confederacy paid "contributions" (*syntaxeis*, singular *syntaxis*). The word *phoros*, "tribute," was studiously avoided, as it brought up bad memories of the Athenian Empire.

10. The Amphictyons (literally, "dwellers around"), or Amphictyonic League, oversaw the oracle of Apollo at Delphi and had the power to declare wars (called Sacred Wars) against those guilty of sacrilege (Part Two, Philip and Athens, p. 71).

11. For proverbial Athenian accusations of Theban stupidity cf. Demosthenes 6.19, 18 *On the Crown* 43.

12. Philip.

13. Cf. §10 with note.

14. Presumably the previous inhabitants of Orchomenus and Coroneia, two Boeotian towns restored to Theban control by Philip (below, §§21–22).

15. Phocians seeking shelter in Athens after the end of the Third Sacred War: see above, §10.

16. Thermopylae. Part Two, Philip and Athens, p. 75.

17. Panhellenic games (on par with the Olympic, Isthmian, and Nemean) celebrated every four years at Delphi in honor of Apollo. See Part Two, Philip and Athens, p. 76.

18. A meeting of the Amphictyonic League (Greek *pylaia*) occurred in the fall and spring of each year.

19. That is, to submit to the demands of the Amphictyonic League.

20. The Peace of Philocrates.

21. Athens claimed the entire Chersonese; Cardia, however, asserted its autonomy, and in the Peace of Philocrates Cardia was listed as an ally of Philip and thus independent of Athens (Demosthenes 19 *On the False Embassy* 174).

22. Idrieus, satrap of Caria. Cf. Demosthenes 1.23.

23. In order to exact (or, from the Athenian point of view, extort) a fee for safe passage. Cf. Demosthenes 4.34; 8.9.

24. That is, over insignificant appearances (such as Philip's membership on the Amphictyonic Council and conduct of the Pythian Games). As pointed out by Harpocration, compiler of a second-century A.D. *Lexicon* to the Attic orators, Demosthenes alludes to a Greek proverb, "to fight over the shadow of an ass," meaning "to fight over something worthless."

# 9. Demosthenes 6

1. The Peace of Philocrates.
2. Toward Philip's victims (below, §2).
3. To the *bêma* (General Introduction, p. 8); i.e., politicians in the Assembly.
4. Part Two, Philip and Athens, pp. 75–76; cf. Demosthenes 5.10 with note, 19–20.
5. In 479 Mardonius, commander of the Persian forces in Greece, made a peace offer to the Athenians, sending as his representative Alexander I Philhellen, king of Macedon. The Athenians rejected the offer, saying (Herodotus 8.143): "as long as the sun travels the same course as it does now, we will never come to terms with Xerxes." Demosthenes' account is somewhat imprecise: the Athenians actually evacuated Attica twice, once in 480 (before the battle of Salamis) and again, following Mardonius' offer, in 479.
6. The medism of the Thebans in 480–479 was a neverending source of bitterness to their fellow Greeks (cf. Demosthenes 1.26). Argos remained neutral during Xerxes' invasion.
7. General Introduction, pp. 11–12.
8. Cf. below, §§28–29.
9. Demosthenes accuses Philip of inconsistency. At the conclusion of the Third Sacred War, Philip backed the Theban hegemony over Boeotia and restored previously independent towns to Theban control (cf. Demosthenes 5.20–22); now, however, he defends the independence of Messenia against Sparta.
10. Cf. Demosthenes 5.22.
11. General Introduction, p. 11.
12. A Phocian city on the border with East Locris. The fortification of Elatea would benefit the Phocians at the expense of Thebes.
13. According to Plutarch (*Moralia* 511a), when the Spartans refused Philip's demand that they recognize the independence of Messenia, Philip sent a threatening letter stating, "If I invade Laconia, I will drive you from your homes." The Spartans responded, "*If*."
14. Particularly the Messenians and Argives.
15. Cf. Demosthenes 5.15.
16. Anthemus, situated north of Olynthus between it and (later) Thessalonice, was given to Olynthus by Philip in 357. For Poteidaea see Part Two, Philip and Athens, pp. 69–70.
17. Cf. Demosthenes 1.5.
18. Lycophron and Peitholaus of Pherae, expelled in 352 (Part Two, Philip and Athens, p. 71).
19. Nicaea was a town in East Locris located southeast of Thermopylae. For Magnesia (the coastal strip of eastern Thessaly) see Demosthenes 1.13, 22; 2.7, 11. Philip granted both to the Thessalians at the end of the Third Sacred War.
20. A board of ten: see Part Two, Philip and Athens, pp. 76–77.
21. See Demosthenes 5.23 with note. Philip returned control of the meetings from Phocis to the Thessalians.

22. The income from the ports and markets of Thessaly. Cf. Demosthenes 1.22.
23. Against Sparta (above, §15 with note).
24. Outside the presence of Philip's envoys.
25. That is, the response to Philip's letter of complaint (Introduction, p. 130). Since the remainder of the speech does not bear out this statement, some scholars have conjectured that Demosthenes read out his proposed response here and its rubric has fallen out of the text; others believe he did so at the end of the speech.
26. To the *bêma* (General Introduction, p. 8).
27. Identified at Demosthenes 19 *On the False Embassy* 12 as Aristodemus, Neoptolemus (see Demosthenes 5.6 with note), and Ctesiphon. These promises are to be distinguished from the promises offered by Aeschines and others upon the return of the second embassy to Philip (below, §§29–30; cf. Demosthenes 5.10).
28. In particular, Aeschines and Philocrates.
29. Philip's oaths ratifying the Peace of Philocrates (Part Two, Philip and Athens, p. 75).
30. Teetotalers were regarded with suspicion in antiquity. In 19 *On the False Embassy* 46 Demosthenes relates that Philocrates stood up in the Assembly and said, "It is no wonder, men of Athens, that Demosthenes and I are of differing opinions: he drinks water; I drink wine." The Assembly broke out in laughter.
31. Thermopylae.
32. General Introduction, pp. 12–13. For the promises concerning Thespiae, Plataea, and Thebes cf. Demosthenes 19 *On the False Embassy* 42.
33. See Part Two, Philip and Athens, pp. 72, 74; cf. Hegesippus = [Demosthenes] 7.39. This would benefit the Athenian colonists on the peninsula by facilitating commerce and protecting them against Thracian invasion.
34. Cf. Demosthenes 5.10.
35. Part Two, Philip and Athens, p. 75.
36. Demosthenes accuses his opponents of mudslinging and implies that he would attract more attention from his listeners if he did the same.
37. Above, §5 with note.
38. Cf. Demosthenes 1.16.
39. Above, §29.
40. Scirophorion 16, 346, the day the second embassy made its report to the Assembly (Demosthenes 19 *On the False Embassy* 58).
41. Philip's naval harassment of Attica actually predated the Peace of Philocrates: cf. Demosthenes 4.34 (capture of the *Paralus* at Marathon, 352).
42. Before the Peace of Philocrates.

# 10. Hegesippus = [Demosthenes] 7

1. The *bêma* (General Introduction, p. 8).
2. The ambassadors sent by Philip to convey his offer.

3. Hegesippus and his fellow anti-Macedonian partisans (including Demosthenes).

4. These three islands were Athenian possessions of long standing.

5. Regarding the semantic arguments of this and the following section see the Introduction.

6. Literally "the Macedonian": cf. Demosthenes 1.23 with note. This prospect would offend an Athenian audience, as Athens was a traditional maritime power, and Macedon was (to say the least) not.

7. Greek *symbola*: agreements between states concerning the jurisdiction over lawsuits arising between their citizens. At Athens there existed a special class of lawsuits called *dikai apo symbolôn*, "lawsuits tried according to *symbola*."

8. In 356 Philip seized Poteidaea, ejected the Athenian colonists, and handed the city over to the Chalcidic League (Part Two, Philip and Athens, pp. 69–70; Demosthenes 4.4, 35; 1.9, 12–13).

9. An inaccurate exaggeration: cf. Demosthenes 3.24 with note.

10. Commercial lawsuits (*dikai emporikai*) were heard at Athens in winter on a monthly basis between Boedromion and Mounychion ([Demosthenes] 33 *Against Apaturius* 23; General Introduction, p. 10).

11. i.e., standard procedure was that cases were tried in the defendant's city of residence (thus making it easier for successful prosecutors to recover fines).

12. As mandated by the Peace of Philocrates: see Part Two, Philip and Athens, p. 75.

13. According to the scholiast, these were Thasian supporters of Philip who had been exiled by their fellow citizens but restored to their homes by the Athenians.

14. General Introduction, pp. 11–12.

15. On the proposed rectification (*epanorthôsis*) of the Peace of Philocrates see the Introduction; Part Two, Philip and Athens, p. 77.

16. According to custom, the ambassadors were invited to a meal at the Prytaneion in the Athenian agora.

17. Python of Byzantium, Philip's chief ambassador to Athens in 343 (Part Two, Philip and Athens, p. 77).

18. The Peace of Philocrates "lost Amphipolis" for Athens insofar as it confirmed Philip's possession of what he held at the conclusion of the peace, including Amphipolis. See below, §§26–29.

19. See below, §43 with note.

20. For the terms of the Peace of Philocrates see Part Two, Philip and Athens, pp. 74–75. Against the argument made here note Demosthenes' admission in 346 (5.25) that the Peace ceded Amphipolis to Philip.

21. Hegesippus refers to the secret agreement of 357 between Philip and the Athenians. Cf. Demosthenes 2.6–7; Part Two, Philip and Athens, p. 69.

22. Philip captured Olynthus in 348 (see Demosthenes 1–3). Several towns bore the name Apollonia, including one in the Chalcidice; Pallene is the western promontory of the Chalcidice.

23. "The Greeks" conceded Amphipolis to Athens at the negotiations regarding the Common Peace of 371 (Aeschines 2 *On the False Embassy* 32);

the Great King did so when he issued his rescript amending the Common Peace in 367 or 366 (Demosthenes 19 *On the False Embassy* 137).

24. For Philip's intervention in Thessaly cf. Demosthenes 6.22 with notes; Part Two, Philip and Athens, pp. 71, 76–77. Ambracia and Cassopia are a city and a region in southern Epirus, where Philip was active shortly before the delivery of this speech. The Elatea mentioned here must be distinguished from Elatea in Phocis (Demosthenes 6.14; Chapter 6, Philip and Athens, p. 82).

25. Alexander of Epirus, brother of Philip's wife Olympias.

26. This passage supports the attribution of the oration to Hegesippus (see the Introduction). The phrase "to the Greeks" shows that the author has delivered speeches relating to Philip outside Athens; Hegesippus had recently taken part in an embassy to the Peloponnese to rouse opposition to Macedon (see Demosthenes 9.72; Part Two, Philip and Athens, p. 78).

27. Above, §2.

28. The Athenian Assembly ratified the Peace of Philocrates on Elaphebolion 19, 346 (Demosthenes 19 *On the False Embassy* 57). The places Hegesippus mentions, located in coastal Thrace, were seized by Philip from the Thracian king Cersobleptes after the ratification of the peace by Athens but before Philip swore the oath of peace to the Athenian ambassadors several months later. See Part Two, Philip and Athens, pp. 75, 78.

29. Carystus is a city in southern Euboea. The individual was the Carystian *proxenus* (representative) of Athens, a Carystian citizen charged with representing Athenian interests in his city.

30. The Athenian presence in the Chersonese (modern Gallipoli) dated back several centuries. The area was vital to Athenian interests because large amounts of imported grain were conveyed from the Black Sea through the Hellespont. See Demosthenes 8.

31. i.e., on the mainland (northeast) side of Agora, a town in the northern Chersonese.

32. Cardia was located just northeast of Agora. For Apollonides, an ally of Philip, cf. Demosthenes 23 *Against Aristocrates* 183.

33. Philip's offer to dig a canal through the Chersonese had been rejected by the Athenians: see Demosthenes 6.30.

34. Hegesippus gets his geography confused here. Cardia was actually northeast of ("beyond") Agora, not southwest ("on this side," i.e., the peninsular side) of Agora. It was, however, "on this side" of the Pteleum–Leuce Acte line where Hegesippus places the boundary of the Chersonese.

35. On the status of Cardia cf. Demosthenes 5.25 with note; Part Two, Philip and Athens, p. 79.

36. In a Greek *polis* the right to own landed property was usually restricted to citizens. Foreigners could not own land except by a special grant, called at Athens (and elsewhere) *enktêsis*. The Cardians, according to Hegesippus, are labeling Athenian possessions in their territory *enktêmata* (possessions granted by *enktêsis*), while their own are simply *ktêmata*, "possessions."

37. Paeania is an Attic deme; the scholiast identifies Callippus simply as "an Athenian politician."

38. The proposer of a decree contrary to existing law was subject to a *graphê paranomôn* (lawsuit for an illegal decree), which could be brought by any Athenian citizen (General Introduction, p. 8; cf. above, §24). Libanius (see the Introduction) assigns this oration to Hegesippus in part because (he says) Hegesippus, not Demosthenes, brought the *graphê paranomôn* against Callippus.
39. General Introduction, pp. 12–13; cf. (e.g.) Demosthenes 4.4.

# 11. Demosthenes 8

1. Athenian general in the Chersonese theater (Part Two, Philip and Athens, pp. 79–80; cf. Demosthenes 9.15).
2. Philip.
3. The Council of 500, whose function was to prepare the Assembly's agenda (General Introduction, p. 8).
4. Athenian citizens sent to settle conquered land.
5. At this point Demosthenes shows the Assembly copies of the decrees.
6. The speaker(s) described in §4.
7. The main harbor of Athens.
8. The logical inconsistency, according to Demothenes, is this: if Philip is considered to be at peace provided that he stays out of Attica, then Diopeithes should be considered to be at peace provided that he stays out of Macedonia.
9. See Demosthenes 5.25.
10. For the contrast between the active policy of Philip and the reactive policy of Athens, cf. Demosthenes 4.36.
11. That is, in addition to the waste of money. Cf. Demosthenes 4.42.
12. See Demosthenes 4.31.
13. The bad Byzantine–Athenian relations to which Demosthenes refers date from the Social War (Part Two, Philip and Athens, p. 70).
14. Due to the etesian winds.
15. Byzantium, like the Chersonese, was vital to the Athenian grain supply due to its location (cf. the Introduction; Hegesippus = [Demosthenes] 7.39 with note). Byzantium commanded the Bosporus, through which grain transports bound for Attica traveled from the Black Sea.
16. That is, the Athenian cleruchs there (§6).
17. The mercenaries under Diopeithes (§9).
18. i.e., with a citizen (as opposed to a mercenary) force.
19. The description of imminent etesian winds in this passage indicates that the speech was delivered in the spring (see the Introduction).
20. Chalcis: cf. Demosthenes 9.74. Megara: see Demosthenes 9.17, 27, 74; 19 *On the False Embassy* 87. Oreus (located on the north shore of Euboea): see Demosthenes 9.12, 59–62.
21. General Introduction, pp. 8–9.
22. The theoric fund is meant: cf. Demosthenes 1.19; 3.11.
23. Greek *syntaxeis*: the contributions paid to Athens by her allies in the Second Athenian Confederacy (cf. Demosthenes 5.13). These were supposed

to fund the activities of the Confederacy but were often kept by Athens for her own domestic use. This often resulted in the dispatch of under-funded or entirely unfunded expeditions, such as Diopeithes'.

24. This was standard policy for Athenian commanders under the Second Athenian Confederacy; cf. §21 with note.
25. Part Two, Philip and Athens, p. 80; Introduction, p. 149.
26. Cf. above, §9.
27. A tablet inscribed with a decree ordering the recall of Diopeithes.
28. On the Athenian procedure of impeachment (*eisangelia*) see Part Three, Athens under Alexander, pp. 189–90.
29. General Introduction, pp. 11–12.
30. One of two state triremes of Athens (the other was the *Salaminia*). These were used only for official business, including the recall of accused generals. Cf. Demosthenes 4.34.
31. A celebrated Athenian general. For his involvement in the Social War, see Part Two, Philip and Athens, pp. 70–71; he also commanded the first Athenian relief expedition to Olynthus in 349/8 (Part Two, Philip and Athens, p. 73).
32. Another leading Athenian politician; cf. Hypereides 4.28. In 346, during the debates over the Peace of Philocrates, Aristophon opposed renouncing Athens' claim to Amphipolis (Theopompus *FGrHist* 115 F 166).
33. The winter of 342/1.
34. Philip's Thracian campaign (Part Two, Philip and Athens, p. 79).
35. Cleitarchus at Eretria and Philistides at Oreus (located on the north shore of Euboea across from the island of Sciathos) respectively. Cf. Demosthenes 9.57–62.
36. Two leading Olynthians who collaborated with Philip. Cf. Demosthenes 9.56, 66; 19 *On the False Embassy* 265; Hypereides fr. 76.
37. Here Demosthenes blatantly ignores over a century of recent Athenian history featuring two attempts at empire, the Delian League (established in 478/7 and disbanded at the end of the Peloponnesian War) and the Second Athenian Confederacy (established in 378/7, significantly diminished as a result of the Social War, but still in existence when Demosthenes delivered this speech).
38. Diopeithes' mercenary force (above, §17).
39. In response to a call for help from an ally. Cf. Demosthenes 4.32.
40. To serve as assistants to the paymasters.
41. Cf. Demosthenes 4.10.
42. In the form of bribes from Philip.
43. The speakers mentioned in §§52–53 above.
44. Cf. Hegesippus = [Demosthenes] 7.41–44.
45. Above, §36; Demosthenes 9.12, 59–62.
46. Hegesippus = [Demosthenes] 7.32; Demosthenes 9.12.
47. See Demosthenes 9.11.
48. Note the contradiction of §42.
49. One of the two standard methods of capital punishment in classical Athens was to nail the condemned man to a board and leave him to die; the other was poisoning by hemlock. Cf. Lysias 13.56 with note.

50. General Introduction, pp. 12–13; Demosthenes 4.3, 1.23; Hegesippus = [Demosthenes] 7.44.
51. On Theban aspirations to reclaim the hegemony of Boeotia, cf. Demosthenes 5.20–21.
52. The Third Sacred War.
53. The Peace of Philocrates.
54. See Hegesippus = [Demosthenes] 7.37 with note; Demosthenes 9.15.
55. That is, bribes from Philip.
56. See Part Two, Philip and Athens, p. 71 for the expulsion of Thessalian tyrants; regarding the Amphictyonic meeting cf. Demosthenes 5.23.
57. Pro-Macedonian speakers. Cf. Demosthenes 3.29.
58. To the *bêma* (General Introduction, p. 8).
59. For Demosthenes' sentiments concerning Fortune cf. 5.11; 6.12.
60. General Introduction, p. 9.
61. In 357: cf. Demosthenes 4.17; 1.8. Timotheus son of Conon was an accomplished Athenian general instrumental in executing the policy of the Second Athenian Confederacy.
62. General Introduction, pp. 11–12.
63. Diopeithes' mercenary army in the Chersonese.

# 12.  Demosthenes 9

1. The Peace of Philocrates (Part Two, Philip and Athens, pp. 74–75).
2. General Introduction, pp. 12–13; cf. Demosthenes 8.62 with note.
3. On the use of italics in the translation of this speech see the Introduction.
4. Cf. Demosthenes 8.34.
5. Cf. Demosthenes 4.2.
6. Such as Aeschines.
7. Athenians; or, more narrowly understood, Demosthenes and his hard-line anti-Macedonian partisans (including Hegesippus, author of [Demosthenes] 7 *On Halonnesus*, and Polyeuctus: see below, §72).
8. On bribes for Athenian politicians; cf. Hegesippus = [Demosthenes] 7.45; Demosthenes 8.66, 8.76.
9. One stade (Greek *stadion*) = 1/9–1/8 mile; thus forty stades is approximately five miles or a little less.
10. Cf. Demosthenes 8.59.
11. Through Thermopylae. Cf. Demosthenes 5.20.
12. Residents of Oreus on the north coast of Euboea. Cf. Demosthenes 8.36, 59.
13. See Demosthenes 8.
14. On these locations in coastal Thrace see Hegesippus = [Demosthenes] 7.37 with note; Demosthenes 8.64.
15. Chares.
16. Demosthenes distorts the facts here. According to the more accurate account at 19 *On the False Embassy* 155–156, Philip seized these locations

after the Athenians swore the oath of peace but before he himself did (in the presence of the second Athenian embassy of 346: Part Two, Philip and Athens, p. 75). Cf. [Demosthenes] = Hegesippus 7.37; Demosthenes 8.64, 18 *On the Crown* 27.

17. It is unclear when, or even if, Persia and the Greeks ceded the Chersonese to Athens. The Thracian king Cersobleptes did so in 352 (Part Two, Philip and Athens, p. 72); Demosthenes may well be embellishing. Cf. Hegesippus = [Demosthenes] 7.29 with note, regarding foreign recognition of the Athenian claim to Amphipolis.
18. Cf. Demosthenes 8.16.
19. Cf. Demosthenes 8.18 with note.
20. Cf. Demosthenes 8.36.
21. In 342 (Part Two, Philip and Athens, p. 79).
22. Philip was in possession of Elis at this time (§27 below).
23. On the importance of the Hellespont to Athens see the Introduction to Demosthenes 8.
24. Diopeithes and his mercenaries: see Demosthenes 8.
25. Here Demosthenes reckons the Athenian hegemony from 478/7 (foundation of the Delian League) to 405/4 (defeat in the Peloponnesian War). Cf. Demosthenes 3.24, where the orator states that the *consensual* Athenian hegemony lasted forty-five years (rounding down from 46: from 478/7 to 432/1, start of the Peloponnesian War).
26. From 405/4 (victory in the Peloponnesian War) to 376/5 (defeat at the battle of Naxos, which returned control of the sea to Athens). Modern historians generally extend the Spartan hegemony to the battle of Leuctra (see next note).
27. In 371; the Theban hegemony lasted until the battle of Mantinea (362).
28. For a detailed treatment of the causes of the Peloponnesian War see book 1 of Thucydides' *Histories*.
29. Thebes serves as the prime example. In 382 the Spartan commander Phoebidas seized the Theban acropolis, called the Cadmeia (Xenophon, *Hellenica* 5.2.25–31); a Spartan garrison remained in Thebes, protecting a pro-Spartan government, until its ejection in 379.
30. Demosthenes appears to date Philip's prominence in the Greek world from his first involvement in the Third Sacred War (see Part Two, Philip and Athens, p. 71).
31. Philip captured Methone in 354 (Part Two, Philip and Athens, p. 70) and Olynthus in 348 (Demosthenes 1–3; Part Two, Philip and Athens, p. 73). For Apollonia cf. Hegesippus = [Demosthenes] 7.28. The thirty-two cities are the members of the Chalcidic League led by Olynthus.
32. Part Two, Philip and Athens, p. 77.
33. See below, §§57–62.
34. See above, §16.
35. In 342: see §§34, 72 below and Hegesippus = [Demosthenes] 7.32.
36. A pro-Philip party had seized control of Elis by 343: see Demosthenes 19 *On the False Embassy* 260, 294.
37. Above, §17.
38. Demosthenes draws an analogy with the Athenian law of inheritance. Mismanaging one's estate could be actionable at law: there existed a

*graphê paranoias* (literally, "public action for insanity") available against those incapable of managing their property responsibly (*Ath. Pol.* 56.6). Such individuals were also barred from addressing the Assembly (Aeschines 1 *Against Timarchus* 30). Cases of disputed inheritance were handled separately, usually via the procedure called *diadikasia* (adjudication between rival claimants).

39. A child fraudulently substituted for the real heir.
40. Philip presided over the Pythian Games in person in 346 (Demosthenes 5.22) and by proxy in 342. Greek writers often refer to the subjects of monarchs as "slaves": cf. below, §43; [Demosthenes] 17 *On the Treaty with Alexander* 10; Hypereides 6 *Funeral Oration* 21.
41. Cf. Demosthenes 5.20.
42. On Philip's relations with the oracle of Apollo at Delphi and the Amphictyonic Council cf. Demosthenes 5.14, 6.22, 8.65.
43. Porthmus was located on Euboea near Eretria. On these events see below, §§57–62.
44. In 343. For Ambracia see above, §27 with note.
45. Echinus was a Theban colony on the north coast of the Malian Gulf.
46. See the Introduction.
47. See Demosthenes 5.25; Hegesippus = [Demosthenes] 7.39–44; Part Two, Philip and Athens, p. 79.
48. The central marketplace of a Greek city. The agora of Athens was located north of the Areopagus and northwest of the Acropolis.
49. General Introduction, pp. 11–12.
50. On the Arthmius decree, probably passed in the 460s or 450s, see Fornara, no. 69; Demosthenes 19 *On the False Embassy* 271; Aeschines 3 *Against Ctesiphon* 258; Deinarchus 2 *Against Aristogeiton* 24–25; Plutarch, *Life of Themistocles* 6.
51. i.e., subject. Cf. above, §32 with note.
52. The Greeks believed that homicide generally brought a ritual pollution upon the perpetrator. Demosthenes interprets the clause he cites (from the homicide legislation of Draco, 621/0) as stating that the killing of an outlaw did not pollute the killer.
53. In the Corinthian War (395–387/6).
54. General Introduction, p. 12.
55. Hoplites (General Introduction, p. 11) were the backbone of the Macedonian army. During the course of the fourth century, however, the hoplite lost some of his prominence as other, more flexible and integrated formations arose under commanders such as Iphicrates of Athens (during the Corinthian War), Epaminondas of Thebes (killed in action at the battle of Mantinea, 362), and Philip and Alexander of Macedon.
56. For the metaphor of illness for civil strife cf. above, §12.
57. Cf. Demosthenes 2.23; [Demosthenes] 11 *Response to Philip's Letter* 17.
58. Cf. Demosthenes 1.25.
59. Cf. Demosthenes 8.61.
60. A leading Olynthian democrat. On the betrayal of Olynthus see Demosthenes 8.40; 18 *On the Crown* 48; 19 *On the False Embassy* 263–267.

61. This occurred in 348 (Part Two, Philip and Athens, p. 73). See Demosthenes 5.5.
62. In 343–342 (Part Two, Philip and Athens, p. 79); cf. Demosthenes 8.36 (for Cleitarchus). Hipponicus was one of Philip's generals. Hipparchus of Eretria is mentioned in a catalogue of Greek traitors at Demosthenes 18 *On the Crown* 295; Automedon is otherwise unattested.
63. Eurylochus may have been one of the Macedonian ambassadors to Athens in 346; he was executed soon after the accession of Alexander. Parmenion was the most prominent of Philip's, and later Alexander's, generals; he was put to death by Alexander in 330 after his son Philotas was convicted of treason.
64. Above, §33; cf. Demosthenes 8.18.
65. Cf. Demosthenes 8.36.
66. Euphraeus had studied under Plato, who then sent him to the royal court of Macedon during the reign of Philip's brother and predecessor Perdiccas III (r. 365–359).
67. In Greek, their *chorêgos* (General Introduction, p. 9): the metaphor implies that they were funded by Philip, as the *chorêgos* funds his chorus.
68. See Demosthenes 8.61.
69. Philistides and his partisans.
70. On this incident see Demosthenes 18 *On the Crown* 79.
71. See §56; cf. Demosthenes 6.20–21. A hipparch is a commander of cavalry; see Hypereides 1.17.
72. For the "ship of state" metaphor cf. Alcaeus fr. 326 Lobel-Page (with Horace, *Odes* 1.14); Aeschylus, *Seven Against Thebes* 1–3; Sophocles, *Antigone* 189–190 (cited by Demosthenes 19 *On the False Embassy* 247–249).
73. As opposed to hired mercenaries.
74. The Athenians took Demosthenes' advice, sending Demosthenes to the Peloponnese (Aeschines 3 *Against Ctesiphon* 97), Hypereides to Rhodes ([Plutarch], *Lives of the Ten Orators* 850a) and possibly to Chios, and envoys to Artaxerxes III Ochus (Philip = [Demosthenes] 12.6).
75. Since Demosthenes repeatedly chastises the Athenians for their dilatory behavior (e.g., above, §35), here he is presumably referring to delays that would be imposed on Philip while he awaited the results of the proposed Athenian embassies.
76. Polyeuctus and Hegesippus were prominent anti-Macedonian politicians allied with Demosthenes. Cf. Hegesippus = [Demosthenes] 7.33.
77. The mercenaries serving under the Athenian general Diopeithes: see Demosthenes 8.

# 13.   Philip = [Demosthenes] 12

1. This is the standard salutation in a Greek letter: "(Sender) to (addressee), greetings." The "Council and people" are the Council of 500 and the Assembly, respectively.

2. Philip is referring to the Peace of Philocrates (Part Two, Philip and Athens, pp. 74–75).

3. The *bêma* (General Introduction, p. 8).

4. The Peace of Philocrates.

5. Two coastal Thracian towns. The exact location of Crobyle is unknown; the scholiast identifies Tiristasis with Peristasis on the northeast coast of the Chersonese. This passage may refer to the same expedition of Diopeithes mentioned at Demosthenes 8.8.

6. General Introduction, p. 10.

7. Heralds were considered sacrosanct in antiquity; abusing heralds was a breach of international law and an offense against the gods.

8. Anthemocritus was an Athenian herald sent to Megara on the eve of the Peloponnesian War (?432/1) with a demand that the Megarians cease cultivating land sacred to the goddesses Demeter and Persephone. See Thucydides 1.139; Plutarch, *Life of Pericles* 30; Harpocration, *Lexicon to the Ten Orators* s.v. Anthemocritus; Isaeus fr. 21 Thalheim.

9. The Eleusinian Mysteries, annual rites in honor of Demeter and Persephone celebrated at Eleusis in Attica.

10. Presumably Callias of Chalcis, who had been friendly with Philip earlier in the 340s but had since aligned himself with Athens (Aeschines 3 *Against Ctesiphon* 85–101 with scholia; cf. Demosthenes 8.36, 9.17). At some point Callias was given Athenian citizenship (Aeschines *ibid.*; Hypereides 5 *Against Demosthenes* 20; Deinarchus 1 *Against Demosthenes* 44); if the award had already been made, it might explain his description here as "the general you sent."

11. Artaxerxes III Ochus, Great King of Persia. Cf. Demosthenes 9.71.

12. Artaxerxes crushed revolts in these satrapies in 345 and 343, respectively.

13. In 490, the troops of Darius I were guided to their landing at Marathon by Hippias son of Peisistratus, who had been ousted from his tyranny at Athens in 511 (Herodotus 6.102).

14. Two Thracian kings. On Cersobleptes see Part Two, Philip and Athens, pp. 72, 79; for more information on Athenian relations with Cersobleptes see Demosthenes 23 *Against Aristocrates*.

15. Decrees of the Athenian people, including treaties and grants of citizenship, were commonly recorded on pillars of stone or bronze. Cf. Lysias 13.71–72; Demosthenes 9.41–42.

16. Philip is twisting the facts somewhat. When the Peace of Philocrates was signed, Cersobleptes was an ally of Athens (see *IG* II² 126 = Tod, no. 151) but not a member of the Second Athenian Confederacy. When the Assembly ratified the peace, Cersobleptes was omitted from the treaty (Demosthenes 19 *On the False Embassy* 174; Aeschines 2 *On the False Embassy* 83–85, 3 *Against Ctesiphon* 73–74). Later the Athenians changed their minds and demanded the inclusion of Cersobleptes (Part Two, Philip and Athens, p. 78; Hegesippus = [Demosthenes] 7.37; Demosthenes 8.64).

17. This passage causes some scholars to question the authenticity of the letter (see the Introduction). The Sitalces most familiar to the Greeks was a Thracian king who was killed in action in 424 (Thucydides 4.101) and was never given Athenian citizenship. Thus it has been suggested that

"Sitalces" here is an error for "Cotys," Cersobleptes' father, whose killers were rewarded with citizenship and gold crowns by the Athenian Assembly (Demosthenes 23 *Against Aristocrates* 119).

18. Evagoras I of Cyprus (d. 374) was tyrant of Cypriot Salamis. Dionysius I ruled Syracuse from 406–405 until his death ca. 367.

19. The relevant descendants, Evagoras II and Dionysius II respectively, had been driven out of their cities.

20. For the Athenian stance on Cardia see Hegesippus = [Demosthenes] 7.41; Demosthenes 8.58.

21. Inhabitants of Peparethos, the island east of Sciathos off the northern extremity of Euboea.

22. The seizure of Halonnesus by the Peparethians, and their subsequent ejection by Philip, occurred after the delivery of Hegesippus = [Demosthenes] 7 *On Halonnesus*. See below, §§14–15.

23. e.g., Hegesippus = [Demosthenes] 7.5.

24. For the assaults on Perinthus and Byzantium (Part Two, Philip and Athens, p. 80).

25. Diopeithes: see above, §3, and Demosthenes 8.

26. Stryme was a colony of Thasos situated near Maroneia (northeast of Thasos on the Thracian coast). Thasos and Maroneia had disputed the possession of Stryme in the late 360s; see Apollodorus = [Demosthenes] 50 *Against Polycles* 20–23; Harpocration, *Lexicon to the Ten Orators* s.v. Stryme.

27. For the long-standing Athenian claim to Amphipolis see Demosthenes 6.17, 8.66; Hegesippus = [Demosthenes] 7.26–29.

28. Philip refers to Alexander I Philhellen (r. ca. 498–452). The account given here is highly dubious. The prisoners were allegedly taken during the Persian retreat from the battle of Plataea in 479. Herodotus (9.89), however, says that the retreating Persians were attacked by Thracians, not Macedonians. Demosthenes (13 *On Organization* 24; 23 *Against Aristocrates* 200) incorrectly assigns the feat to Perdiccas II, Alexander's successor.

29. In 424/3 Amphipolis surrendered to the Spartan general Brasidas. When Brasidas was killed in action in 422, the Amphipolitans transferred to him the founder-cult with which they had previously honored Hagnon of Athens (Thucydides 4.105–106, 5.11). Philip captured Amphipolis in 357 (Part Two, Philip and Athens, p. 69).

30. Philip is correct in his statement that the Peace of Philocrates confirmed his possession of Amphipolis (Part Two, Philip and Athens, pp. 74–75; cf. Demosthenes' admission at 5.25 and Hegesippus' attempt at obfuscation at 7.26–29). However, Philip's implication that the treaties of peace and alliance were separate is an attempt to gild the lily; the Peace of Philocrates included both.

# Part Three: Athens under Alexander

1. According to [Plutarch], *Lives of the Ten Orators* 841e, Lycurgus was such a determined prosecutor that, according to one saying, "Lycurgus inked his pen against the wicked not with ink but with death."

2. Such a fine already existed in *graphai* (General Introduction, p. 5); before the fine was adopted in *eisangeliai*, prosecutors were motivated to bring an *eisangelia* instead of a *graphê* by the fact that the former did not involve financial risk (Hypereides 1.12).

## 14. Hypereides 1

1. A universally accepted editorial supplement, not present in the actual text of the fragment.
2. The heliastic oath (Hypereides 4.40; General Introduction, p. 5).
3. Three manifestations of treason that formed statutory grounds for an impeachment (*eisangelia*). Cf. Hypereides 4.7–8; Part Three, Athens under Alexander, p. 189.
4. Presumably a relative or friend of the woman's first husband.
5. Phlya is an Attic deme located northeast of the city of Athens.
6. Greek *ex autou*: perhaps "by him"; cf. "pregnant by him (*ex autou*)" below.
7. i.e., if the child died: a common Greek euphemism.
8. The will left by the deceased husband.
9. General Introduction, p. 6.
10. General Introduction, p. 10.
11. General Introduction, pp. 6–7.
12. The first stage of an impeachment was the lodging of an accusation before the Assembly; this could be followed (as in the present case) by a trial before a jury-court (Part Three, Athens under Alexander, p. 189).
13. On Dioxippus see the Introduction, p. 193.
14. In a part of the speech that has been lost.
15. Orestes, son of Agamemnon and Clytemnestra, avenged Clytemnestra's killing of Agamemnon by killing her and her lover Aegisthus, and subsequently went insane. Margites was a proverbial idiot and the protagonist of a poem commonly ascribed to Homer in antiquity.
16. The defendants' *synêgoroi* (advocates: General Introduction, p. 5).
17. General Introduction, p. 6.
18. The word I have translated "public lawsuits" is *graphai*: see General Introduction, p. 5. No doubt Hypereides had in mind the *graphê moicheias* (public lawsuit for seduction, which fell under the jurisdiction of the *thesmothetae*: *Ath. Pol.* 59.3). Another possibility may have been the *graphê hybreôs* (public lawsuit for hubris: see General Introduction, pp. 12–13). The *thesmothetae* (lawgivers) were the six junior archons, who presided over jury-courts.
19. At the time of this trial there was no punishment for malicious prosecution by *eisangelia*; however, prosecutors by *graphê* who received less than twenty percent of the jury's votes were fined 1,000 drachmas (Part Three, Athens under Alexander, p. 190 with note.
20. On the identity of Euphemus see above, fr. 4. Athenian brides were customarily dowered unless they came from destitute families: cf. Lysias 12.21.

21. Horse-raising was a favorite pastime of wealthy Greeks. Sons of prosperous families were commonly given names including the element *hippos*, "horse"; e.g., Xanthippus (father of Pericles), Glaucippus (father of Hypereides), Hippias and Hipparchus (sons of the tyrant Peisistratus), and, of course, Philippus (= Philip).

22. Crowns (of leaves or gold) were commonly given as awards for merit. In a military context a crown was the equivalent of a medal today.

23. Cf. §1 with note. Here the jury (as representative of the Athenian people) gets credit for votes of the Assembly.

24. Commanding officer of a tribe's contingent of cavalry. Cf. Lysias 16.6.

25. The island of Lemnos had long been an Athenian possession. The office of hipparch (cavalry commander: cf. Demosthenes 9.66) for Lemnos is mentioned at *Ath. Pol.* 61.6.

26. Hephaestia and Myrine were two cities on Lemnos.

27. Defendants convicted by *eisangelia* faced an aggravated death penalty: they were executed and their bodies could not be buried in Attica.

28. A *synēgoros* (advocate) for Lycophron; there may have been others. Another defense speech from this trial has survived in fragmentary form (*Oxyrhynchus Papyri* no. 1607; translated by Burtt in his Loeb edition of *Minor Attic Orators 2*); it is tentatively ascribed to Hypereides and may be the speech given by Theophilus.

# 15.  Hypereides 4

1. Commanding general of the Athenian fleet at Thasos in 361/0, impeached for treason (Apollodorus = [Demosthenes] 50 *Against Polycles* 14ff.; Demosthenes 19 *On the False Embassy* 180; 23 *Against Aristocrates* 115; 36 *For Phormio* 53; Aeschines 1 *Against Timarchus* 56 with scholia).

2. Commanding general of the Athenian fleet at Peparethos in 361/0, impeached for treason (Diodorus 15.95.1–3; Aeschines 2 *On the False Embassy* 21, 124).

3. A leading Athenian politician of the 370s and early 360s; one of the architects of the Second Athenian Confederacy. He was impeached but acquitted in 366/5 for the loss of Oropus to Thebes; Hypereides must be referring to a later impeachment and conviction (cf. Lycurgus 1 *Against Leocrates* 93). Since the impeachments at the beginning (Timomachus, Leosthenes) and end (Theotimus) of Hypereides' list come from 361/0 (or possibly 360/59), it is probable that Callistratus and Philon of Anaea were also impeached in 361/0.

4. Unknown. Anaea was a town on the Ionian coast opposite Samos.

5. Sestos was a town in the Chersonese. In 361/0 or 360/59 Sestos withdrew from alliance with Athens and went over to the Thracian king Cotys; the blame apparently fell on an Athenian general named Theotimus.

6. Callistratus.

7. General Introduction, p. 7.

8. Flute-girls were slaves commonly hired out by their masters to provide sexual services as well as musical entertainment. Athenian law set the maximum price a pimp could charge for a flute-girl at 2 drachmas (*Ath. Pol.* 50.2).

9. Halimous was an Athenian deme; Agasicles was charged with falsely claiming Athenian citizenship.

10. Greek *antigraphê*: the statement drafted by the defendant in response to the prosecutor's indictment.

11. The *archon basileus* (king archon) presided over the *graphê asebeias* (public lawsuit for impiety), which was tried in a jury-court: see *Ath. Pol.* 57.2.

12. The eponymous archon was often simply called "the archon." The legal action would be a *graphê*, or perhaps *eisangelia*, *kakôseôs goneôn* (public lawsuit, or impeachment, for abuse of parents: see *Ath. Pol.* 56.6). Cf. Lysias 13.91.

13. The *thesmothetae* ("lawgivers": the six junior archons) presided over the *graphê paranomôn* (public lawsuit for proposing an illegal decree): General Introduction, p. 8; *Ath. Pol.* 59.2.

14. Summary arrest (Greek *apagôgê*) was available against certain malefactors caught in the act. Covered offenses included homicide (cf. Lysias 13), seduction, and certain thefts. A suspect arrested by *apagôgê* was brought before the Eleven, who superintended the state prison and oversaw executions. If he confessed, he was immediately executed; if he disputed the accusation, he was tried by jury in a *dikastêrion*. See General Introduction, p. 5; Lysias 13.67 with note.

15. In an Athenian trial the prosecutor spoke first, followed by the defendant. On the prosecutor's tactic of anticipating the defense cf. Hypereides 1.9–10.

16. Hypereides addresses Polyeuctus.

17. Greek *synêgoros* (General Introduction, p. 5). Hypereides is one of Euxenippus' *synêgoroi* in this trial; §41, and possibly §15, indicate that there were more.

18. Each litigant had a platform (*bêma*) from which he (and his *synegoroi*) delivered their speeches (General Introduction, p. 6).

19. This individual cannot be identified. There were two Attic demes named Oion, Oion Dekeleikon and Oion Kerameikon.

20. The jurors.

21. To spend the night in the temple and await a sign from the god. The temple in question is that of Amphiaraus at Oropus (see below, §16).

22. Polyeuctus.

23. This shows that Hypereides was not the first speaker for the defense; the wording suggests that the man who spoke immediately before Hypereides was not the defendant Euxenippus but another *synêgoros*.

24. In this case "the god" is not Amphiaraus (as above in this paragraph) but Apollo, whose oracle was located at Delphi.

25. The citizens of Athens were divided into ten tribes. The two tribes meant here are Acamantis and Hippothoöntis (see below, §16).

26. A city on the Boeotian border whose possession was long disputed between Athens and Thebes. Oropus was awarded to Athens by Philip in

338/7 (Part Two, Philip and Athens, p. 83) and again by Alexander the Great after his destruction of Thebes in 336.

27. i.e., the price of any agricultural produce from the land in question which had already been sold.

28. That is, Polyeuctus was convicted in a *graphê paranomôn* (General Introduction, p. 8) for proposing a decree that violated existing law.

29. See Hypereides 1.20 with note.

30. Olympias was one of the wives of Philip II and the mother of Alexander the Great. Hygieia (Health) was worshiped as a goddess; the statue mentioned here was located in Athens.

31. That is, to a meeting of the League of Corinth. See Part Two, Philip and Athens, p. 84; Part Three, Athens under Alexander, p. 188.

32. The central marketplace of Athens.

33. Above, §19.

34. Dodona, located in the region of Epirus called Molossia, was the site of an oracle of Zeus centered around a sacred oak tree.

35. The goddess with whom Zeus shared the sacred site of Dodona.

36. In less grandiose terms, they repainted the statue and added expensive jewelry.

37. Olympias was the daughter of Neoptolemus, king of Molossia from 370 to 368; cf. Demosthenes 1.13 with note. For centuries the region produced a famous breed of large dog called the Molossian: see, e.g., Aristophanes, *Thesmophoriazusae* 416; Horace, *Satires* 2.6.114–115.

38. By serving as their advocate (*synêgoros*: see above, §11 with note), as he is doing here for Euxenippus.

39. Aristophon of the deme Azenia was prominent in Athenian politics for some seven decades following the restoration of the democracy in 403. Hypereides probably refers to a *graphê paranomôn* (public lawsuit for proposing an illegal decree) that he brought against Aristophon in 363/2; cf. Hypereides fr. 40–44.

40. An Athenian active in politics in the 340s (not to be confused with the general Diopeithes mentioned in Demosthenes 8 and 9, whose deme was Sounion).

41. The namesake of the Peace of Philocrates (Part Two, Philip and Athens, pp. 74–75, 77–78). Hypereides impeached Philocrates in 343; Philocrates fled Attica rather than standing trial and was sentenced to death *in absentia* (Aeschines 2 *On the False Embassy* 6, 3 *Against Ctesiphon* 79; Demosthenes 19 *On the False Embassy* 116).

42. See §4 with note.

43. These two men cannot be securely identified.

44. Cf. Hypereides 1.9.

45. General Introduction, pp. 6–7; Hypereides 1.1.

46. General Introduction, pp. 10.

47. Teisis used a procedure called *apographê* ("registration"): he compiled an inventory of property in private hands that he claimed belonged rightfully to the city of Athens, and he sought to confiscate it. The successful prosecutor in an *apographê* was rewarded with one-third of the sum confiscated (Apollodorus = [Demosthenes] 53 *Against Nicostratus* 1). None of the individuals involved here can be securely identified.

48. That is, the jurors in the respective cases: see General Introduction, p. 6.

49. Public lawsuits (including not only *apographê* but also *graphai* and, by 330, *eisangelia*: Part Three, Athens under Alexander, p. 190; Introduction to Hypereides 1, pp. 193–194) involved sanctions for prosecutors who failed to obtain twenty percent of the jurors' votes. Such failed prosecutors were fined 1,000 drachmas and barred from bringing similar suits in the future; Hypereides refers to the latter sanction when he says that Teisis was "disenfranchised."

50. That is, inside the boundary of a neighboring mine. The Athenian state leased silver-mining concessions at Laurium in southern Attica to private individuals or (as here) corporations (for another mining case see Demosthenes 37 *Against Pantaenetus*). Trespassing on a neighboring mine thus constituted a public offense. Lysander used a procedure called *phasis* ("denunciation"), in which the prosecutor charged the defendant with illegally withholding public property.

51. Hypereides 1 fr. 1; General Introduction, p. 5.

52. Apparently additional *synêgoroi* were prepared to speak for Euxenippus. Athenian defendants commonly displayed their children in order to arouse the sympathy of the jury.

# 16. Hypereides 5

1. Cf. the beginning of Hypereides 4.

2. Often, but not exclusively, by challenges to torture slaves. Under Athenian law slaves could only give valid evidence under torture, which required the consent of both litigants. Thus challenges issued by a litigant to his opponent offering to torture his own slaves, or demanding that the opponent submit his slaves for torture, occur commonly in the orators (e.g., Lysias 4 *On an Intentional Wounding* 10–11; Apollodorus = [Demosthenes] 59 *Against Neaera* 124). A litigant could also challenge his opponent to swear an oath regarding the facts of the case (e.g., Demosthenes 54 *Against Conon* 40–41).

3. From the money brought to Athens by Harpalus: Part Three, Athens under Alexander, pp. 191–192. A talent was a unit of weight and coinage (General Introduction, p. 10); from col. 3 below we learn that Harpalus' funds were in gold.

4. Deinarchus, another of the special prosecutors (Part Three, Athens under Alexander, p. 192), also mentions Demosthenes' challenges in regard to the investigation of the Harpalus affair (Deinarchus 1 *Against Demosthenes* 4–6, 61–63).

5. That is, the trials of the other defendants accused in connection with the Harpalus affair.

6. One of Alexander's officials in Asia Minor.

7. An incision in the rock of the Pnyx hill, where the Athenian Assembly met, possibly dividing the lower from the upper seats.

8. The stater was a gold coin issued by various states, including Persia. Cf. Lysias 12.11.

9. Harpalus'.

10. A fund from which disbursements were made to allow poor Athenians to attend religious festivals (Part Two, Philip and Athens, p. 72). Demosthenes' contention (according to Hypereides) is that he borrowed the money from Harpalus and then lent it to the Athenian state, assuming the risk of default himself.

11. The Council of the Areopagus.

12. Demosthenes.

13. At Athens a shipowner could take out an interest-bearing loan for the value of his ship, its cargo, or both. If the ship and cargo survived the trip safely, the borrower paid back the loan plus the interest; but if the ship or cargo were lost, the borrower kept the money.

14. Hypereides refers to the abortive Greek revolt of 335, bankrolled by Darius III and led by Thebes and Athens (Part Three, Athens under Alexander, p. 188).

15. The Exiles Decree (Part Three, Athens under Alexander, p. 190), proclaimed by Nicanor at Olympia in 324.

16. Governors of provinces (called satrapies) in the Persian Empire. As he conquered Persia, Alexander retained the system of satrapies, sometimes confirming existing satraps, sometimes appointing replacements.

17. Olympias is Alexander's mother (cf. Hypereides 4.19). On Callias of Chalcis see Philip = [Demosthenes] 12.5 with note.

18. The channel separating Euboea from the mainland; its current changed direction frequently.

19. Hypereides and Demosthenes had previously been political allies; see Part Two, Philip and Athens, p. 77.

20. Hypereides (b. 390/89), who was older than Demosthenes (b. 384 ± 1), is obviously referring not to himself but to one or more of his fellow prosecutors.

21. A phrase borrowed from Homer (e.g., *Iliad* 22.60).

22. i.e., a fine equal to the misappropriated sum. Cf. *Ath. Pol.* 54.2.

23. Another prominent Athenian politician and defendant in the Harpalus affair: Part Three, Athens under Alexander, pp. 191–92.

24. *Proxenos* was the title given to a man appointed by a foreign power as its official representative in his home city. At Athens, proxeny grants were awarded by decree of the Assembly.

25. Darius III. See above, col. 17.

26. Solon, often venerated by the Athenians as the founder of their democracy, had banned the practice of pledging one's body (that is, his freedom) as security for a loan (*Ath. Pol.* 6.1).

27. Paeania is the name of Conon's (and, incidentally, Demosthenes') deme. Five drachmas was the annual theoric payment (see above, col. 13 with note) granted to an Athenian (cf. Deinarchus *1 Against Demosthenes* 56).

28. The Academy was the school of philosophy founded by Plato, located northwest of the city of Athens in a grove named after the hero Academus.

29. From what follows it is safe to infer that this clause began with a negative, such as "It was not the case that...". This fragment begins with a

discussion of events following the battle of Chaeroneia in 338; "the war"
at the beginning of col. 39 is that fought between Athens and Philip. See
Part Two, Philip and Athens, p. 83.

30. "It" is the Assembly; "him" refers to Lycurgus, who was appointed to administer the Athenian treasury in 336 (Part Three, Athens under Alexander, p. 189).
31. The jury. General Introduction, p. 6; cf. Hypereides 4.34.
32. Probably the decree mentioned in col. 1.
33. Above, col. 5.
34. On Alexander's pretensions to divinity see Part Three, Athens under Alexander, p. 191.
35. The Assembly.
36. One of Demosthenes' fellow defendants.
37. An instrument of torture.
38. These fragments do not survive on the papyrus but are transmitted by other authors; their locations in the speech cannot be securely determined.
39. General Introduction, pp. 12–13.
40. Greek *akratokôthônas*; literally, those who drink their wine undiluted. On Demosthenes' reputation for sobriety see Part Two, Philip and Athens, p. 75.

# Bibliography

The following bibliography includes texts, commentaries, translations, and other secondary scholarship I have used in preparing this volume, as well as recommended readings for those interested in pursuing further study.

C. D. Adams, ed., *Lysias: Selected Speeches* (Norman, OK 1970)

E. Badian, "Harpalus," *Journal of Hellenic Studies* 81 (1961) 16–43

C. W. Blackwell, *In the Absence of Alexander: Harpalus and the Failure of Macedonian Authority* (New York 1999)

F. Blass, *Die attische Beredsamkeit*, 4 vols. (repr. Hildesheim 1979)

A. Boegehold, *The Athenian Agora* vol. 28: *The Lawcourts at Athens* (Princeton 1995)

A. B. Bosworth, *Conquest and Empire: The Reign of Alexander the Great* (Cambridge 1988)

J. O. Burtt, ed., *Minor Attic Orators II: Lycurgus, Dinarchus, Demades, Hyperides* (Cambridge, MA 1954)

J. B. Bury–R. Meiggs, *A History of Greece to the Death of Alexander the Great*[4] (New York 1975)

C. Carey, *Trials from Classical Athens* (London 1997)

E. E. Cohen, *Ancient Athenian Maritime Courts* (Princeton 1973)

J. K. Davies, *Athenian Propertied Families 600–300 B.C.* (Oxford 1971)

R. Develin, *Athenian Officials 684–321 B.C.* (Cambridge 1989)

M. R. Dilts, ed., *Scholia Demosthenica*, vol. 1 (Leipzig 1983)

M. R. Dilts, ed., *Scholia in Aeschinem* (Leipzig 1992)

M. R. Dilts, ed., *Demosthenis Orationes*, vol. 1 (Oxford 2002)

K. J. Dover, *Lysias and the* Corpus Lysiacum (Berkeley and Los Angeles 1968)

J. R. Ellis, *Philip II and Macedonian Imperialism* (London 1976)

M. Faraguna, *Atene nell' età di Alessandro* (Rome 1992)

N. R. E. Fisher, *Hybris* (Warminster 1992)

C. W. Fornara, ed., *Archaic Times to the End of the Peloponnesian War* (Cambridge 1983) [Fornara]

M. Gagarin and D. M. MacDowell, tr., *Antiphon and Andocides* (Austin, TX 1998)

C. Habicht, *Athens from Alexander to Antony* (Cambridge, MA 1997)

N. G. L. Hammond, *A History of Greece to 322* B.C.³ (Oxford 1986)

N. G. L. Hammond–G. T. Griffith, *A History of Macedonia*, vol. 2: 550–336 B.C. (Oxford 1979)

M. H. Hansen, *Eisangelia* (Odense 1975)

M. H. Hansen, *Apagoge, Endeixis, and Ephegesis Against Kakourgoi, Atimoi, and Pheugontes* (Odense 1976)

M. H. Hansen, *The Athenian Democracy in the Age of Demosthenes*² (Norman, OK 1999)

P. Harding, ed., *From the End of the Peloponnesian War to the Battle of Ipsus* (Cambridge 1985) [Harding]

A. R. W. Harrison, *The Law of Athens*², 2 vols. (Indianapolis 1998)

C. Hignett, *A History of the Athenian Constitution to the End of the Fifth Century B.C.* (Oxford 1952)

S. Hornblower–A. Spawforth, edd., *The Oxford Classical Dictionary*³ (Oxford 1999)

C. Hude, ed., *Lysiae Orationes* (Oxford 1911)

F. Jacoby, *Die fragmente der griechischen Historiker* (Leiden 1957–) [*FGrHist*]

C. Jensen, ed., *Hyperidis orationes sex cum ceterarum fragmentis* (Stuttgart 1917)

J. J. Keaney, ed., *Harpocration* Lexeis *of the Ten Orators* (Amsterdam 1991)

F. G. Kenyon, ed., *Hyperidis Orationes et Fragmenta* (Oxford 1906)

P. Krentz, *The Thirty at Athens* (Ithaca, NY 1982)

W. R. M. Lamb, ed., *Lysias* (Cambridge, MA 1930)

D. M. Lewis et al., edd., *The Cambridge Ancient History*, vol. 6² (Cambridge 1994)

J. H. Lipsius, *Das attische Recht und Rechtsverfahren* (Leipzig 1905–1915)

W. T. Loomis, *Wages, Welfare Costs, and Inflation in Classical Athens* (Ann Arbor 1998)

D. M. MacDowell, *The Law in Classical Athens* (Ithaca, NY 1978)

D. M. MacDowell, ed., *Demosthenes On the False Embassy* (*Oration 19*) (Oxford 2000)

J. M. MacGregor, ed., *The Olynthiac Speeches of Demosthenes* (Cambridge 1926)

R. Meiggs–D. Lewis, edd., *A Selection of Greek Inscriptions to the End of the Fifth Century B.C.* ., rev. ed. (Oxford 1992) [Meiggs–Lewis]

J. Ober, *Mass and Elite in Democratic Athens* (Princeton 1989)

D. D. Phillips, "Homicide, Wounding, and Battery in the Fourth-Century Attic Orators" (unpublished Ph.D. dissertation, University of Michigan, 2000)

A. W. Pickard-Cambridge, tr., *Demosthenes' Public Orations* (London 1963)

P. J. Rhodes, *A Commentary on the Aristotelian* Athenaion Politeia (Oxford 1993)

J. E. Sandys, ed., *The First Philippic and the Olynthiacs of Demosthenes* (London 1897)

J. E. Sandys, ed., *Demosthenes On the Peace, Second Philippic, On the Chersonesus and Third Philippic* (London 1913)

A. Schäfer, *Demosthenes und seine Zeit*, 4 vols. (repr. Hildesheim 1966)

C. J. Schwenk, ed., *Athens in the Age of Alexander* (Chicago 1985)

R. Sealey, *A History of the Greek City-States ca. 700–338 B.C.* (Berkeley and Los Angeles 1976)

R. Sealey, *Demosthenes and His Time* (Oxford 1993)

R. J. A. Talbert, *Atlas of Classical History* (London 1985)

M. N. Tod, ed., *Greek Historical Inscriptions* (repr. Chicago 1985) [Tod]

S. C. Todd, "The Use and Abuse of the Attic Orators," *Greece and Rome* 37 (1990) 159–178

S. C. Todd, *The Shape of Athenian Law* (Oxford 1995)

S. C. Todd, tr., *Lysias* (Austin, TX 2000)

J. Travlos, *Pictorial Dictionary of Ancient Athens* (New York 1971)

S. Usher, *Greek Oratory: Tradition and Originality* (Oxford 1999)

J. H. Vince, ed., *Demosthenes*, vol. 1 (Cambridge, MA 1930)

H. Weil, ed., *Les Harangues de Démosthène* (Paris 1912)

D. Whitehead, *The Demes of Attica* (Princeton 1986)

D. Whitehead, *Hypereides: The Forensic Speeches* (Oxford 2000)

A. G. Woodhead, *The Study of Greek Inscriptions*[2] (Norman, OK 1992)

I. Worthington, ed., *Persuasion. Greek Rhetoric in Action* (London 1994)

I. Worthington, ed., *Greek Orators II: Dinarchus and Hyperides* (Warminster 1999)

I. Worthington, ed., *Demosthenes: Statesman and Orator* (New York 2000)

H. Yunis, ed., *Demosthenes On the Crown* (Cambridge 2001)

# Index